Sound Business

AMERICAN BUSINESS, POLITICS, AND SOCIETY

Series Editors: Richard R. John, Pamela Walker Laird, and Mark H. Rose

Books in the series American Business, Politics, and Society explore
the relationships over time between governmental institutions and the
creation and performance of markets, firms, and industries large and
small. The central theme of this series is that public policy--understood
broadly to embrace not only lawmaking but also the structuring presence
of governmental institutions--has been fundamental to the evolution of
American business from the colonial era to the present. The series aims to
explore, in particular, developments that have enduring consequences.

A complete list of books in the series is available from the publisher.

Sound Business

Newspapers, Radio, and the Politics of New Media

Michael Stamm

PENN

UNIVERSITY OF PENNSYLVANIA PRESS

PHILADELPHIA

Published by
University of Pennsylvania Press
Philadelphia, Pennsylvania 19104-4112
www.upenn.edu/pennpress

Printed in the United States of America
on acid-free paper
10 9 8 7 6 5 4 3 2 1

Library of Congress Cataloging-in-Publication Data
Stamm, Michael.
    Sound business : newspapers, radio, and the politics of new media / Michael Stamm.
        p.   cm. — (American business, politics, and society)
    ISBN 978-0-8122-4311-6 (hardcover : alk. paper)
    Includes bibliographical references and index.
    1. Radio broadcasting—Ownership—United States—History—20th century. 2. Radio
broadcasting—Political aspects—United States—History—20th century. 3. Newspaper
publishing—United States—History—20th century. 4. Newspaper publishing—Political
aspects—United States—History—20th century. I. Title. II. Series
HE8698.S755   2011
384.54/3097309041—dc22
(PU) 4853015   2010047579

For my mother,
and for the memory of my father

Contents

Underwriting the Ether: Newspapers and the Origins of American Broadcasting

Reminiscing in 1951, *Detroit News* publisher William E. Scripps recalled that he was something of an experimenter as a young man and mused that, had he not had the calling of a family publishing business, his interests "probably would have led me into engineering had I been growing up today." Instead, William started working at the *News* because he was "ambitious to try to help my father," James E. Scripps, who had founded the paper in 1873. In the summers, William worked for the paper as a "messenger boy or any other job that there was to do" and soon, he recalled, "I went through every department in the plant, through every one of the mechanical departments." William E. Scripps expressed no regrets over his decision to enter publishing. He was happy working for the family business and was always "interested in the newspaper." And yet, he claimed, he retained a fascination with technology and confessed that he "couldn't entirely forget scientific and mechanical things." During the early years of his career at the *Detroit News*, Scripps found no way to combine these professional and personal interests. This would change, however. William E. Scripps had an old friend named Tom Clark who liked to experiment with wireless communication, an early form of what later became known as radio broadcasting.[1]

Thomas E. Clark was a Detroit inventor who owned an electrical service and supply company. Clark met the teenage William E. Scripps after Scripps and his friends began, as Clark recalled, buying equipment from his shop to "build a telegraph circuit" connecting their homes. William often visited Clark's shop, and the two "became quite well acquainted." In addition to his shop, Clark rented space in Detroit's Banner Laundry Building, where he had set up experimental wireless communication equipment. He also arranged to use a small space nearby "on the top floor of the Chamber of Commerce building," and by 1900 was successfully transmitting wireless messages between the two buildings. Clark offered to show William how he sent "Morse code without wires," and soon after gave William and his father James a demonstration that left the pair "quite enthused and pleased."[2]

Thomas Clark and William E. Scripps remained friendly in the ensuing years as Clark grew his electrical business and William came to take over the *Detroit News* and raise a family. William E. Scripps noticed that his son, William J. Scripps, had developed his own interest in technology and encouraged the boy to experiment. In 1919, William E. Scripps bought his son a wireless set, and later recalled that the boy "had great sport with it. He would spend into the wee hours of the morning, when he should have been in bed, listening to try to pick up messages. One night about two o'clock in the morning, he came tearing downstairs and woke me up. He said, 'Dad, come upstairs. I heard a voice on the air.' Of course I didn't believe it, but I couldn't doubt his word so I went up to his little workshop and I sat there for half or three quarters of an hour, listening, listening. Finally I did catch one word. I don't know what it came from or who it was addressed to, but it demonstrated anyway that there was a voice in the air." His son's wireless demonstration made William E. Scripps recall Tom Clark's similar feat almost two decades before. "My mind flashed back to that demonstration given to my father and me. Would wonders never cease!" Here was a way, Scripps surmised, of merging his career as a newspaperman with his hobbyist's interest in wireless. Standing in his son's room in the middle of the night, the thought occurred to William E. Scripps that "perhaps the *News* should become interested in wireless telephony."[3]

With Tom Clark's help, William E. Scripps had a small studio built in the *Detroit News* building and the station began experimental transmissions on 20 August 1920. Satisfied that everything was in working order, the *News* announced on 31 August that the results of the day's state primary elections would be aired in the evening, and the broadcast was successful. On 1 September, the *Detroit News* described its four-hour block of election coverage as a miraculous event "fraught with romance." As the station was "hissing and whirring its message into space," the *News* claimed, "few realized that a dream and a prediction had come true. The news of the world was being given forth through this invisible trumpet to the unseen crowds in the unseen marketplace." Newspapers, the dominant providers of Americans' daily information, now had a new medium with which to address the public, if they chose to pursue the opportunity.[4]

Many soon followed the *News*' example, and Scripps's experimental venture into radio was an early and important example of an evolving relationship that would come to shape the futures of both newspapers and radio. Historian Alan Trachtenberg argues that a process of "incorporation" characterized the decades after the Civil War, as America became a "changed, more tightly structured society with new hierarchies of control." For Trachtenberg, the rise of the modern business enterprise was central to this process. Firms grew dramatically in size, scope, and influence, and America became "incorporated" in the sense that corporations permeated the lives of ordinary citizens in more ways and to greater degrees. The arrival of broadcasting extended this pattern of incorporation through the twentieth century, as media corporations gathered Americans into increasingly large and dispersed groups as audiences for radio programming. That programming was often the product of newspaper firms that were incorporating radio into their existing business enterprises. In many ways, radio's growth was a story of successful exploitation and incorporation by existing elites and institutions, and at virtually every turn the newspaper was at the center of this story.[5]

This book focuses on the relationship between newspapers and radio— the old media and the new—during the period stretching from the origins of radio broadcasting through the early years of commercial television, roughly 1920 to 1953. In so doing, it makes two related arguments. First, it argues that newspapers used radio broadcasting to create a new kind of media corporation that utilized multiple media to circulate information and generate profits. And second, it argues that these multimedia corporations were central to the legal and political processes structuring the American public sphere in the twentieth century. These corporations participated in virtually every significant media policy debate, and they were strongly influential on the outcomes. Ultimately, these were the corporations that made the business of information a multimedia endeavor, and their actions transformed the ways that Americans received ideas about culture, society, and politics in the twentieth century.

Radio was in many respects transformative in the ways that it expanded the public sphere and enabled new ways of imagining the world through sound. Through radio, ideas circulated in the United States with more variety and with greater immediacy. After 1920, American homes became filled with the sounds of news, speeches, music, and church services, all broadcast live from what were to listeners unseen and often distant sites. Though it was compelling for many to have new experiences of the world through listening, however, it is important to remember that radio did not simply or seamlessly displace the long-standing practice of apprehending the world through print. A nation of radio listeners remained as well a nation of readers, and as they added radio sets to their homes in vast numbers in the 1920s and 1930s, Americans never stopped reading newspapers. In fact, they read more. Between 1920 and 1955, daily newspaper circulation nearly doubled, a rate that well outpaced a concurrently dramatic population growth, and the newspaper remained a major part of daily life in the era of electronic broadcasting.[6]

In the late 1930s and early 1940s, sociologist Paul Lazarsfeld conducted extensive empirical research on the relationship between radio and reading and found that the "greatest single change which radio has helped to bring about is the greatly-increased interest in news all over the country." Radio, Lazarsfeld argued in 1941, stimulated people to read newspapers. "For a number of psychological reasons, persons who *hear* a news item are often inclined to want to *read* it just because radio has brought it to their attention." Lazarsfeld concluded that radio listening in the interwar period had become a widespread supplementary practice to newspaper reading, but he also argued that print remained foundational. "There are many ways to communicate serious ideas," Lazarsfeld argued, and even after Americans had become active radio listeners, reading still "occup[ied] a place of peculiar primacy and virtue in the world of ideas. Print is the lever, we have come to feel, that can move the world. Whatever other media of communication we may use, we tend to fall back upon reading as the inescapably necessary supplement." After almost two decades of living with radio, Americans showed no signs of abandoning their relationship with print.[7] This is not to suggest that there was nothing new or peculiar about early radio listening, nor is it to ignore the profound strangeness that was part of the early radio listening experience.[8] But it is to suggest that the experience of listening to radio was impossible to bracket completely from the experience of reading printed texts, and to argue that the growth of radio (and later television) broadcasting took place within the context of a vibrant reading culture. All the while, strategic corporations profited from activities in all media.

In the early 1920s, the reasons that people and institutions had for starting a radio station varied. Some simply were attracted by the novelty of having an outlet to reach the public using a new technology. Others had vague ideas about how to sell time to advertisers to generate money through radio.[9] Churches and universities wanted to use broadcasting to expand their public presences beyond their physical locations.[10] Department store owners believed that radio offered a way to attract customers.[11] Manufacturing companies like the Radio Corporation of America (RCA), Westinghouse, and Zenith foresaw great profits in the sale of radio sets and began broadcasting in order to give listeners appealing content that would induce them to purchase receivers. Newspapers' broadcasting was motivated by a combination of these impulses. On the one hand, newspapers looked at radio as universities did and saw it as a new technology that could expand the institution's public presence and geographic reach. Newspapers also saw in broadcasting some of the things that department stores did, believing that it could promote the paper and attract more customers. And, in the long term, newspapers believed that radio was a means to greater profits for their businesses.

Though newspapers owned a small portion of the total stations on the air in the 1920s (an average of about 7 percent for the years 1923–1929), these stations were among the most powerful and significant of any across the country, and their influence on the industry structure and public policy for radio vastly outpaced their numbers. The number of newspaper-owned stations rose steadily after 1929, and by 1937 newspapers owned 25 percent of American radio stations. By 1940, newspapers owned almost a third of the stations broadcasting in the United States, and this trend continued into newly licensed FM stations after 1941 and television stations after 1948 (see Appendix). Across eras, newspapers played strong roles at formative moments in broadcasting, and over time their activities in broadcasting created a nationwide phenomenon that shaped the media in towns and cities of all sizes. As one author noted in the magazine *Radio Broadcast* in 1925, the "future of the press lies in the air," and the multimedia business model developed by newspapers became the dominant one for American media corporations in the twentieth century. In the decades when the basic corporate and legal structures of American broadcasting were being constituted and entrenched, to use sociologist Paul Starr's terms, newspapers were among the most significant institutional actors. Through radio, newspaper corporations participated in the institutional transformation of the mass media as they began creating new media corporations whose products were not just printed sheets, but instead branded information communicated through multiple media from a single corporate source.[12]

Despite newspapers' significance as station owners during the formative era of broadcasting in the United States, historians have largely overlooked the roles that they played in this history.[13] This is a significant oversight, as the history of American broadcasting needs to be understood as the history of radio's adoption by and relationships with newspapers. This is an approach emphasizing continuity over discontinuity in media history and focusing on the relationships between the "new media" of the time and its most significant precursor.[14]

Ultimately, the history of newspaper involvement in broadcasting is a history of the transformation of the institutions that defined the public sphere in the United States in the transitional period between the era in which printed materials were the dominant media of mass communication and the evolution of our own electronically mediated environment. Though the public sphere changed dramatically after the introduction of radio broadcasting, this is a complex story of adaptation rather than a simple story of decline. In his classic formulation of the public sphere concept, Jürgen Habermas presented radio as part of a constellation of new twentieth-century media that transformed an active "rational-critical" reading public into a passive collection of spectators, a process that created an inferior public culture and provided a weak foundation for informed political participation. "The world fashioned by the mass media is a public sphere in appearance only," Habermas argued, drawing a stark contrast between a public culture mediated through print and one created through the electronic media. When one examines the roles played by newspapers as institutions in shaping the new public sphere created by radio broadcasting, this clear distinction between eras and media seems less tenable. In many cases, the corporations that shaped the print-based public sphere remained the institutions shaping the public sphere that included broadcasting.[15]

This is a history with a mixed legacy. It is on the one hand a story of media consolidation with origins in the early days of radio broadcasting. On the other hand, it is also a story of strategic behavior by newspapers as business firms legitimately believing that they were uniquely qualified to be good broadcasters. One of the main goals of this book is to provide an account of media history that neither celebrates nor condemns corporate broadcasting, but instead one that demonstrates how newspapers were key institutional actors in shaping the history of American broadcasting.[16]

Newspapers and New Technologies

The lack of attention given to newspaper involvement in American broadcasting by historians has several causes. At a broad level, it is attributable to the simple fact that many historians treat newspapers as source material rather than as institutions or as agents of change. In many historical accounts, newspapers dwell in the footnotes as evidence of events rather than in the main text as institutional agents.[17] Another factor explaining newspapers' abscences from media history has to do with the fact that, in most cases, historians write that history from the perspective of a single medium rather than by exploring relationships between various media.[18]

In the specific case at the heart of this book, historians of broadcasting rarely discuss newspapers because their attention is instead directed at describing radio's revolutionary characteristics and effects as a medium. In some respects, there are good reasons for taking this approach, given the themes in some of the source material. Press accounts of early radio are filled with utopian and millennial claims about the effects of radio. As one journalist wrote in 1922, "For thousands of families, life has acquired new savor through radio. It is hard to imagine the splendor of the vistas which radio must have opened to many of these people." In 1928, National Broadcasting Company (NBC) president Merlin Aylesworth similarly told an audience at Princeton University that radio was the "greatest means of personal communication invented by man" and described it as something with an appeal far surpassing that of the "impersonal and cold printed word." Those analyzing the social significance of radio have often taken this kind of language at face value. For example, in 1935 in one of the first significant academic studies of radio, psychologists Hadley Cantril and Gordon Allport remarked that radio was "epochal in its influence upon the mental horizons of men" and "something new under the psychological sun."[19]

Many contemporary broadcast historians have been similarly concerned with explaining what they perceive as radio's novel effects. Even while avoiding technological determinism, many historians argue that radio created a break with the print-dominated past as a radically new aural medium that initiated a series of major historical changes: radio redrew the lines between public and private life, rapidly accelerated the speed at which news and information could be disseminated, and broke down geographic boundaries by allowing listeners to hear the voices of distant others. In comparison, the daily newspaper can seem plodding and provincial, the product of an era in which people were somehow far less modern, less informed, and less interconnected.[20]

Media historians David Thorburn and Henry Jenkins caution against taking this sort of "medium-specific" approach, arguing that it tends to overstate novelty and "risk simplifying technological change to a zero-sum game in which one medium gains at the expense of its rivals." In reality, there are "complex synergies that always prevail among media systems, particularly during periods shaped by the birth of a new medium of expression."[21] Historian Warren Susman similarly suggests that historians should probe the connections and interrelations between contemporary media rather than study particular media in isolation from each other. This "ecological approach," as Susman describes it, reminds us that every particular medium, regardless of how novel it may appear, is "perforce related to others, sharing in some greater whole." To forget this, Susman cautions, is to "miss the crucial issue of *relationships*, perhaps the most essential of all cultural questions." Susman's ecological metaphor suggests that historians ought to consider different media as related elements of the daily life of particular historical moments. Thus, to understand radio history one must interrogate how it related to other media, and in interwar America, none were more important than the daily newspaper.[22]

Prior to radio, newspapers provided people with the daily information enabling them to imagine themselves as part of a larger public through the ritual of reading. Newspaper reading, as anthropologist Benedict Anderson argues, was a "mass ceremony . . . performed in silent privacy, in the lair of the skull." In a variety of public and private settings—subway cars, living rooms, and cafes, for example—millions of people spent parts of their days with a collation of printed sheets identified by the name of the publisher and the exact date of publication (this distinguished it from book reading in some important respects), from which they selectively read information about current local, national, and international events. The following day, the mass ritual repeated, this time with a new copy of a newspaper with a later date. But, as Anderson also reminds us, a newspaper was more than just the focus of a regular mass ritual, as its production process came to resemble that of an industrial commodity. The newspaper was not just a foundation of "print culture," Anderson argues, but a motivator of what he calls "print-capitalism." A newspaper was for readers the focus of a daily activity at the same time that it was for its publishers a consumer good produced and sold on a mass scale.[23]

The demands of producing a newspaper in an industrial economy have meant that the adoption of new technology has always been a part of the newspaper business. At its most basic level, this began when publishers modified and improved upon hand-powered printing presses based on Johannes Gutenberg's fifteenth-century invention. In the early nineteenth century, the adoption of new industrial printing technologies such as the steam press allowed enterprising publishers to produce more copies at cheaper prices, thus encouraging the development of the penny press in the 1830s. This trend continued in the 1840s with the telegraph, as newspaper publishers such as Philadelphia's William Swain and New York's Horace Greeley and James Gordon Bennett became major investors supporting Samuel Morse's Magnetic Telegraph Company.[24]

In the early twentieth century, wireless telegraphy and later wireless sound transmission and broadcasting extended this process of newspaper experimentation with new technologies. After James Gordon Bennett, Jr., took over the *New York Herald* from his father, he helped found a company in 1883 dedicated to establishing a transatlantic telegraph line. Bennett also became intrigued by and supportive of experimental wireless transmission. In 1899, Bennett hired radio pioneer Guglielmo Marconi to provide coverage of the America's Cup Yacht Races using wireless telegraphy, and through this arrangement in October the *Herald* gave Marconi's invention one of its most high-profile demonstrations to date as it was used to provide live updates of the race. During the next decade, the *Herald* began experimental sound broadcasting from a transmitter at the Battery in New York City.[25]

Radio broadcasting presented different sorts of challenges and opportunities than new printing technologies or even the telegraph, as it opened up a separate mass distribution channel to the public and threatened newspapers' roles as the dominant providers of daily news and information in the United States. In choosing how to approach radio, publishers grappled with a new kind of choice about how to incorporate technology into their businesses. This was not an issue of weighing the adoption of a more efficient kind of printing press but was instead a question of how to respond to a technology that might supplant the entire newspaper business and create a new set of information providers. In the views of many publishers, radio threatened to transform the basic commodity being sold by the news business.

The question of what to do about radio was one that confronted newspaper firms of all sizes throughout the country. In Parkersburg, West Virginia, for example, the owners of the *Parkersburg Sentinel* and *Parkersburg News* had long been exploring ways of expanding their services to the public, even before radio. In 1941, W. E. Ingersol, the papers' business manager, recalled that "We happen to have a large yard beside our newspaper plant" that could be used to distribute news quickly to a physically assembled public. "Every year we would engage the benches at the city park from the City Administration, which, naturally, they couldn't turn down to the newspapers, and we carried large advertisements, and got a man with a good voice, and a megaphone and we thought we had invented a sort of procedure to give the ball scores to the people and we always had more people than we could accommodate. So it has been in our blood to do those things." His company, Ingersol stated, had "always tried to do our best and have always had that reputation in the community, as giving the news at the earliest possible moment," and looked at this reputation as a well-earned civic responsibility and privilege. In the 1920s, radio began challenging the newspaper as the first reporter of news, and Ingersol argued that this made his papers want to use it as an extension of what they were already doing. Ingersol pointed out that the desire to broadcast was not motivated by "any large commercial reason or a matter of profits." Rather, this was a question of civic authority in Parkersburg, something that Ingersol felt that his company had earned and something that it wanted to protect by getting involved in radio. Ingersol pointed out that the papers' management "have been natives in Parkersburg all our lives, spent our money and our investment there, and if someone else has the . . . privilege of giving the homes and the people that news, we feel that it is a matter of pride in the community, that we should be entitled to render the same service."[26]

Papers like those in Parkersburg looked at radio as both a threat and an opportunity, and these increasingly common newspaper forays into broadcasting not only showed older corporations trying to stave off new competition but also established institutions trying to direct what they perceived might be a force for significant change in their communities. The adoption of radio broadcasting thus motivated a process whereby publishers began altering their understandings of the kind of business that they were in. Those that had created institutions selling content and advertising in printed newspapers began evolving into institutions selling content and advertising in multiple media.

William Randolph Hearst's corporate empire is perhaps the best-known example of this kind of new media corporation. Starting in the late 1880s with a San Francisco newspaper, Hearst in subsequent decades built a multimedia corporation with strong and even dominant positions not just in newspaper publishing but also magazines, film, and broadcasting. Whenever possible, Hearst used one arm of his media empire to advance another. "Decades before synergy became a corporate cliché," historian David Nasaw remarks, "Hearst put the concept into practice." Hearst's newspapers and radio stations employed a variety of synergistic strategies throughout the early years of broadcasting. For example, Hearst's *San Francisco Examiner* began printing charts in the late 1920s that football fans could use as visual accompaniment to the company's radio broadcasts. "With this form," the company noted, "the football fan is able to sit at his receiver and chart the game as it comes directly from the field. It gives him an extra interest in the game and provides a mental picture of what is transpiring on the gridiron." With so many tuning into the broadcasts, the printed chart proved to be a "great promotion stunt."[27]

These practices were not limited to sports, nor were they limited to major metropolitan newspapers like those published by the Hearst Corporation. Electoral politics also offered opportunities to use print and radio together to provide multimedia coverage, and papers of all sizes took advantage. In 1936, for example, the *South Bend Tribune* printed a "radio primary election scorecard" and encouraged listeners to tune in to its radio station on election night to "get the official picture of the exact standing of each candidate in the primary" with unprecedented speed.[28]

What these kinds of strategies demonstrate is the evolution of the "newspaper business" into the "news business," the latter conception being based on using multiple media to provide the public with information in various forms. Don Elias, an executive with the *Asheville Citizen-Times* and its station WWNC, made this clear while testifying before a Senate subcommittee in 1947. "We are an electronic journal," Elias described his North Carolina corporation. "Some people like to get their information and entertainment through their optic nerve, and some want to get it through their auditory nerve, and some want to get it through both. But the principles involved are identical from start to finish. There is no difference between operating a radio station and operating a newspaper." Strategic about adopting new media, Elias expressed a conception common among newspaper corporations starting in the 1920s.[29]

Not all newspapers responded as eagerly and strategically to broadcasting. Some, in fact, tried to obstruct radio at every turn and initiated intermedia

Figure 1. "Freedom of the Hot Air." Cartoon. *Editor & Publisher* 66 (21 April 1934): 18.

competition that became so acrimonious in the early 1930s that it became known as the Press-Radio War. A cartoon published during this period in the leading newspaper trade journal *Editor & Publisher* encapsulated the feelings of these anti-radio publishers. In the cartoon, an eager newsboy from a paper called the *Herald Statesman* delivers a newspaper into the cramped quarters of the "Chiseling Broadcasting Company." As the harried radio announcer reads another newspaper into his microphone, he identifies the incoming young newspaper representative as "our Zanzibar correspondent," presumably just before reading this new newspaper over the air. And thus, as some publishers believed, radio "chiseled" profits away from their newspapers.[30]

As twenty-first-century publishers are trying to find ways to generate revenue when their content is accessed via the Internet, some of their predecessors worried about what would happen if people accessed news content via the radio. Many thought that those who had heard the news over the radio would not then buy a newspaper, believing themselves already adequately informed. In some instances, newspapers' responses to this competition took the form of court cases barring radio stations from simply reading the news on the air, as the "Chiseling Broadcasting Company" was doing.[31] In others, this involved formal agreement with the national networks to abstain from broadcasting news. At one point in late 1933, the newspaper industry succeeded in getting the NBC and Columbia Broadcasting System (CBS) networks to refrain from all news broadcasting save for five-minute summaries aired after 9:30 A.M. and 9:00 P.M., times that were presumably well after Americans had already purchased and read their morning and evening papers. From the perspective of a contemporary era in which the newspaper business is quite beleaguered, it is a striking testament to their corporate power in the 1930s that they could force the radio networks to agree to this sort of arrangement, even though it ultimately proved to be only a temporary solution. The newspaper-radio pact did not include stations that were not network affiliates, and new wire services like Transradio Press Service began gathering news to sell to these stations. Many other broadcasters, including some of the network affiliates, began searching for alternatives to their agreement with the newspaper industry, and by 1935 the press-radio accord had effectively collapsed. The motivations behind the drive to squash radio came from publishers who were looking at the new medium not as something to be strategically adopted, but as something to be crushed. This group of publishers ultimately lost the Press-Radio War, as many others ignored it as much as they could and simply waited for the agitation by the defenders of the old order to pass. For strategic newspapers, radio was not the enemy, it was the prize.[32]

In the 1920s and 1930s, though some were anxious and skeptical about radio and its effects on the newspaper industry, publishers on the whole became increasingly receptive to and partnered with broadcasting. Papers across the country of all sizes began operating radio stations and many made radio ownership a key element of a successful media corporation. *Editor & Publisher*, just three years earlier a critic of the "Chiseling Broadcasting Company," gave glowing coverage to newspaper-owned stations in 1937, as columnist Frank Arnold remarked how "closely knit together" press and radio were, citing the *Detroit News* and its station WWJ as an example of the "perfect unity of purpose and operation between a broadcasting station and a newspaper." Similar success stories, Arnold stated, could be found across the country in partnerships like the *Fort Worth Star-Telegram* and WBAP, the *St. Louis Post-Dispatch* and KSD, and the *Dayton Daily News* and WHIO.[33]

Throughout the history of broadcasting in the United States, newspapers created institutional continuities between old and new media. Roy Roberts of the *Kansas City Star* recalled in 1941 how his paper began operating station WDAF in the early 1920s, remarking that some publishers were afraid that radio "was going to kill their circulation" and lower their revenues and thus looked at radio with a great degree of "hostility." The *Star*, Roberts argued, took a different view of radio and saw it not as a threat but as an opportunity. Radio was "something new coming along, it was interesting . . . to the public, and we thought we had better join and go with it," even if this meant losing money. Though some among the paper's management felt that "radio was a parasite," creative staffers developed strategies to generate revenue, including offering to advertisers an innovative "combination rate—a discount rate if you take both the paper and the radio." Roberts felt that WDAF started as a "stepchild," but as time went on, "it kept growing and suddenly the stepchild became a beautiful debutante, and we love it now." Roberts was certain not only that the economics of joint ownership made sense, but also that companies like his provided better service to the public. Looking back from the vantage point of 1941, Roberts felt that radio was a natural extension of the newspaper, and remarked that "it was my view then and it is my view now, that newspapers with long traditional training in public service, in operation—I think the two go right hand in hand, I think they are the best operators you can get for radio." In terms of management, public service, and program quality, the newspaper was simply the best kind of owner, Roberts asserted, and he thought radio "would be better off if you had more newspapers running it."[34]

Testimonials by newspapers about their commitment to public service were constant throughout the early days of radio as publishers presented themselves as uniquely fit to broadcast. As Americans came to terms with radio as a new technology, newspapers were regularly reassuring them that well-intentioned publishers were prudently directing its course. In 1943, newspaper attorney Sydney Kaye told Congress that newspapers were better "than the leading manufacturer or the butcher or the candlestick maker or any other people who would go into the broadcasting business. In many towns the only interest that does crusade for and does concern itself in the public interest is the local newspaper." Though Kaye left open the possibility that bakers might be good broadcasters as well, he made a point echoed by newspapers throughout the period by claiming the superior qualifications of newspapers to operate quality radio stations.[35]

Similarly, the *St. Louis Post-Dispatch* under publisher Joseph Pulitzer, Jr.'s, leadership made numerous attempts to tout newspapers' radio stations as providing superior public service. In 1936, the paper claimed in an advertise-

Figure 2. Protecting Against "Association with the Unworthy." *St. Louis Post-Dispatch* advertisement, *Broadcasting Yearbook, 1936* (10 February 1936): 4. Reprinted with permission of *St. Louis Post-Dispatch*, copyright 1936.

ment that it "exercises an inflexible censorship over all programs offered for broadcasting." By acting as the arbiter of public discourse, the newspaper-owned station guarded "listeners and advertisers against association with the unworthy."[36] In essence, the *Post-Dispatch* claimed to be running a radio station that was both for-profit and concerned with the public interest. As the business of selling ideas and information became increasingly profitable through radio, prominent companies like the *Post-Dispatch* found these kinds of public service claims increasingly successful ways to promote the quality of their products.

Pulitzer made persistent claims about his public-oriented commercialism in the mid-1940s as he promoted his project to eliminate the middle commercial on the *St. Louis Post-Dispatch* station KSD's news broadcasts. To Pulitzer, sponsored news was not in itself a problem, but rather "the middle commercial represents neither good news broadcasting nor good advertising. News is news and the public is entitled to hear it without interruption." The listener, Pulitzer argued, "simply does not want to be compelled to listen to drool about vitamins and laxatives" while listening to the news, and he forced KSD to stop using a middle commercial during its newscasts. Pulitzer later expanded this effort into a major editorial campaign to encourage the entire radio industry to follow his lead and eliminate the middle commercial that he termed the "plug-ugly" from newscasts. Though the campaign was never successful on a national level, it attracted support from Justin Miller, a federal judge who in 1945 became the president of the National Association of Broadcasters (NAB). In a letter published in the *Post-Dispatch*, Miller lauded the paper for its campaign, noting that it was "particularly encouraging that this insistence upon higher professional standards should come from a newspaper—a representative of the profession which has most intelligently through the years defended the guarantees of the first amendment." In the long run, Miller argued, such activities would help broadcasters in any campaigns against what might be onerous regulations. "Only by intelligent anticipation of public reaction and by equally intelligent self-discipline can we prevent legislative intemperance," Miller argued.[37]

Miller's boosterism encapsulated a significant trend in the rhetoric that publishers and broadcasters used to frame radio in its early days. As Miller presented it, newspapers brought professionalism and a commitment to public service to the new medium, and he aimed to make radio not only financially successful but also socially legitimate. At the same time though, however much Miller may have believed his statements, they also belied a deeper strategic purpose. As radio became an increasingly profitable endeavor after 1920, the fear of "legislative intemperance" increased as well, and the newspaper as a public service-oriented institution became an ideal connection for broadcasters to cultivate in order to minimize the state's regulatory power while maximizing their own profits.

Radio and the Expanding Marketplace of Ideas

Some of the reasons for the persistence of the kind of public service discourse employed by people like Roy Roberts, Joseph Pulitzer, Jr., and Justin Miller had less to do with sincerity than with self-promotion, business strategy, and the desire to bolster public opinion about newspapers. Though millions of Americans read and trusted newspapers, public attitudes about publishers were never uniformly positive during the interwar period. In 1934, for example, journalist Isabelle Keating mocked press boosters for what she believed to be the persistent argument that "God handed down all news rights to Gutenberg and his professional progeny, the publishers, and let him who dares disbelieve beware." In 1939, almost 50 percent of respondents to a *Fortune* magazine survey stated that radio gave news "freer from prejudice" than newspapers, while only 17 percent believed that newspapers provided fairer coverage than radio. Almost a quarter of respondents believed that newspaper stories were "not accurate in many instances." To many critics, newspapers' commitment to public service was sporadic, selective, and invariably of secondary concern to generating profits.[38]

In addition to skepticism about publishers' self-congratulatory and self-serving rhetoric, many also expressed concerns about the implications of newspapers owning radio stations and potentially monopolizing the distribution of public information. Concerns about media concentration have become increasingly common in contemporary America, and have been made perhaps most prominently by journalist Ben Bagdikian. In 2004, Bagdikian in *The New Media Monopoly* decried the fact that a small handful of corporations controlled the vast majority of American media outlets. Monopoly was bad in general, Bagdikian claimed, but media monopoly endangered democracy because these corporations were "unique in one vital respect. They do not manufacture nuts and bolts: they manufacture a social and political world." Though profound, the anxiety that Bagdikian expressed about media consolidation was not at all new, as concern about newspaper ownership of radio was a steady part of American public life between 1920 and the 1950s, forming a discourse about the perils, promise, and effects of new media. When Americans talked about newspaper ownership of radio stations, what they were talking about were the political and cultural consequences of media consolidation, which many felt would be negative.[39]

Newspaper ownership of radio stations became a strenuously contested issue in interwar American political culture. Elite and ordinary Americans were often highly skeptical of publishers' public service rhetoric, and many were staunchly opposed to allowing newspapers to own radio stations. One such citizen wrote to the Federal Communications Commission (FCC) in 1941 that a "separation of ownership and control would provide the most effective means for maintaining the freedom of the press which is essential to our form of government." Another was furious at the owners of newspapers and radio stations who acted as if they were "beyond regulation" and always invoked the "old theme when cornered, 'freedom of the press'. It's a real joke. Certainly free to the special interests who are willing to pay the price but not to the general public, unless they happen to be gullible and swallow their propaganda hook, sinker and line. It is the hope of these syndicates through the medium of positive control of press and radio to exploit and control the common people of this country. They have become so powerful that they challenge the government to thwart them; they have adopted the policy of rule or ruin." This criticism of the media shares much with the statement made by *New Yorker* press critic A. J. Liebling in 1960 that "Freedom of the press is guaranteed only to those who own one" in the ways that it not only portrayed media consolidation as harmful to society but also as the result of corporations that were both manipulative and cynical. Liebling's remark, often given without context, was in an article bemoaning increasing media concentration and the declining number of cities with competing newspapers. "Diversity—and the competition that it causes—does not insure good news coverage or a fair champion for every point of view," Liebling argued, "but it increases the chances."[40]

More than twenty years before Liebling's remarks, the desire to keep media ownership diverse had become a regular part of American political discourse. Joy Elmer Morgan, the editor of the *Journal of the National Educational Association*, advocated a complete ban on newspaper ownership of radio stations in order to promote a more diverse and democratic media. "If monopoly is bad in the material realm," Morgan asserted, "it is infinitely worse in the realm of instruments for the formation of public opinion." The Central Labor Council of New Haven, Connecticut, denounced cross ownership "In the interests of Democracy, a free press and a free radio." Senator Josh Lee, a Democrat from Oklahoma, remarked in 1938 that the "power of the press combined with the power of the radio is too great a concentration of power, too great a concentration of control of public opinion to be in keeping with democracy." In 1944, Utah Supreme Court Chief Justice James Wolfe claimed that allowing newspapers to own radio stations was "detrimental to the growth of democracy."[41]

What these sentiments ultimately formed was a discourse about the concept of a "marketplace of ideas" in an era when the amount and variety of ideas available increased dramatically. To many, this phrase signifies an ideal zone of free intellectual exchange and debate among citizens who have access to a comprehensive body of information enabling them to form knowledgeable opinions and make rational decisions and choices. This concept has proven durable in American writing about free expression despite the fact that its origins are often misunderstood and the connections between its ideal and actual iterations ignored. As communications scholar John Durham Peters argues, the concept is often misattributed to John Milton, Adam Smith, and John Stuart Mill, none of whom actually used "economic metaphors to talk about liberty of communication." This connotation is instead a twentieth-century invention that often elides the increasing ability of corporations to put information into the public sphere at rates and quantities far exceeding that of ordinary citizens.[42]

Despite the obscurity of the term's origins and its occasional misuse in contemporary discourse, the "marketplace of ideas" concept was in fact a significant influence on the debate over radio broadcasting starting in the 1920s. Radio became a mass phenomenon in the period immediately following Oliver Wendell Holmes's 1919 dissent in *Abrams v. U.S.*, in which Holmes promoted a vigorous circulation of ideas as an essential element of a democracy. The "ultimate good," Holmes asserted, "is better reached by free trade in ideas . . . the best test of truth is the power of the thought to get itself accepted in the competition of the market." Only Louis Brandeis joined Holmes in dissenting from the majority opinion, as the other seven justices upheld the imprisonment of five Russian-born radicals charged with circulating antiwar leaflets in violation of the Sedition Act of 1918. Holmes's dissent, cultural historian Louis Menand argues, is often misunderstood as a libertarian protection of the rights of individuals to express themselves, but what Holmes was actually concerned with was not the individual citizen but rather the integrity of this metaphorical "market." What

Holmes believed America needed, and what his *Abrams* dissent promoted, was a public culture shaped by as many competing ideas and perspectives as possible.[43]

Radio transformed the tenor of this competition in three significant ways beginning in 1920. First, radio introduced a new variety of expression into this metaphorical marketplace in the form of the broadcast sounds that became a part of the everyday reality of millions of Americans. Second, the profits to be made by corporations in the commercial media marketplace increased dramatically as broadcasters developed successful strategies to sell airtime to advertisers. And third, the barriers to entry into this multimedia marketplace grew because of the inherently limited number of radio frequencies. As radio expanded the amount of ideas available after 1920, it also constrained the number of potential producers of these ideas, and it led to a situation where the federal government controlled access to this market.

The political struggles over how to regulate this newly emerging marketplace of ideas took place against the backdrop of *Abrams* and a broader expansion of protections of free expression in the United States. The First Amendment was ratified as part of the Bill of Rights in 1791, but its application for more than a century after bears little resemblance to many contemporary understandings of it. Though Oliver Wendell Holmes remarked in *Abrams* that it was the "theory of our Constitution" that truth was best arrived at through the "competition of the market," this does not square with First Amendment jurisprudence prior to 1919. It would, however, increasingly come to define understandings of free expression during the radio era.[44]

State level prohibitions on free expression were routinely enforced throughout the nineteenth century, and prior to World War I the Supreme Court upheld only one First Amendment claim against a state law for the entirety of American history. During the First World War, the federal government used the Espionage Act of 1917 to deny second-class postal privileges to radical publications like *The Masses* because of their content, effectively making it prohibitively expensive for these publications to circulate, and in 1919 in *Schenck v. U.S.*, the Supreme Court upheld the conviction of members of the Socialist Party who had distributed leaflets critical of wartime conscription. After the 1919 *Abrams* decision, however, judicial understandings of the scope of the First Amendment became more protective of free expression. In 1925 in *Gitlow v. New York*, the Supreme Court ruled that the Fourteenth Amendment protected individuals against infringement of their First Amendment rights by state governments, and in 1931 in *Near v. Minnesota*, the Court ruled that prior restraint of publication was unconstitutional. In many respects, Supreme Court jurisprudence in the 1920s reflected broader antipathy toward wartime suppression of expression, and the creation of American radio regulation took place within the context of the development of an expansive understanding of the First Amendment.[45]

In addition, radio law was a product of an evolving legal climate for popular entertainment and new media. Most significantly, in 1915 in *Mutual Film Corporation v. Industrial Commission of Ohio*, the Supreme Court upheld the constitutionality of a state film licensing board that had the authority to approve or deny the exhibition of motion pictures based on their perceived "moral, educational or amusing and harmless character." Film exhibition, the Supreme Court ruled, was a "business pure and simple, originated and conducted for profit" and was "not to be regarded . . . as part of the press of the country." This was a troubling statement for broadcasting corporations in the 1920s that aspired to earn profits through new media. The development in the United States of a broadcasting system in which radio frequencies were made public property that was licensed to private users was a compromise among several competing policy alternatives, and it was a system whose architecture was influenced by both the example of the newspaper as a legal entity and by newspapers' participation in the policy process.[46]

For broadcasters, a common strategy in the 1920s was to insinuate themselves into ongoing debates about press freedom and the First Amendment by employing libertarian language, and many took it as their task to show that they were more like the press than they were some sort of commercial amusement. As RCA president David Sarnoff argued in 1924, the "same principles that apply to the freedom of the press should be made to apply to the freedom of the air," and he claimed that the "danger to freedom of speech by radio is not the danger that any one interest will ever be able to monopolize the air. The real danger is in censorship, in over-regulation." As publishers were pursuing legal avenues to expand First Amendment protections in the period around *Gitlow*, broadcasters like Sarnoff hoped to be pulled along in that direction rather than categorized with the motion picture industry as a "business pure and simple." As Sarnoff testified before Congress in 1924, "America to-day may justly be proud of the freedom of the press" and he hoped that "the freedom of broadcasting will be maintained in the same American spirit." For many broadcasters, deploying this rhetoric was less about high-minded civil liberties crusading than it was about keeping their businesses as free as possible from regulation. Regardless of motivation, during radio's development this sort of antistatist discourse was pervasive among industry representatives. As Sarnoff had connected press and radio in the 1920s, the trade journal *Broadcasting* editorialized in 1938 that "protection of radio is really the first line of defense for the press," and it praised publishers who were "ready to fight shoulder to shoulder with broadcasters" to protect what many media industry representatives claimed were their constitutional rights.[47]

Debates about radio regulation took place not only within the context of a reinterpretation of the First Amendment, but also within the context of debates about the future of American democracy in an era of advanced industrial capitalism. In both arenas, Supreme Court justice Louis Brandeis and the philosopher John Dewey contributed particularly influential perspectives on how to resolve the seeming contradictions between modern capitalism and democratic citizenship. Throughout his career as a lawyer and judge, Brandeis developed an antimonopoly perspective based on a belief that the concentration of private corporate power threatened society. As his biographer Melvin Urofsky argues, Brandeis's antimonopoly philosophy "relied far more on principles of morality and political theory than on economics. Brandeis opposed large businesses because he believed that great size, either in government or in the private sector, posed dangers to democratic society and to individual opportunity." Though against monopoly, Brandeis was not anti-business, and his intellectual sympathies and proposed solutions to the problem of monopoly remained firmly rooted in a faith in private property and private initiative. What he advocated, political scientist Gerald Berk argues, was a "republican experimentalism" in which the state "regulated competition" in such a way that it would encourage innovation by keeping markets open to new participants. The most effective way to democratically manage twentieth-century capitalism, Brandeis believed, was to create industrial regulations that kept all industries open, competitive, and free from monopoly.[48]

A contemporary of Brandeis, John Dewey also wrote extensively on the relationship between capitalism and democracy in the 1920s and 1930s. In 1935, Dewey argued that the classical liberalism articulated by John Locke and John Stuart Mill was an antistatist philosophy holding that the "great enemy of individual liberty was thought to be government because of its tendency to encroach upon the innate liberties of individuals." By the twentieth century, this philosophy effectively provided large corporations with the kinds of rights and protections that had been designed originally to protect individuals. Once the historically specific tenets of classical liberalism were "formulated as eternal truths," Dewey claimed, they came to be used as "instrument[s] of vested interests in opposition to further social change." Those who still deployed this philosophy in the twentieth century were, in Dewey's view, ignoring or ignorant of the differences between the economy and society of the eighteenth and nineteenth centuries and those of the twentieth. "Wittingly or unwittingly," Dewey concluded, defenders of the old liberal philosophy in the twentieth century "still provide the intellectual system of apologetics for the existing economic régime, which they strangely, it would seem ironically, uphold as a régime of individual liberty for all."[49]

If broadcasters like David Sarnoff wanted a marketplace of ideas unrestricted and unregulated by the state, others expressed skepticism at the possibility of this being democratic in an era of electronic broadcasting. For attorney Morris Ernst, an acolyte of Brandeis (in 1944, a journalist profiling Ernst for *Life* wrote that "Ernst's feeling for Brandeis . . . is akin to that of a small boy for his favorite baseball hero") and an active participant in media policy debates beginning in the 1920s, the state had to develop regulations to correct imbalances created in the marketplace of ideas by large corporations. Writing in *The Nation* in 1926, Ernst proposed that ownership of radio stations should be limited to one for each "corporation, individual, or related interests" in order to prevent undesirable concentration. Ernst extended this critique in 1941, arguing in language taken directly from Oliver Wendell Holmes that "I don't believe you can maintain the theory which this country is dedicated to, that truth wins out in the marketplace, unless the marketplace has some integrity." In order to accomplish this, Ernst argued, regulators had to approach the problem with a Deweyan historicism rather than with a legal absolutism. Protecting the new marketplace of thought demanded new regulations, and this demanded new understandings of free speech and of the role of the state in securing it for all Americans, not just large media corporations. It demanded, he concluded, that the "contours of constitutional guarantees today—of free speech and free press and the others—must be rounded out in the terms of the market place today—not in terms of the market place as it existed in 1787."[50]

When the federal government began to consider adopting the kinds of new regulations on media ownership that Ernst was suggesting, some prominent civil libertarians protested the policies by employing Dewey's old liberal terms. For example, American Civil Liberties Union (ACLU) attorney Arthur Garfield Hays asserted in 1941 that the state should not impinge on what he claimed were absolute individual rights, even if the "individuals" in question were national media corporations. Proposals to prevent newspapers from owning radio stations were offered by people like Ernst to affirmatively institute diversity in the media, but they were for Hays "an interference with free speech." If the state followed this line of policymaking, Hays argued, "you will have a government that is trying to shift and change your economic institutions in order that people may have equal opportunities. In other words, it is a sacrifice of what I regard as fundamental rights in order to bring about a kind of economic society where people had equal opportunities and, as soon as the government does that, you have more or less a vicious kind of government." While ignoring the fact that multimedia corporations and ordinary people had unequal opportunities to practically exercise their right to free speech, Hays still advocated protecting absolute rights as a defense against what he believed to be an overreaching state.[51]

Those sympathetic to Louis Brandeis and John Dewey remained critical of this absolutist defense of private rights over the public good and began developing philosophies of state action attempting to diversify media ownership. Dewey's historically grounded twentieth-century liberalism was based on "the idea that the state has the responsibility for creating institutions under which individuals can effectively realize the potentialities that are theirs." Dewey's point, in other words, was that democracy demanded a commitment to seek freedom through government, not freedom from government, and many applied this philosophy as they attempted to regulate media corporations in the public interest.[52]

One of this book's central concerns is with the evolution of the discourse about a "marketplace of ideas" as it was shaped by the structures of advanced industrial capitalism, the administrative state, and the emerging new media system that was embedded within both. At the policy level, FCC chairman James Lawrence Fly tried to apply some of these ideas into media ownership regulations in the late 1930s and early 1940s. In a 1944 speech, Fly argued that the American newspaper business had become increasingly consolidated and that many papers had been "absorbed by national chains." Nationally, control of the press was slipping into fewer hands, and radio was similarly concentrated, as it had been taken over by newspapers to the degree that a "third of the radio stations are owned by the varied press interests. Most of these are closely affiliated with the national networks." What Fly worked for on the FCC was the kind of diverse marketplace of ideas that Morris Ernst advocated, and his methods were inspired by the conception of positive state power that Dewey and Brandeis suggested. "We live in an age of machines, mass production, and high-pressure merchandizing, monopolies and near-monopolies,"

Fly argued. "The present-day threat—the increasing domination of the media of communication by a few economic entities, and the resultant lessening of opportunities for the full, free spread of all kinds and shades of opinion—is the begotten child of technology and big business." While quoting Holmes's *Abrams* decision in his speech, Fly argued that "we must cling to the theory that ideas, good and bad, must have access to the market-place of thought, clashing in open competition in the bid for popular acceptance." Democracy, Fly concluded, was "most faithfully served by *diversity*."[53]

This marketplace of ideas metaphor is far from perfect in its application to media policy, and some economists and legal scholars argue that its defects have prevented the FCC from creating either consistent or judicially sustainable regulations on media ownership.[54] This book is not an attempt to demonstrate the metaphor's unqualified virtue. Rather, it aims to show how central the idea was to thinking about the relationship between press, radio, and democracy at a particularly significant and transformative historical moment. Less than a year after Oliver Wendell Holmes had made the "free trade in ideas . . . in the competition of the market" the ideal standard for a society wanting free expression and democracy, this was the language that the *Detroit News* used to describe its first broadcast in August 1920: an "invisible trumpet to the unseen crowds in the unseen marketplace."[55]

As the federal government tried to develop policies designed to protect diversity of ownership at the local and national levels, Brandeisian and Deweyan proponents of a competitive "marketplace of ideas" kept the concept at the center of virtually all of the debates. At times, these debates can seem arcane and mundane, as regulators and industry representatives have argued endlessly over such issues as the exact number of FM, AM, or television stations a particular corporation may own at the local and national levels and whether a newspaper should be permitted to own a broadcasting station in the same city in which it publishes.[56] Ultimately, however, the substance of the debates about media ownership is grounded deeply in American ideals about politics and society. As legal scholar C. Edwin Baker notes, these debates in fact "reflect competing ideals of democracy and the value placed on them," and they have determined the basic structures of the industries creating the ideal "informed citizen" at the heart of our conception of a free society. In interwar America, the debate over newspaper ownership of radio was ultimately over who would have the power to shape public opinion and the emerging new public sphere that included radio alongside newspapers, and who would have the power to create the institutions undergirding American society and politics.[57]

Politics and Society in the Age of Commercial Multimedia

In 1922, journalist Frederick Allen wrote that World War I had "made us realize that the problem of newspaper conduct is larger and more fundamental
than we had supposed it to be." For many intellectuals and critics like Allen,
the ease with which public opinion toward the war had been swayed by propaganda and public relations efforts aided or at least unchecked by journalists
was disconcerting, and some were skeptical about the future of American
democracy and the capacity of the mass media to sustain it. Democracy, Walter Lippmann argued in 1922, depended on a public composed of citizens
who were "theoretically omnicompetent," but all he saw was a public whose
ignorance and culpability allowed for the easy "manufacture of consent" to
matters as serious as total war. The press was complicit in this process, Lippmann argued, and publishers' and journalists' conduct during the war led
him to believe that they were doing a poor job of nurturing a democratic
public composed of informed, rational, and critical citizens. "My conclusion,"
Lippmann stated, "is that public opinions must be organized for the press if
they are to be sound, not by the press as is the case today."[58]

As newspapers built multimedia corporations starting in the 1920s, these
corporations changed the ways that Americans learned about the world around
them during a period in which particularly significant debates about citizenship and democratic theory took shape. From post-World War I fears about the
effects of domestic wartime propaganda and public opinion to 1930s concerns
about the global spread of totalitarianism to post-World War II anxiety about
the Soviet Union, Americans were occupied to the point of obsession with the
possibility of informed citizenship in an era in which the creation of irrational
opinion on a mass scale seemed possible through the mass media.[59]

The reaction from publishers and journalists to this criticism was immediate after World War I and persistent afterward, as those in the business
and profession of news and journalism struggled to redefine their mission
and values. Editors formed the American Society of Newspaper Editors in
1923, the group that created the first formal code of ethics for journalism.
Journalists also began to develop a vigorous campaign to promote their professional "ideal of objectivity" in news reporting. This practice of alleging a
vigorous commitment to public service occasioned steady criticism of many
radio practices as well, as journalists not only defined and codified standards
for print journalism after World War I but also began to develop a broader
sense of media ethics as they applied the ideas behind these nascent codes to

radio. As journalist Frank Parker Stockbridge argued in 1930, broadcasting was a "mess," but it was a "situation which the newspapers, as such, can clean up." Newspapers, Stockbridge argued, had "cleaned our own houses," and he claimed that radio could also benefit greatly from their leadership.[60]

For the newspapers that owned or wanted to own radio stations, the need to publicly profess their new ethical standards was even more compelling. Radio, some critics felt, was an antidote to the bias of the press, and it offered the promise of being a new medium that might correct the problems of public opinion formation that surfaced during World War I by giving listeners more direct access to important people and events without the often willfully deceptive influence of the press. Some critics were never convinced by newspapers' postwar contrition, looking instead to radio as something that might offer Americans, "instead of partisan prejudice, as imperfectly reflected in the newspapers . . . the facts and opinions of each side direct from the mouths of the leaders." Radio, that new communications medium that could deliver the voices of political leaders directly into the home, free of omission or biased interpretation, might fail to live up to its promise if it could not develop independently of the press, and newspapers with an interest in radio realized that they had to defend their participation in broadcasting. This book is a study of how newspaper corporations accomplished this as they entered into and shaped radio broadcasting as it emerged after World War I.[61]

The kind of public culture that emerged after the introduction of radio broadcasting had a great deal to do with the activities of these new multimedia corporations that newspaper publishers began to develop in the 1920s. This corporate transformation did not take place in a political vacuum, as in government and among ordinary citizens these new corporations seemed to be not manifestations of strategic decisions by firms in the media business but instead institutions that could potentially do serious harm to American society and politics by gaining too much power to shape public discourse and public opinion. Competing understandings of these corporations shaped the path of their development and in turn the contours of American life in an age of commercial multimedia.

In November 1947 a New Yorker named Harry Kursh wrote to the *New York Times* expressing his opposition to media consolidation in language that drew on some of the major intellectual trends in contemporary press criticism. "The spirit of the free press principle," Kursh wrote, "means that people living in a democracy have the right to receive information from as many and diverse sources as possible." Kursh's letter invoked not only Oliver Wendell Holmes but also Louis Brandeis in its opposition to centralized corporate power. As Kursh saw it, if publishers were "allowed to own and operate radio stations, the domination of radio would be complete." Diverse and oppositional voices would be stifled, Kursh asserted, if the FCC continued to grant licenses to newspapers. The "circle of transmitting information will be disastrously closed with dangerous consequences for the spirit of the free press principle," Kursh claimed. "The license to operate a free press does not carry with it the right to dominate the means of communications." Kursh and likeminded media critics inside and outside government composed one side of a debate that ran through the entire span of radio history.[62]

On the other side were the publishers who created some of America's first media monopolies by owning radio stations, and who saw themselves not as monopolists but as heirs to the noble tradition of public service created by leaders in the American press. Six months after Harry Kursh wrote his letter to the *Times*, William J. Scripps, publisher of the *Detroit News* and owner of station WWJ, one of the first and most important American radio stations, testified before the FCC that he was a proud "newspaper man, in the third generation of a family which has published a great metropolitan daily since 1873," when his grandfather began publishing the *Detroit News*. Following directly in the footsteps of his father, William E. Scripps, William J. Scripps claimed that "freedom of the press" was "something I believe in just as firmly as I believe in God and democracy. That feeling I have carried over with me into radio." To understand radio history requires a consideration of the Scripps family and the hundreds of other publishers who became broadcasters and imported their ideas about newspapers into radio, as well as the Americans—elite and ordinary—who tried to stop them from doing so. These publisher-broadcasters and their critics were the people that created the structures into which radio arrived and the people that helped determine the course of radio's development.[63]

Power, Politics, and the Promise of New Media: Newspaper Ownership of Radio in the 1920s

After broadcasting the Michigan primary election results in August 1920, the *Detroit News* station WWJ continued to deliver a regular slate of programming to an expanding listening audience. WWJ aired weekday concerts in the late morning and early evening, often by playing phonographs but occasionally by securing live singers and musicians. Later that fall, WWJ broadcast the results of the 1920 World Series and the 1920 presidential election. On 1 January 1921, the *News* claimed that WWJ was the first station to have broadcast a "human voice singing a New Year's melody of cheer" as the clock struck midnight the previous evening. Press accounts lauded the *News* for being "first newspaper in the United States and, so far as is known, in the world, to perceive the possibilities of increasing its usefulness by furnishing the public with radio service." The *Detroit News* activities inspired publishers around the country, and many soon followed the paper's example and established their own radio stations. This original group included such prominent urban papers as the *Kansas City Star*, *St. Louis Post-Dispatch*, *Chicago Tribune*, *Chicago Daily News*, *Atlanta Journal*, *Milwaukee Journal*, *Hartford Courant*, *Minneapolis Tribune*, *Dallas News*, and three different New Orleans dailies (the *Item*, *States*, and *Times-Picayune*). Many newspapers in smaller cities quickly took to radio as well, for example, Indiana's *South Bend Tribune*,

Georgia's *Rome News*, and New York's *Rochester Times-Union*. Though not all early newspaper stations stayed on the air permanently (the three New Orleans papers had stopped broadcasting by the end of 1923, for example, as had the *Minneapolis Tribune*), those that did believed in the tremendous promise of radio, and they eventually established themselves as some of the most important stations in the country.[1]

As radio developed in the 1920s, the new medium promised many things. To some, it promised a better politics, as Americans had more direct and personal access to candidates through the sounds of their voices. As one writer put it in the *New Republic* in 1924, radio "does reproduce to some degree, for the first time in the United States, the conditions of the Athenian democracy where every voter, for himself, could hear and judge the candidates . . . . The listener can form his own opinion from the candidate's utterance, before the press or the parties can instruct him." Radio also promised all Americans regardless of geography, race, or class access to a new and greater variety of cultural goods in the form of music, religious programming, and educational talks. "Grand opera, news expensively and quickly gathered, the words of political and religious leaders, instrumental music by great artists" could, as one journalist noted, now be "carried by the house-top antennas down into dingy rooms for the comfort of persons for whom such things simply did not exist a year ago." To corporations, radio promised great profits if consumer desire for sets could be stoked. RCA's David Sarnoff predicted in 1920 that, with proper promotion and marketing, the company could sell one million of what he called "Radio Music Boxes" by 1925. The company actually exceeded this benchmark, and its success attracted other firms to the market seeking similar returns. To newspapers, radio promised a way of expanding circulation, profits, and public influence. As an author in *Radio Broadcast* in 1923 noted, "if the radio news items are properly worded, they will convey not only news but also the impression that it is well worth while to buy the paper to get the rest of the facts. This use of radio, putting real news on the air . . . is probably one of radio's most promising fields."[2]

Though radio's promise was widely believed, the power to make use of that promise was not as widely distributed. In radio broadcasting, the concept of "power" meant several things. At its most basic level it meant wattage, as stations with higher power transmitters could reach larger audiences. A low-power station in a remote area might reach mere hundreds of listeners. Conversely, as one author noted in 1922, a "powerful station in the vicinity of a large city like New York would reach at present perhaps one or two hundred thousand persons." Power in early radio was also measured in terms of a station's capital and ability to develop and present engaging programming. Stations run by schools and churches found that securing adequate funding to support the equipment and staff necessary for broadcasting was difficult and often impossible to do. Stations run by corporations with prosperous existing businesses such as radio set manufacturers and newspapers had smoother experiences with radio broadcasting because they had easier access to capital to back the station. And most importantly, having power in early radio meant having political connections and influence. At the moment when the basic corporate and legal structures for radio were being developed, broadcasters with easier access to Congress and to the Department of Commerce, the regulatory authority for radio from 1912 to 1927, found themselves better able to protect their interests than those who were not political insiders. Newspapers in the 1920s often had these strong political connections, and they effectively parlayed these positions to direct the development of radio broadcasting.[3]

Having the power to succeed in radio ultimately meant having the capacity to act effectively in technical, economic, and political realms. For all that radio promised in the 1920s and for all that was new and exciting about broadcasting, it was most often the already powerful who built the industry's basic structures in the 1920s. Radio became a big business in the 1920s not just because investors and entrepreneurs created a new and appealing product, but also because newspapers wanted it to develop that way.

Building Institutions and Creating Content

In many ways, the content of radio broadcasting in its embryonic stage was simply sound itself. Programming was irregular and inconsistent in the early 1920s, but this was of little concern to radio enthusiasts, most of whom were thrilled by the act of exploring the airwaves on homemade sets. For many radio fans, tuning in mysterious and often random sounds was the most appealing part of the experience, and many listeners were attracted less by the actual substance of what they heard over the airwaves than they were by the experience of hearing sounds that seemed to come out of the air on their own from obscure points of origin.[4]

A radio station had no masthead and, unlike a newspaper, lacked a way of constantly and visually announcing its identity. Broadcasters who wished to distinguish their stations had to be creative, and some stations soon developed strategies to forge distinct identities for themselves. In 1921 in Chicago, for example, Westinghouse station KYW aired opera exclusively, including live broadcasts from the Chicago Opera Company, a practice designed to create goodwill for Westinghouse and consumer demand for its receiving sets. One journalist reported that KYW's broadcasts had in one year "established a radio audience of thousands" and helped to push "the number of sets in use in Chicago . . . from 1,300 to something like 20,000." By establishing itself as a regular source of operatic music on the air, Westinghouse's KYW quickly demonstrated that an audience could be drawn to specific stations for specific kinds of content. Though listeners might explore the airwaves, many also liked to have stable stations as regular destinations and even anchors.[5]

Newspapers found other ways to create distinct identities for their stations and to promote the idea that a single institution was providing information in both media. One strategy that newspapers employed was to use the call letters of their stations to constantly invoke the identity of the common corporate producer. For example, the *Milwaukee Journal* obtained the call letters WTMJ, acronym for "The *Milwaukee Journal.*" Another strategy was for announcers on newspaper owned radio stations to mention the paper when giving the station identification. *Detroit News* managing editor W. S. Gilmore reported great success with this tactic on WWJ, remarking that it "offered a new and startling method of putting our name before the public," and claiming that listeners had responded to the constant invocation of the institutional connection between the two media. "We know that in thousands of homes our station is spoken of as '*The News*' rather than as WWJ," Gilmore stated, "and that the letters WWJ and *Detroit News* are synonymous." Even in cases where the call letters were not an acronym, the announcement clearly connected the station to the newspaper, creating a kind of brand identity for the radio sound. What these strategies allowed newspapers to do was to give the impression that their stations were related to established providers of news and information. As early radio listeners explored the dial for new sounds, what they often heard were the names of newspapers.[6]

As newspapers strove to connect their radio sound to their printed pages and create a common identity that encompassed both media, they were exploring ways of using radio as a way to increase the overall public presence of their companies. In some cases, successful strategies were developed from adaptation to accidental circumstances. In Atlanta in late 1922, for example, what became a huge fire broke out in the city's downtown area near the *Atlanta Journal*'s building while in-house station WSB was broadcasting its evening music program. Station announcer Lambdin Kay stopped the music and began narrating the scene, in the process providing a live news report of unfolding events more than a decade before this became a common radio practice. The station earned praise from the city's fire chief for quickly alerting residents to the fire and from other newspapers for its news reporting, as the *Philadelphia Inquirer* later reported that it learned about the event not through the "more conventional medium of the telegraph instrument," but from a "speaking voice" that "came floating through the air, a distance of approximately 760 miles." Other newspapers around the country covered the story using WSB's broadcast as the source, and the event ultimately provided an early demonstration of the news reporting capabilities of a medium that could instantly reach a mass audience from a single transmitter. The *Kansas City Star*, a paper that had started broadcasting in May 1922, wrote the day after the fire that "radio 'beat the world' last night as a medium for broadcasting news."[7]

If Kay's broadcast over WSB demonstrated the news reporting potential of radio in urgent circumstances, newspapers also proved adept at finding appealing content under more ordinary conditions. By virtue of established reputations in their communities, many newspapers were connected to local institutions such as symphonies, universities, churches, and sports teams, and were thus well positioned to broadcast interesting events. Edwin Lloyd Tyson, a teen radio enthusiast who went to work at WWJ, recalled how he used the local prestige of the *News* when he negotiated with Detroit Tigers owner Frank Navin to broadcast the team's games in 1927. Tyson convinced Navin that the broadcasts would not adversely affect the Tigers' attendance, and soon WWJ was the "first station to broadcast a full baseball schedule of any league team over the whole year." Newspapers were also able to lure public figures onto the air with the promise of additional press coverage. WWJ's Rex White recalled that he would always "watch the news columns; and if someone was in town, a scientist for instance, or a great artist or musician—anyone of any note—I would try to contact them and persuade them to come over and do something on the radio." White attracted potential guests with the promise that an appearance on WWJ would give them extra publicity, as the paper would report on it as well. This early form of multimedia marketing appealed to many potential guests, though White remarked that "nearly all of them" were "in a state of nerves" in the unfamiliar surroundings of a 1920s broadcast studio. At a time when finding programming was a major challenge for all broadcasters, newspapers held an advantage as they had extensive experience finding content to fill their printed columns, and many readily drew upon this experience to fill time on their stations.[8]

Newspapers were also well suited for broadcasting because they were already in the business of selling information. One of the most pressing problems facing all pioneer broadcasters was the fact that radio broadcasting could be a costly endeavor showing few signs of generating any revenue. Someone involved with each early station had to have the money and resources to build and maintain a studio, employ a staff, and create programming. This process could often prove costly, and some stations in the early 1920s reported spending $50,000 annually (about $520,000 in 2009 dollars) on developing stations that were returning only a fraction of that investment, at best. In the case of WWJ, setting up a station and making the early broadcasts in 1920 and 1921 cost the paper about $9,000 total (about $90,000 in 2009), and expenses soared to $80,000 in 1922 (about $850,000 in 2009) as the station began expanding its facilities and programming. The station ultimately operated at a loss until 1930, and one WWJ staffer estimated that the total expenditures during the decade prior to the station becoming profitable were $500,000 (about $5.1 million in 2009). Before broadcasters learned to use paid advertisements to generate revenue in the mid-1920s, operating a station was an expensive activity the main commercial benefit of which was to promote the broadcasters' other business. Radio manufacturers (the largest group of station owners in the 1920s) like Westinghouse and Zenith were willing to tolerate operating losses from their stations since they were offset by enormous profits from radio set sales. Department stores were similarly active as early broadcasters as they used their stations to attract and inform potential customers about the radio sets and equipment that they had for sale, and to advertise for the store itself.[9]

Newspapers were some of the few other parties involved in early broadcasting that had both the capital and self-interest to operate a broadcasting station in this business climate. In many ways, newspapers had the greatest need for radio given the more direct influence that radio might have on the newspaper business than on others. Newspapers were not in the business of selling radio sets nor did they operate retail establishments selling other kinds of goods. Newspapers sold information in the form of print, and radio offered the chance to extend and expand this business through the use of sound. In the case of the *Detroit News*, WWJ's Herbert Ponting stated, broadcasting was a "promotional event to attract the attention of the readers of the *News* and the people of Detroit to what the *News* was doing," and the paper searched for ways to expand its listening audience.[10] Quality factory-made radio receivers were expensive and not widely available in the early 1920s, and the *News* printed numerous articles instructing readers how to build radio sets.[11] The paper also developed outreach programs with potential listeners to introduce them to radio, including hosting local high school students on Saturday mornings to teach them how to make receiving equipment.[12] WWJ's promotional utility soon stretched far beyond the limits of metropolitan Detroit as its signal traveled to a much wider listening audience. By 1922, the station had received letters from across North

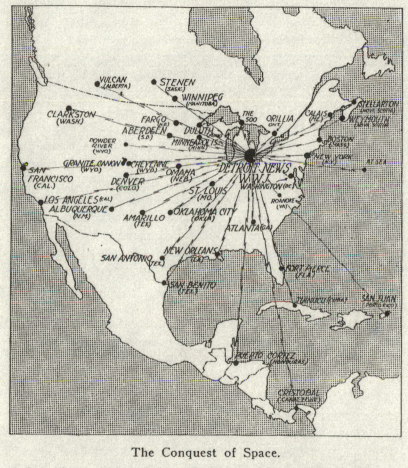

The Conquest of Space.

A few of the remote points which have heard WWJ Broadcasts.

Figure 3. "The Conquest of Space." Radio staff of the Detroit News, *WWJ— The Detroit News: The History of Radiophone Broadcasting by the Earliest and Foremost of Newspaper Stations; Together with Information on Radio for Amateur and Expert* (Detroit: Evening News Association, 1922), 11.

and Central America from listeners who had tuned in its signal. The creation of this more widely dispersed listening audience was not immediately profitable for the *Detroit News*, but it demonstrated an intriguing strategy for local newspapers to expand their reach. Through radio, a local newspaper might cultivate a regular regional, national, and even international presence.[13]

Like the *Detroit News*, the *Chicago Daily News* operated its station, WMAQ, with a similar mixture of experimentation and self-promotion, but it demonstrated some key differences in its organizational structure. While the *Detroit News* began broadcasting at the behest of its owner, William E. Scripps, the impetus at the *Daily News* came from managers and midlevel employees working within an emerging corporate structure in which salaried employees took advantage of entrepreneurial opportunities that the enterprise afforded them and helped their newspaper diversify into new media.[14] At the *Daily News*, the catalyst was William S. Hedges, a newspaper correspondent who later became one of the most significant corporate executives in American broadcasting. Hedges had worked for the paper beginning in 1915, and recalled that he was summoned into news editor Henry Justin Smith's office one day in the early 1920s and informed that he had been put "in charge of the radio activities" of the newspaper. When Hedges inquired about the specifics of his new job, Smith replied simply that it involved "anything that you think we should do in the field of radio." Hedges began writing a column in the *Daily News* devoted to "telling readers how to make their own sets" and keeping them apprised of new technological and programming developments.[15]

Hedges quickly sensed greater opportunities for the paper and went to Walter Strong, then the business manager and later the publisher of the paper, to suggest that they should not "be using all our good space in the paper talking about someone else's radio station." Strong agreed, and the *Daily News* partnered with the owners of Chicago's Fair Department Store, which had some wireless equipment left over from pre-World War I experimental transmissions. Station WMAQ began broadcasting in April 1922. Like WWJ, WMAQ groped for appealing programming to air and found that the newspaper provided an ideal source. Staffer Judith Waller recalled that programming was a question of "getting what you could get," and admitted that she often had *Daily News* columnists give talks to fill airtime. Waller also regularly visited "music schools, and lyceums, Chautauqua agencies and places of that kind," asking them to come on the radio and "offering them some publicity in the paper" in return. By 1924, William S. Hedges was confident that WMAQ had developed into a beneficial adjunct to the *Daily News*, as he told the magazine *Radio News* that radio helped the paper with the "creation of good will, that intangible, yet nevertheless invaluable asset for quasi-public institutions, such as newspapers . . . Dollars may not directly follow from the pleasures experienced by listeners to programs broadcasted by newspapers, but the feeling of friendliness is there, and the friendship of the masses makes strength for the newspaper." Even though the station was not yet profitable, Hedges felt that it was paying for itself with the promotional work that it did, as the "radio broadcasting station of the newspaper pours inoffensively its name into the willing ears of thousands of listeners."[16]

Executives at the burgeoning broadcast networks took note of WMAQ's success, and the station became one of the National Broadcasting Company's first network affiliates in 1927, an arrangement that allowed the station to become profitable for the first time. WMAQ also experienced a bit of luck in its quest for programming, as the station was the beneficiary of the *Chicago Tribune*'s decision to let Freeman Gosden and Charles Correll leave the *Tribune*-owned WGN with their nationally popular program *Sam 'n' Henry*. After a contract dispute with WGN in 1928, Gosden and Correll signed with the rival *Daily News*, changed their show's name to *Amos 'n' Andy*, and soon extended the program into a long-running national hit that became one of the most important and controversial programs in radio history.[17]

The *Tribune*'s loss of Gosden and Correll was one of the few setbacks the paper suffered in its early years of broadcasting as it sought to compete with its print rivals over the airwaves. As Robert McCormick explained to Hulbert Taft, the editor and publisher of the *Cincinnati Post*, the *Tribune* began broadcasting for three primary reasons: "To promote the *Tribune* . . . 'To sit in the game' since it is our business to keep out in front in a medium which has such a close relationship to the newspaper . . . [and] Because the other newspapers in Chicago either own or operate radio stations or are closely identified with radio stations." Radio changed the nature of competition in the newspaper business as rivalries previously based around the circulation of the printed page shifted into newer media. The *Tribune* had long been immodestly describing itself as the "World's Greatest Newspaper" and took advantage of the fact that stations east of the Mississippi River began their call letters with "W" rather than "K." Soon after it began broadcasting in 1924, the paper was able to transfer this slogan onto the radio after successfully requesting from the Department of Commerce that it be given the call letters WGN, the acronym for "World's Greatest Newspaper."[18]

The *Tribune* spared few expenses broadcasting a regular programming schedule as well providing radio coverage of popular public events that would attract wide audiences. Between 1924 and 1930, in fact, the company spent $1.5 million (about $15 million in 2009) on radio. In 1924, WGN began broadcasting the games of the local baseball teams, the Cubs and White Sox, and in October aired a live broadcast of the Illinois-Michigan football game. The following year, the station broadcast the Rose Bowl, Kentucky Derby, and Indianapolis 500, among other events.[19] Perhaps the most famous of WGN's early broadcasts was its coverage of the Scopes trial in 1925. John T. Scopes, a Tennessee biology teacher arrested for teaching the theory of evolution in a public school classroom, went on trial in July in a case that became one of the defining events of the decade. The Scopes trial, WGN officials believed, offered the station a chance to cover a legal proceeding that elicited great public

Figure 4. William Jennings Bryan at the trial of John T. Scopes. The WGN microphones are in the foreground and to Bryan's left. W. C. Robinson Collection of Scopes Trial Photographs, circa 1925, MS-1091, Folder 1, University of Tennessee Libraries, Knoxville, Special Collections. Used with permission.

fascination and presented the possibility of great oratory from William Jennings Bryan and Clarence Darrow. WGN set up microphones in the courtroom and obtained an exclusive wire connection back to Chicago, where it used its powerful transmitter to broadcast the proceedings of the trial across the country. As the hundreds of print reporters on site transmitted by telegraph what were estimated to be 150,000 to 200,000 words each day to their home newspapers, WGN broadcast live courtroom proceedings for the first time in American history, including Darrow's now legendary examination of Bryan as a witness for the prosecution. Tragically, no recordings of any of the broadcasts have surfaced, but in photographs on the silent pages of newspapers and magazines, the WGN microphone is present in the frame, providing a sign that events in the Dayton, Tennessee, courtroom were being sent live across the country. The WGN microphone was also the mark of a brand and an announcement that the self-proclaimed "World's Greatest Newspaper" was bringing the news to the people over the new medium of radio. Newspapers, the WGN microphone signaled, were present at and instrumental in the creation of American broadcasting.[20]

Throughout the formative period of American broadcasting, newspapers were instrumental in developing radio into a viable medium with appealing programming. As part of the process of protecting their businesses from new competition, newspapers also promoted themselves to the American people as high-quality broadcasters and as known entities in an unknown new media environment. Some of this rhetoric was sincere and some of it was blatant self-promotion, but at a moment when radio's future and effects were uncertain, this rhetoric was successful with both ordinary Americans and broadcast regulators. Newspapers as broadcasters promoted not just themselves, but also their own ideas about what respectable broadcasting might sound like.

Promoting the Desirable Class of Broadcasters

Radio's first decade coincided with the end of a period that saw the creation of a mass consumer society in the United States. Between the 1880s and the 1920s, Americans found themselves both able to purchase a vastly greater array of consumer goods and confronted with increasingly voluminous and sophisticated advertising. Many came to shop more often in department stores and to purchase more nationally branded goods. Radio offered intriguing new ways to reach consumers through broadcast advertising, but finding ways to do this effectively and profitably was for broadcasters an occasionally perilous process. Radio carried the voices of the public directly into the home, and many station owners were wary of angry responses from listeners if messages were not calibrated properly to have what could be understood as a family appeal. As a new and influential component of a consumer society, American broadcasting grew throughout the 1920s into a highly profitable industry, largely on the sale of time for advertisements. Station owners were ecstatic when they could turn radio into a profitable endeavor, but as they did this many were also faced with substantial public criticism of their commercials.[21]

American social thought in the 1920s was rife with fears that the country was steadily and sadly becoming an advertising-saturated consumer society and those hoping to profit through commercials thus faced some serious challenges. In March 1925, pioneer radio engineer Lee De Forest remarked that radio advertising was "nauseating and vulgar," and he advocated public opposition to it. That same year, a New York congressman suggested that legislation should be enacted to make radio advertising illegal. Newspapers involved in broadcasting thus faced something of a quandary, as they had to find ways to generate profits with radio without sullying their self-styled reputations as community-oriented institutions and to balance commercialism and respectability on the air.[22]

A large part of the solution that they arrived at involved setting what newspaper representatives believed were higher standards for advertisements, both in terms of the types of products for sale and the tone of the sales pitches. Judith Waller recalled that operating WMAQ as part of the *Chicago Daily News* meant that the station could only air advertisements that reflected positively on the owner, and the station thus refused to accept spots for patent medicines or liquor. This was a practice that Waller and other representatives of newspaper-owned radio stations claimed was not followed by all broadcasters. In 1929, *St. Louis Post-Dispatch* publisher Joseph Pulitzer, Jr., implemented strict standards for accepting advertisements on the paper's station KSD, hoping to set an example that others might follow in approving their advertising. The *Detroit News* had similar policies and often portrayed itself as a check on what its staffers claimed was the rampant commercialization of radio broadcasting. WWJ employee Edwin Tyson stated that the *Detroit News* always asserted control over radio advertising lest its reputation be tarnished by what staffers and many listeners felt were tawdry advertisements on other commercial stations. Tyson stated that the paper exerted "absolute control over the type of advertising taken and the kinds of products promoted." Sponsors were required to submit advertisements for review, and the paper routinely rejected ads. "The station has objected to a number of things," Tyson stated. "There's been a lot of business that has not been accepted just on that account. Then the sponsor either has to modify his announcements, or get off."[23]

Many of these claims were self-serving and the newspaper-owned stations' attitudes toward advertising were by no means entirely altruistic, though publishers were fond of describing their motivations in that way. Many publishers who had taken to commercial broadcasting found their practices assailed by their corporate brethren. *Editor & Publisher*, the leading newspaper trade journal, constantly criticized radio advertising, editorializing in October 1924 that there was a "legitimate place in the scheme of life for the home radio. Plainly its function is not as an advertising medium." In 1925, the magazine devoted its cover story to the issue of whether it was "good business and good public policy" for a newspaper-owned radio station to sell time for advertisements. After surveying a "fair cross-section of the thought of newspaper executives," the great majority of whom stated that they were opposed to the practice, the magazine suggested that aspiring publisher-broadcasters take great care and proceed cautiously if they chose to sell advertising. While the feature article's criticisms of commercial radio were rather muted, the accompanying editorial was far less ambivalent and conciliatory, calling radio advertising a "stunt performance," remarking that some of it was "very crude," and concluding that "raw radio broadcasting will ultimately disgust the average listener."[24]

Critiques of radio's commercialism intersected with several other strands of press criticism that were being articulated by some of America's leading journalists and intellectuals in the 1920s. Radio broadcasting emerged at a particularly anxious moment in the history of the American newspaper, as publishers and journalists were being subjected to unprecedented levels of public scrutiny in the period immediately following World War I. Among the most high profile of these critics was Upton Sinclair, a journalist, novelist (his widely influential *The Jungle* was published in 1906, galvanizing public opinion as the federal government debated the legislation that became the Pure Food and Drug Act), and activist (a longtime socialist, he ran a controversial but ultimately unsuccessful campaign for governor of California in 1934). In 1920, Sinclair published *The Brass Check*, a scathing indictment of what he called a "class-owned press, representing class-interests, protecting class-interests with entire unscrupulousness, and having no conception of the meaning of public welfare." One historian notes that the book was "Sinclair's biggest hit since *The Jungle*," and it sold over 150,000 copies to a public receptive to criticism of the press after World War I.[25]

In the 1920s, newspapers defended themselves from these sorts of criticisms by developing self-promotional campaigns touting their public service and objective reporting, in the process presenting themselves as stable and trustworthy institutions in a media environment that seemed in flux in the 1920s. Newspapers across the country claimed historical connections to the communities and regions where their papers circulated and asserted that they had long taken prominent roles in civic affairs and that they knew best what their communities wanted. Newspapers claimed, in short, to be the best possible class of broadcasters, and they readily absorbed radio into these ongoing

Figure 5. WTMJ transmitter, 1929. Records of the Milwaukee Journal Stations, Milwaukee Manuscript Collection, Golda Meir Library, University of Wisconsin-Milwaukee, Box 3, Folder 7. Copyright 2009 Journal Sentinel, Inc., reproduced with permission.

Figure 6. "First by Merit." WTMJ transmitter, 1929, detail.

public relations efforts. This ideology was exemplified when the *Milwaukee Journal* built a tall radio transmitter for its station WTMJ just west of the city. The sign at the base of the structure, located on a major interstate road, read "First By Merit."

These campaigns appeared throughout the country in the 1920s as newspapers moved into radio broadcasting, and by the end of the decade they had proven successful in many areas. In Buffalo, New York, the *Buffalo Evening News* portrayed its entry into broadcasting as an attempt to break up the monopoly that local evangelist Clinton H. Churchill held over the local airwaves. Churchill began broadcasting in 1925 with station WKBW (the call letters stood for Well Known Bible Witness) and by 1929 had formed the Buffalo Broadcasting Corporation, consolidated his ownership of four of the five local stations, and become the dominant broadcaster in the city. (The fifth station Churchill did not own was a marginal 100–watt outlet that was almost entirely ignored in press coverage of and federal hearings about broadcasting in Buffalo.) *News* employee Joseph Haeffner later recalled that the paper began receiving letters from local citizens claiming that Churchill's stations had "too many commercials," ignored local concerns, and generally provided poor service. The newspaper began a campaign to "obtain its own station and to break what it called a monopoly in the Buffalo broadcasting field," and in 1929 the *News* applied to the Federal Radio Commission (FRC) for a license to broadcast over one of the frequencies currently used by the Buffalo Broadcasting Corporation. Representatives from the paper went to Washington, D.C., for hearings on 31 October, assuming that the matter would be a one-day affair. Instead, Haeffner recalled, the hearings "extended into six days and attracted national attention." Alfred Kirchhofer, a longtime *News* employee, recalled that the paper received a great deal of support for its application because of "the promise that the *News* would try to introduce the standards of its newspaper operation into the radio field in Buffalo." *Editor & Publisher* reported that the station received "100 affidavits from farm interests" in New York, and the *New York Times* reported that "Students of national radio problems" were closely monitoring the proceedings, which were the "first case . . . raising the question of monopoly, by a single corporation, of the entire radio facilities of a city." The FRC was ultimately persuaded that the *Buffalo Evening News* would be a good broadcaster, and it granted the paper a license in December 1929, in effect reducing the Buffalo Broadcasting Corporation's local holdings. *Editor & Publisher* lauded the new station (which was given the new call letters WBEN to stand for *Buffalo Evening News*) soon after for bringing a "new and a free note to an area in which all radio facilities had for some years been held and exploited by a purely commercial monopoly," and noting that this case should be an encouragement for other newspapers to follow suit. "The successful battle that the *Buffalo News* fought," the magazine argued, "should have a score of counterparts, if the newspapers do not wish to foster by neglect an instrument which has tremendous powers for good or evil in political and business affairs."[26]

Throughout the 1920s, newspapers around the country claimed that they were the best and most desirable candidates to own radio stations. In some cases, as with the *Milwaukee Journal*'s roadside signage, these were public proclamations. In others, such as in Buffalo, newspapers promoted themselves in official settings to obtain radio licenses. In all cases, newspapers promoted themselves as the most ethical, community-oriented, and civically responsible parties on the air, and they proudly touted their institutional histories and their records of community service as evidence to back up these claims. Increasingly, these campaigns proved successful in justifying and even encouraging newspaper participation in radio, both to the public and to skeptical publishers and, just as importantly, to those shaping the emerging regulatory policy for radio. As the government struggled to determine how to allocate scarce radio frequencies in the mid-1920s—a process of considering in practice who really were the most desirable station owners—newspapers were among the key parties involved in the legal cases and congressional debates that led to the creation of modern broadcast regulation.

Not All Can Have a Station

All who wish to be broadcasters cannot do so. Broadcasting is a governmentally granted and revocable privilege, and there have always been more aspiring broadcasters than there are authorized broadcasters. The basic structures of this regulatory system were put in place when Congress passed the Radio Act of 1927, which declared the airwaves public property that would be licensed to private users for fixed, renewable terms. The 1927 Act was a necessary revision of the Radio Act of 1912, a law that had been passed four months after the *Titanic* sank amid widespread allegations that interference from thousands of amateur radio operators had prevented the ship's distress calls from being heard by other vessels in nearby waters. The 1912 Act required all wireless operators to obtain licenses from the Department of Commerce but initially allocated the majority of spectrum space to military and commercial users making direct point-to-point wireless transmissions. When stations like WWJ, WGN, and WTMJ began building powerful transmitters that could broadcast great distances in the early 1920s, the limited amount of space that they shared soon proved inadequate.[27]

Herbert Hoover, then secretary of the Commerce Department, searched for an "associative" solution that would provide the basis for a regulatory system built through public-private cooperation. In radio as with other industries, Hoover believed that economic development could best be achieved by using the federal government to promote voluntary cooperation among industrial leaders. To this end, he held four National Radio Conferences between 1922 and 1925 that brought together broadcasters, government officials, and other experts to craft a solution to allocating the spectrum. Radio raised a series of new regulatory questions, and representatives from established and aspiring participants in the new industry strove to ensure that regulatory solutions were as favorable to their interests as possible.

Representatives from newspapers were actively involved in each conference and proved highly influential in shaping the discussions and policy recommendations. Publicly and privately, many newspapers pledged their assistance to Hoover and, in terms supportive to the point of being sycophantic, portrayed themselves as both Hoover's allies and the sort of broadcasters that Hoover should want to encourage. For the publishers who had already started public relations campaigns to tout their public service and profess their desirability, these conferences offered a chance for them to make these claims in policy circles at the moment when all of the fundamental questions in radio law were open for debate.[28]

In his opening statement at the First National Radio Conference in February 1922, Herbert Hoover remarked that radio was "one of the most astounding things that has come under my observation of American life," and he asserted that it was "inconceivable that we should allow so great a possibility for service, for news, for entertainment, for education, and for vital commercial purposes, to be drowned in advertising chatter." In response, newspapers touted their abilities to broadcast according to Hoover's high standards. At the conference, the *Detroit News* actively tried to present itself in terms that comported to Hoover's hopes for radio. The paper sent as its representative Frank Doremus, who had just finished his fifth term as a congressman from Michigan and who in 1923 became the mayor of Detroit. "A newspaper," Doremus remarked, "bears an intimate relationship to the community it serves. I doubt if you could find an agency anywhere equipped with better facilities to handle the broadcasting service than the modern American newspaper." Responding directly to Hoover's desire to keep the balance between commercialism and public service in favor of the latter, Doremus stated that there was a "very radical distinction" between newspapers and other sorts of broadcasters. In the case of the *News*, he claimed, the paper "gets nothing out of it . . . except as it may increase the public good will" toward it. "I think I can speak for the newspapers of America," Doremus concluded, in asking "that we be unmolested and permitted to continue what we really believe to be a meritorious public service."[29]

At the Second National Radio Conference a year later, the Commerce Department welcomed newspapers' further input. *Editor & Publisher* noted that "Representatives of twelve newspapers attended the conference as delegates and the newspaper viewpoint and the needs of the newspaper broadcasting station played an important role in the agreement reached by the Conference for voluntary cooperative action designed to eliminate confusion and congestion in the air." *Kansas City Star* radio editor Leo Fitzpatrick (the

paper-owned station WDAF) played a particularly active role at the conference and was a key member of the committee that drafted the new policy
recommendations that came out of the conference.[30]

Newspaper representatives increased their participation at the Third National Radio Conference in 1924, as Fitzpatrick was joined by Lambdin Kay
of the *Atlanta Journal*, Walter Strong of the *Chicago Daily News*, and Joseph
Knowland of the *Oakland Tribune*, all of whom played substantial roles in
framing policy discussions. In his opening statement to the third conference,
Hoover acknowledged the need to "classify and study the ownership" of radio
stations to better understand the industry. Noting that concentration of media
ownership was a widespread public concern, that preliminary estimates were
that newspapers were the second largest group of commercial station owners
after radio set manufacturers, and that he had recently received "thousands
of letters from men, women, and children all over the country" expressing
in various ways that they "fear a monopoly of the air," Hoover again stressed
that he would work to prevent this. Radio, Hoover remarked, "is free to-day,
and free it will remain. There is no man nor body of men strong enough to
monopolize it even if there was any desire to do so."[31]

Newspapers through aggressive self-promotion succeeded in obscuring
the fact that their entrance into broadcasting might create undue media concentration. As Joseph Knowland remarked at the Third National Radio Conference, newspapers with radio stations were "anxious, through the use of the
public press, and willing through the use of the public press, which is a power
throughout the nation, to aid you, in cooperating in every way possible . . . to
solve amicably the problems which face the American people in this new
radio development." American newspapers, Knowland claimed, especially
"those who are conducting newspaper stations," were "willing and anxious, in
every way possible, to cooperate in the proper solution."[32] This sort of rhetoric
was never uniformly successful, as some, most prominently organized labor,
vigorously protested against newspaper ownership of radio. It was, however,
successful in deflecting most criticism and in keeping newspapers from being
considered monopolists in radio. Throughout early debates about broadcast
regulation, newspapers remained highly influential in the most important
policymaking circles, and were a welcome group of participants at the Fourth
National Radio Conference in 1925.[33]

Through the four conferences, Hoover supervised a debate over a policy
to allocate the radio spectrum in a way that was efficient and at the same time
promoted what he believed to be quality radio service for the American

people. With more aspiring broadcasters than available stations, however, Hoover had difficulty bringing order to the airwaves, as some station owners refused to abide by the rules of the Commerce Department, whose actual authority to regulate broadcasting under the Radio Act of 1912 was open to debate. Some papers responded to this gap in authority with ingratiating statements pledging assistance, hoping to sway regulations that way from within the context of official Department of Commerce debates.

Other papers were less cooperative, though their actions were no less influential on the development of federal radio policy. Some station owners ignored or challenged Hoover and the Commerce Department and began broadcasting on frequencies other than those set aside by the government. Others started broadcasting on frequencies so close to existing stations that many listeners could get nothing but static interference on their sets. Still others began broadcasting at such high wattages that they blotted out all other stations in the area. As these rogue broadcasters wreaked havoc on the airwaves, Hoover tried in vain to police individual offenders but found his legislative authority challenged and finally overturned in three legal cases in the 1920s, all of which involved stations associated with metropolitan newspapers. The presence of newspapers in this litigation attests both to their level of involvement in radio broadcasting and the tenacity with which they held their positions in the new industry.

The first major decision against Hoover came in the 1923 *Intercity* case, a matter that stemmed from radio transmissions by the Intercity Radio Company, a New York enterprise partnered with William Randolph Hearst's newspapers. In 1921, Intercity built a powerful station in lower Manhattan that it used to receive news directly via wireless from Europe that could then be forwarded to other stations owned by the company in Detroit, Cleveland, and Chicago. The power and location of the Intercity operation proved to be highly disruptive and caused so much interference that it made it hard for most listeners in the New York area to pick up any other transmissions on their sets. The Commerce Department revoked the license, a move that Intercity challenged and won on appeal, the court asserting that Hoover's duty to issue licenses to all aspiring broadcasters was "mandatory" regardless of the potential interference that their transmitters might cause. In effect, the court's decision raised significant doubts about whether the Commerce Department could deny any broadcaster a license, even for technologically necessary reasons.[34]

Intercity was soon followed by a case involving WJAZ, a station owned by the Zenith Corporation that had been broadcasting part-time on a frequency it shared with stations in Cincinnati and Denver. In 1925, Zenith sold a partial ownership in the station to the *Chicago Herald Examiner* and began clamoring for a full-time license. Throughout this period, Eugene McDonald, president of Zenith and one of the founders of the National Association of Broadcasters, became increasingly frustrated with Commerce Department policy and its effects on his station. After *Intercity* established that Hoover could not deny licenses, McDonald seized the opportunity to challenge the Commerce Department's authority to assign wavelengths as well. McDonald wrote to the Commerce Department that his newspaper competitors, the *Chicago Daily News* and the *Chicago Tribune*, both had full-time stations and that WJAZ should be given the same privilege. "It is obvious that we cannot adequately serve the public" given the existing part-time, shared frequency arrangement, McDonald told the Department, which denied his requests. In January 1926, McDonald grew exasperated at these denials and WJAZ simply began broadcasting at a different frequency that was at the time reserved exclusively for Canadian broadcasters. The Commerce Department tried to stop Zenith and the *Herald Examiner* but lost in court. The decision cut to the heart of the Commerce Department's authority, as it stipulated that the Department had no power under the Radio Act of 1912 to assign frequencies or specify what hours stations could broadcast. Radio was soon engulfed in a situation that *Editor & Publisher* described as "anarchy" and "chaos," as stations jumped all over the dial in the wake of the decision, and many listeners were frustrated throughout 1925 and 1926 by continual interference and poor reception.[35]

The third and final court decision limiting the Commerce Department's authority came in a 1926 case involving the *Chicago Tribune*. The *Tribune*-owned station WGN broadcast on 990 kHz and had aired programming that the paper claimed was of a consistently "high-class character" and that had "built up a good will with the public." In the process, the company had "enhanced the value of the newspaper and increased the profits" through WGN, and it saw the radio station as an integral part of its business. In September 1926, Louis Guyon, the owner of station WGES, moved his transmitter from suburban Oak Park to a downtown Chicago dancehall that he owned and began broadcasting at 950 kHz. This not only caused signal interference with WGN's broadcasts but also attracted unintentional listeners to WGES who thought they were tuning in to WGN, and the *Tribune* saw this as a violation of what its management believed were the property rights that it had earned for its station. The paper filed a suit in state court alleging that WGES had "interfered with and destroyed" WGN's broadcasting as listeners "have been unable to hear the programs" because of interference. If the court did not force WGES to move, the *Tribune* claimed, the upstart station would not only "work incalculable damage and injury to the good will" of WGN, but would actually "injure the circulation . . . so far as its newspaper is concerned and deprive it of great profits." WGN, the *Tribune* asserted, had become so intertwined with its business and its service to the people of Chicago that harm to the radio station was tantamount to harm to the newspaper.[36]

The *Tribune* gave front-page coverage to its own case, hailing its campaign to defend what it believed were the property rights of established stations and narrating every development in the proceedings. The court felt that the *Tribune* had a persuasive case and upheld its property rights claim, ruling that, "under the circumstances in this case, priority in time creates a superiority in right." The court then ordered WGES to move far enough away from WGN so as to not cause interference. The case received national publicity, and when a New York station filed a similar lawsuit almost immediately afterward, the possibility of a property rights system emerging in radio pushed members of Congress to step in to create a stable system of radio regulation.[37]

Congress had been debating the issue of radio regulation throughout the 1920s, often animated by concerns about the monopolization of the airwaves. The limited number of radio frequencies meant that, unlike newspaper publishing, radio broadcasting might come to be dominated by a small group of owners, with critics and competitors excluded from the air and unable to start outlets of their own. In order to prevent this from happening, some believed that they had to craft a policy to allocate the spectrum in a way that discouraged concentration of broadcast ownership. Attorney Morris Ernst put the issue plainly to the Interstate Commerce Committee in 1926. "There is here a unique situation," he claimed. "You have got a limited territory to divide. In the newspaper game you have not got that problem at all." Congress could not create a radio law "with no limitation on the number of stations" that one corporation could own, as to do so would be "putting into the hands of the men who have the stations a power infinitely greater than the power of the newspaper. Any man can start a newspaper and develop his public if he has the ingenuity and the money to run his paper." This was simply not the case in radio, Ernst argued.[38]

Many policymakers shared Ernst's understanding of the newspaper as an analogy and used it as an example to demonstrate the stakes of the debates over radio legislation.[39] Representative Luther Johnson, a Texas Democrat, argued that the government urgently needed to prevent radio monopolies in order to promote democracy on the airwaves. "For publicity is the most powerful weapon that can be wielded in a Republic, and when such a weapon is placed in the hands of one, or a single selfish group is permitted to . . . acquire ownership and dominate these broadcasting stations throughout the country, then woe to those who dare to differ with them." Johnson pointed out that, even if "some trust or combination" bought up every existing newspaper in the country, "independent and competing" newspapers could still be established. The same was not true in radio, since if the "necessarily limited" number of frequencies was monopolized in the hands of a few owners, "then the public will be helpless to establish others."[40]

What united Ernst and Johnson was the belief that if radio frequencies were not specifically protected from monopolization, large corporations could, and perhaps would, eventually come to control all of them, to the detriment of the public. The monopoly of radio in a small number of private hands, they believed, was a dangerous concentration of political and economic power, and what they advocated was strict federal oversight and explicit antimonopoly provisions. In this way, they believed, radio station ownership could be kept diffused and democratic.[41]

Newspapers were important not only as analogies for understanding the political significance of radio but also as participants in legislative debates. Publishers curried favor with Congress as aggressively as they had with Hoover during the Radio Conferences, and the American Newspaper Publishers Association (ANPA) had representatives at virtually all the significant congressional hearings on broadcasting. More importantly and influentially, newspapers also led what became the major organizational campaign to shape the emerging regulatory structure. *Chicago Daily News* publisher Walter Strong became chairman of the National Radio Coordinating Committee (NRCC), an organization with representatives from all the major trade groups involved in broadcasting: the National Association of Broadcasters, Radio Manufacturers Association, Federated Radio Trade Association, National Electrical Manufacturers Association, American Newspaper Publishers Association, Radio Magazine Publishers Association, American Radio Relay League, and Newspaper Broadcasters Committee. Of all of the various industry groups represented by this organization, Strong as a publisher-broadcaster emerged unanimously as the authoritative figure among and public representative of the broadcasting industry, and his subsequent lobbying was intended to continue the project he began during the Radio Conferences: cooperate with lawmakers and make newspapers seem to be part of the solution to radio regulation, not part of the problem.

Press coverage of the ongoing debates about radio regulation consistently cited the publisher-headed NRCC as the leading industry authority. In late 1926, the *New York Times* gave front-page coverage to an NRCC report imploring Congress to reach a regulatory solution, as "further delay in dealing with the radio problem will jeopardize a national industry involving $600,000,000 a year and disappoint 20,000,000 people in a very vital and personal family interest."[42]

Within months, the campaign that Walter Strong directed proved largely successful in its policy aims. As federal officials debated the legislation, they had various options to consider. These included proposals to expand the Commerce Department's authority, to create a private monopoly system as proposed by representatives of the communications giant American Telephone and Telegraph Company (AT&T), and to institute a publicly controlled system based on the British model, under which the federal government would operate a national radio system in the place of licensed private broadcasters. Though passage of this latter sort of legislation faced tremendous opposition, proponents of the British model tapped into a powerful current of transatlantic policy discourse in the 1920s, as American policymakers drew upon European models for solutions to domestic problems in areas as diverse as social welfare policy, urban planning, and agricultural resource management. Throughout the policymaking process, publishers and broadcasters lobbied strenuously against a federally operated radio system, and as they opposed national control of radio, newspaper publishers revived the criticisms they developed after World War I. During the war, the federal government took over all wireless transmission, an authority that secretary of the navy Josephus Daniels sought to extend after 1918. Given radio's importance to the military and to national security, Daniels believed, federal control was a better solution than allowing the industry to be developed by private or corporate interests. The press vigorously opposed Daniels's plans, which were defeated in Congress in 1919, and in the 1920s publishers and opponents of national control of radio were again successful. Adopted in other areas, European-influenced policies for broadcasting were rejected by Congress in 1927, both because of concerns about the political and constitutional implications of state-run broadcasting and because of strenuous lobbying on the part of private corporations.[43]

The law that Congress ultimately passed as the Radio Act of 1927 declared the airwaves to be public property that would be licensed to private users of specific frequencies who would have to regularly reapply to continue broadcasting. Those with more libertarian conceptions of free speech found elements to criticize in the Radio Act, as some claimed that the provisions giving the new FRC the authority to deny license renewals to broadcasters who had not operated with sufficient attention to the nebulously defined "public interest" gave the federal government too much supervisory control over broadcast content. Despite these reservations, broadcasters on the whole were satisfied with the outcome, especially given some of the other possibilities. As leaders in a variety of industries had worked with the federal government to craft regulatory policies during the Progressive Era, the owners of newspapers and radio stations cooperated with public officials to develop a radio policy that preserved the positions of the dominant private interests in broadcasting.[44]

The antimonopoly provisions in the Radio Act of 1927 ultimately created a mixed legacy. On the one hand, the Act contained explicit provisions calling for the revocation of licenses held by broadcasters found guilty of monopoly in federal court, a clear warning to corporations involved in the business of broadcasting to refrain from anticompetitive practices. It also forbade any corporation involved in the telegraph or telephone business from owning a radio station. Though not mentioning AT&T by name, the Radio Act's provision against dual ownership of a radio station and wired communication network unambiguously kept the corporation from owning a broadcast station. Looked at from one angle, the Radio Act of 1927 explicitly barred federally convicted monopolists from broadcasting and kept the country's most powerful communications company from becoming a radio broadcaster. But, on the other hand, the Radio Act's antimonopoly provisions were also written in such a way as to open the door for future consolidation in the industry. The Act in effect transferred the authority to rule on monopoly issues in broadcasting from the FRC to the courts. And, while barring AT&T and convicted monopolists from broadcasting, the Act contained no positive statements about the desire or mandate to protect diversity of station ownership, and most of the more aggressive antimonopoly sentiments of people like Morris Ernst and Luther Johnson were left out. The Radio Act excluded owners of the existing communications network infrastructure from broadcasting, but it was an inclusive policy for owners of existing and often powerful newspaper businesses. Overall, federal officials crafted a policy amenable to many of those that were already in dominant positions in broadcasting and, given the range of available policy options, the Radio Act of 1927 was both moderate in tone and appealing to existing corporate broadcasters.[45]

The eventual policy outcome reflected the desires of many newspapers. Publishers "took a hand in influencing the formulation" of the Radio Act of 1927, as one observer noted, and contributed greatly to the process of policy development. It is difficult to state with certainty that radio regulation would have placed more restrictions on broadcasters or done more to curb media consolidation if newspapers had not been as active as they were in policy debates, but judging from Walter Strong's statements, publishers warmly welcomed the outcome, as Strong publicly touted the roles played by newspaper publishers in crafting the Radio Act. Strong proudly claimed that newspapers played "an important part in shaping the destinies of the art and science of radio during the past year," and he boasted that the Radio Act "to a very large extent follows the recommendations" the NRCC had made. Other industry leaders noted this influence as well, as an executive with the National Electrical Manufacturers Association claimed that the Radio Act "embodies many of the suggestions of the National Radio Coordinating Committee and is, therefore, representative of the entire industry." Ultimately, representatives of the old medium of the newspaper were profoundly influential in shaping the new regulations that governed the new medium of radio. Radio promised much in its early years, but its development largely followed the path laid out by those with the most power, particularly the press.[46]

Entrenching Newspaper-Radio Joint Ownership

The Radio Act of 1927 was certainly not the final step in radio regulation, and both reform advocates and defenders of corporate media became increasingly active in shaping the policy direction of the new (and in its first two years, ill-funded and disorganized) FRC. Publishers continued to remain deeply involved in shaping emerging policy, often appearing before the FRC to help develop specific regulatory provisions. Walter Strong remained in regular contact with Herbert Hoover and offered unwavering support as coordinated by one of America's leading publishers. For those interested in broadcast reform, the general confusion about the new regulatory environment also opened a space for active opposition to corporate broadcasting. Antimonopolists in Congress continued to push for stronger regulations, and in 1928 House Democrat Ewin Davis, a Tennessee Representative, succeeded in getting the eponymous Davis Amendment passed, forcing the FRC to "generate a permanent and general reallocation plan that would necessitate a complete reshuffling of stations and frequency assignments" in order to equalize the number of stations available throughout the country and try and break the stranglehold that powerful urban stations held over broadcasting.[47]

The Davis Amendment might have meant that the growing broadcast reform movement had a chance at getting some of their suggestions passed. However, the FRC's selection to oversee the reallocation, Louis Caldwell, effectively mitigated that threat. Caldwell was the head of the American Bar Association's Standing Committee on Communications and, more importantly, the *Chicago Tribune*'s representative in Washington. *Tribune* publisher Robert McCormick had personally sent Caldwell to Washington to "protect the *Tribune*'s radio interests and to assist in the development of broadcast legislation and regulation," and that is exactly what he did.[48] Caldwell took a temporary leave from his position at the law firm Kirkland, Fleming, Green & Martin and took over as the first general counsel of the FRC. Caldwell did so well for the *Tribune* while on the government's payroll that M. C. Martin, one of the partners at Caldwell's firm, asked McCormick to compensate the firm for the partner fees it paid government employee Caldwell while he was not engaging private clients. Caldwell, Martin pointed out, had been "carrying out most efficiently his functions as chief counsel of the Radio Commission, during which time he has effected very constructive accomplishments for the *Tribune* which otherwise could not have been had." Caldwell was "in effect being loaned to the Federal Radio Commission by our firm for the purpose of promoting the radio interests of the *Tribune*," and Martin asserted that, "were such efforts being rendered by him as a lawyer in private practice," they "would be very productive of substantial fees." It was only fair, Martin argued, that McCormick should "at least cover the actual cost to the firm by reason of Mr. Caldwell's absence, plus a reasonable fee for accomplishment." Caldwell soon returned to private practice and went back to being paid directly by the *Tribune* for work on their behalf.[49]

While working for the FRC, Caldwell not only helped the *Chicago Tribune*'s radio business but also helped defeat the proposals of the Chicago Federation of Labor (CFL), the group that had developed one of the most vigorous critiques of corporate and newspaper domination of the airwaves in the period immediately following the passage of the Radio Act of 1927. CFL secretary Edward Nockels became organized labor's leading radio representative in the 1920s and began aggressive lobbying efforts aimed at promoting diverse ownership of radio stations.[50] In January 1929, Nockels and CFL President John Fitzpatrick pleaded to Senator Clarence Dill that something had to be done to protect radio from corporate domination. "Radio broadcasting is the most effective means known to man for influencing public opinion," Nockels and Fitzpatrick argued, but it was in danger of being monopolized by "about 25 to 30 of the great metropolitan newspapers" that were "granted licenses to operate broadcasting stations on very choice channels." The CFL was acutely conscious of this problem, representatives pointed out, as the two largest local papers, the *Chicago Tribune* and the *Chicago Daily News*, both had powerful radio stations. The CFL felt that neither paper treated labor issues with anything resembling fairness and asked Dill to help it get a full-time broadcasting license for its station WCFL, which at the time had a license to broadcast at the comparably meager power of 1,500 watts, and only during the daytime. "This is the last great public domain," the CFL asserted, and it should not be allowed to be "sucked into the maw of great metropolitan newspapers, already in uncontrolled possession of power that threatens the welfare of the country."[51]

Nockels and the CFL found bipartisan support in the Senate from Burton Wheeler, a Democrat from Montana, and Smith Brookhart, a Republican from Iowa. In the House, Representative Frank Reid of Illinois took up their cause and charged newspapers with trying to monopolize radio. "Never in the history of the Nation has there been a bold and brazen attempt to seize control of the means of communication and to dominate public opinion as is now going on in the field of radio broadcasting," Reid fulminated, and "Never in our history has an agency of the Federal Government shown such favoritism or such a crass disregard for the interests of the workingmen and women of the Nation." Newspapers were being given powerful frequencies that they could use to broadcast their views beyond their immediate localities, he claimed, while groups like the CFL were being shut out. "Metropolitan newspapers," Reid asserted, "which already have a powerful means of communication, but which are nevertheless local institutions, have been given the choicest wave lengths, with ample power and unlimited time of operation." Despite the attempts of figures like Wheeler, Brookhart, and Reid, the CFL was not ultimately able to achieve many of its goals for WCFL, nor was it able to curtail newspaper involvement in radio.[52]

In the 1920s newspapers participated actively in the creation of American broadcasting as an industry and an object of government regulation, in the process laying a foundation that would prove very difficult to dislodge or fundamentally alter in the future. Sociologist Paul Starr argues that major developments in communications present political actors with what he calls "constitutive choices" about what can be done to shape the future of new media, and that the choices made create "mechanisms of *entrenchment*" that make it very difficult to take a completely different path later. At key moments, for example the creation of early radio regulation, "ideas and culture come into play, as do constellations of power, preexisting institutional legacies, and models from other countries" in shaping possible courses of action. As Starr sees it, there are very few ruptures in media history, as these "constitutive choices" create a "cumulative, branching pattern: Early choices bias later ones and may lead institutions along a distinctive path of development." The decision to license broadcasters, for example, foreclosed the possibility of station owners obtaining permanent property rights to their frequencies. The decision to allow newspapers to own important and powerful radio stations likewise created a class of owners that would grow rapidly starting in the 1930s, and which allowed the growth and prosperity of the multimedia corporations that came to dominate the media business for decades after. Legal scholar Yochai Benkler notes that the choice of how to regulate radio was the "only serious potential inflection point, prior to the emergence of the Internet, at which some portion of the public sphere could have developed away from the advertiser-supported mass-media model," and the decisions made by policymakers on the subject of newspaper ownership of radio stations in the 1920s in many ways set the terms of the debate over the basic structures of the broadcasting industry for the rest of the century.[53]

By the end of the 1920s, newspapers had firmly entrenched themselves in broadcasting, to the point that staffers at the FRC were openly promoting the benefits of cross-ownership. As FRC attorney Ben Fisher remarked in 1930, radio had "become one of the most useful adjuncts to the newspaper," and many industry insiders hoped to see their presence in radio increase further. Journalists similarly extolled these commercial benefits of radio for newspapers. Frank Parker Stockbridge remarked that radio was a "bigger bulletin board than any newspaper office can erect on the front of its publication office. Bulletins sell papers." Newspaper ownership of radio not only made good commercial sense but also good political sense, Stockbridge argued, as the press could act as a bulwark against undue encroachment over radio content by the state. "One reason why newspapers must take over broadcasting in America," Stockbridge argued, "is to forestall government censorship." Ongoing newspaper-radio partnering was a "consummation devoutly to be wished," Stockbridge concluded, and this would ultimately "mean better programs, more intelligent advertising, and greater prosperity for the newspapers."[54]

NBC President M. H. Aylesworth offered some of the most potent endorsements of cooperation between press and radio as the 1920s drew to a close. Under Aylesworth's leadership, NBC developed a policy to "encourage the newspapers to purchase radio stations and to bring them into our networks, and in this way cooperate with the press with the hope that we would become friends and work together in our related fields of endeavor." In so doing, Aylesworth felt, broadcasters might partner with newspapers that were entering radio both out of interest and out of caution. Aylesworth delivered an ingratiating message to the American Society of Newspaper Editors in April 1930. "When we organized the National Broadcasting Company about three years ago," Aylesworth began, he was in constant contact with a "large number of newspaper men" who "formed a sort of unofficial advisory council which guided me in all matters which had to do with the relationship of broadcasting to the publications industry." By 1930, NBC had some twenty affiliates owned by newspapers. Aylesworth gave a glowing assessment of their broadcasting, and he urged his audience to expand the relationship. "Radio is here to stay," Aylesworth concluded. "It exists as a force capable of producing unlimited results by those who utilize it. It provides a listening audience which includes readers of your newspaper, and non-readers of your newspaper, as an outlet for promotion." Aylesworth implored publishers "not to worry about radio as a competitor, but to recognize in radio a powerful ally, and to take advantage of its tremendous power. We in radio are always eager to cooperate with you. We have many problems in common. We are all on the same side of the fence."[55]

Chapter 2

New Empires: Media Concentration in the 1930s

In November 1930, *Chicago Tribune* executive W. E. Macfarlane traveled to Sea Island Beach, Georgia, to address the fall convention of the American Newspaper Publishers Association. The pleasant climate did little to calm some of the assembled newspaper representatives. The U.S. economy was sliding into depression, newspapers' advertising revenues were declining, and the upstart new business of radio seemed to be capturing not just publishers' disappearing incomes but also the American popular imagination. For publishers already skittish about the country's economic situation, fears of losing money and readership were pushing some into open hostility toward broadcasting. Macfarlane went down to Georgia to tell them they had nothing to worry about. Do not fear or fight radio, he urged. Work with it, and everything would be just fine.

Macfarlane was not just a newspaperman but also the manager of WGN, the radio station owned by the *Chicago Tribune*. As the representative of a successful media corporation, Macfarlane told the assembled ANPA members that newspapers and radio were much better understood as partners, not adversaries. Macfarlane believed that the business of broadcasting "bore a striking resemblance" to the newspaper business, and he claimed that newspapers and radio were "naturally and logically supplementary to each other." Macfarlane saw the newspaper-radio partnership not just as a sound business strategy for publishers but also as something of a duty. "I believe that there is no industry better qualified to operate a successful broadcasting station than the press," Macfarlane stated. Newspapers had established relationships with their communities, and they had talent and experience "unequalled by" any other type of broadcaster that they could "put at the disposal of a station for the benefit of the public." If it were up to him to choose who should be radio broadcasters in the United States, Macfarlane stated, he had "no hesitation in saying that newspaper publishers should be preferred."[1]

Though some publishers remained anxious about radio and its effects on newspaper publishing, Macfarlane's speech represented views shared by many in the newspaper business in the formative era of American broadcasting. Papers across the country, from large metropolitan dailies to smaller local papers, had begun operating radio stations in the 1920s. Though their absolute numbers were relatively low as of 1930, the stations that were on the air played significant roles in developing the foundation of American broadcasting. These publishers developed radio into a viable commercial medium, shaped the content of early radio by developing influential programs, and helped to create the structures of American broadcast regulation. In the 1930s, this vanguard group motivated an increasingly large following of newspapers to begin radio broadcasting. After 1930, when Macfarlane gave his speech promoting radio ownership among newspapers, ownership rates went up steadily every year throughout the 1930s, and by the end of the decade newspapers owned 252 of the 770 stations on the air, almost one-third of the total (see Appendix).

Macfarlane's speech was not an immediate success in all corners of the newspaper industry. Some left his talk unpersuaded that radio was anything other than a threat to their businesses, and these publishers responded with attempts to contain broadcasting rather than exploit it. Radio, as some publishers thought of it, was enemy rather than adjunct.

These efforts at containment proved unsuccessful, however, as publishers across the country built multimedia corporations of such increasing size and influence that many began invoking the metaphor of "empire" to describe them. Karl Bickel, president of the wire service United Press, celebrated the achievements of these corporations in his 1930 book *New Empires: The Newspaper and the Radio*. "The press of America," Bickel argued, was "the greatest in the world," and he described it as an unqualified force for good in the country. "The newspaper industry is similar in many ways to the light and power business. The newspaper is a power plant. It creates an energy as real and as definite as electricity—advertising power. It sells this power just as the power plant sells its 'juice.' It offers a news service just as the power plant offers an illuminating service." Radio extended this, Bickel claimed, and would prove to be "a most decidedly favorable factor in the growth and development of the newspaper." Radio would "lift and widen the boundaries of men's minds" by exposing listeners to a host of new ideas that they would then "desire to read about" in the newspaper. Assessing newspaper-radio relations in 1930, Bickel saw nothing but promise, and he claimed that the only publishers that were agitated about radio were those that did not own a station. For those that did, "the feeling . . . is that the two can and should prove to be co-operating factors," and he envisioned a bright future for the partnership.[2]

Many Americans in the 1930s were fascinated by the increasing power of media corporations, and others also used the trope of empire to describe them. Not all, however, used it in such a positive manner as Karl Bickel. One such critic, *Ventura Free Press* publisher H. O. Davis, wrote a blistering critique of radio in 1932 entitled *The Empire of the Air: The Story of the Exploitation of Radio for Private Profit*, in which he predicted the "inevitable" drive toward "monopolistic control over broadcasting" by corporations that would "wield a power greater than that of the Caesars." Perhaps the most prominent use of the "empire" concept during this period came in 1941, when director Orson Welles opened *Citizen Kane*, a thinly veiled portrait of media mogul William Randolph Hearst, with a fictional newsreel announcing that "Kane's empire in its glory held dominion over thirty seven newspapers, two syndicates, a radio network, an empire upon an empire." This was only a slight exaggeration of Hearst's real holdings, and Welles's point was clear: during the 1930s, media moguls like Hearst built multimedia conglomerates of such power and scope that their influence seemed imperial.[3]

To some, this linking of media and the concept of empire did not just mean economic power, but also the power to shape politics and society on a mass scale. Economic historian Harold Innis, for example, saw world historical significance in the connections between communications media and political power, claiming in 1950 in *Empire and Communications* that "communication . . . occupies a crucial position in the organization and administration of government and in turn of empires and of Western civilization." For Innis, particular regimes' abilities to control the media of communication kept them in power while new forms of media posed challenges to and could hasten the decline of empire.[4]

Pioneer radio engineer Lee de Forest invoked the idea of empire to describe the power and potential of radio, claiming in his 1950 autobiography that he had "discovered an Invisible Empire of the Air, intangible, yet solid as granite, whose structure shall persist while man inhabits the planet; a global organism, imponderable yet most substantial, both mundane and empyreal; fading not as the years, the centuries fade away—an electronic fabric influencing all our thinking, making our living more noble." For critics throughout the early decades of radio, the metaphor of empire reflected the degree to which communications seemed connected to economic, political, and social power.[5]

Though the Great Depression posed serious financial challenges for American businesses of all sorts, the media industries fared well given the circumstances. Despite declines in advertising revenue, newspaper circulation continued to rise. Radio set sales increased even as the Depression deepened, and broadcasting became an increasingly powerful element in the ongoing creation of a national mass culture during the 1930s. During the Depression, the industries that Karl Bickel described as "new empires" prospered and converged into powerful multimedia corporations despite the broader economic climate. In the 1920s, newspapers had established a model for creating these sorts of enterprises, and the use of this model extended throughout the 1930s. Throughout the decade, newspapers in increasing numbers used radio to increase corporate profits and expand their public presences using multiple media. This process was not seamless, but it was unmistakable. As American culture became increasingly a mass culture in the 1930s through the press and radio, corporations developed what many saw as "new empires" that used both media to produce, disseminate, and sell that culture.[6]

Containing New Media

The stock market crash of October 1929 and the onset of the Great Depression precipitated a steep drop in newspaper advertising revenues. Some observers rightly saw this decline as symptomatic of broader economic factors, as many companies went bankrupt while others tightened promotional budgets and decreased spending on newspaper advertisements. Some publishers, however, looked at the simultaneous rise in radio advertising revenue and perceived the early stages of a major competitive threat. While newspapers' advertising revenues declined from $800 million in 1929 to $490 million in 1932 before rebounding to $600 million in 1937, radio revenues climbed steadily from $40 million in 1929 to $80 million in 1932 to $145 million in

1937. Newspapers between 1929 and 1937 experienced a 25 percent decline in advertising revenue, while radio experienced a 263 percent increase.[7]

Though newspapers remained far ahead of radio in the total amount of advertising revenue generated, many publishers found these trends deeply troubling. Trade journal *Editor & Publisher* claimed in 1931 that radio was "the greatest competitor [newspapers] have ever faced," and asserted that the industry was "being picked to pieces, unit by unit, by an integrated, centralized, vigorous radio competitor."[8] In response to this perceived new competition, publishers in the early 1930s employed a variety of tactics to compete with radio. Some papers stopped printing specialty sections devoted to the new medium. Others, like the *New York Times*, stopped publishing regular news items about radio. Many papers dropped radio program listings or demanded that stations that wanted their listings printed pay for the space like any other advertiser. In New Orleans, for example, the city's newspapers cooperated to ban free program listings beginning in June 1932. Some publishers, like William Pape of Waterbury, Connecticut, agreed to print program listings in his *Republican* and *American* only with the names of program sponsors omitted, so as to discourage advertisers from thinking that they could get their name in the paper for free by sponsoring a radio program.[9] Others pursued legal avenues to challenge radio and accused broadcasters of "pirating" news by simply reading newspaper articles over the air.[10]

By late 1932, the newspaper campaign against radio peaked in an episode known to contemporaries and historians as the Press-Radio War.[11] According to newspaper publishers, the conflict stemmed from both competition over advertising revenue and the larger struggle over which medium would be America's primary source of information. Concerned about the economics of the newspaper business and with maintaining their professional authority and prestige, some publishers repeatedly attacked the allegedly inferior news reporting done by the "Showmen who control radio." The radio coverage of the kidnapping of Charles Lindbergh's infant son in March 1932 elicited a particularly vigorous response from publishers, many of whom believed that the coverage had been irresponsible. Newspapers never would have acted as such, *Editor & Publisher* claimed. "Staffed by men selected for voice quality and program skill, the broadcasters were confronted with a flood of information, some of it palpably false, some plausible, some 'officially' vouched for and the lack of trained news judgment was often evident in its selection and presentation. Some stories circumstantially related over the air were still 'exclusive' for several days, or until the police officially denied them." These claims were to a great degree self-serving, as publishers also feared that radio coverage of significant breaking stories might lower the demand for printed extras, but they also reflected beliefs among publishers and journalists that radio was an inferior medium for news. "The lack of a permanent record," *Editor & Publisher* concluded, "often referred to in these columns as a major and inherent disability of radio, makes . . . charges easy to bring and hard to refute."[12]

This mixture of commercial concern and professional resentment motivated the Press-Radio War. The conflict culminated in late 1933 at the Biltmore Hotel in New York City, where representatives from the radio and newspaper industries gathered in December to negotiate a settlement. After two days of meetings in what one journalist called "smoke and hate-filled rooms," the groups arrived at the so-called Biltmore Agreement. The agreement created the Press-Radio Bureau, a committee with representatives from the American Newspaper Publishers Association; the press agencies United Press, Associated Press, and International News Service; the National Association of Broadcasters; and the radio networks NBC and CBS. Under the Agreement, radio stations would get two daily press reports from the wire services and would be allowed two daily five-minute news broadcasts, one in the morning and one in the evening. The morning report could not be given before 9:30 A.M., and the evening report could not be given before 9:00 P.M. The goal of the Biltmore Agreement was to limit radio's ability to compete directly with newspapers in the distribution of news, as the ANPA reported that the "bulletins will be written and broadcast in such a manner as to stimulate public interest in the reading of newspapers," which in practice meant that radio "news" consisted of announcers reading headlines and giving brief outlines of key stories.[13]

For anti-radio newspapers in the 1930s, and for a number of historians since, the Biltmore Agreement was a defining event in radio history. For newspapers that owned radio stations, however, it had little long-term significance, and their opposition to it prevented the agreement from ever attaining any lasting legitimacy. In 1931, for example, *Editor & Publisher* noted that radio station ownership had become a wedge issue in the newspaper industry and an impediment to collective action against radio by newspapers. This was "due of course to the active participation of many newspapers in the present radio systems," and the magazine claimed that there was a "sharp cleavage between newspapers which have such connections and those which have adhered strictly to the newspaper business." Once the agreement was in place, newspaper-radio combinations were among the primary agents working against the maintenance of a coalition of publishers and the main obstacles to making the pact durable.[14]

To publishers who were already broadcasting, opposition to radio seemed profoundly misguided. In one instance shortly after the 1932 presidential election, *St. Louis Post-Dispatch* publisher Joseph Pulitzer argued to L. K. Nicholson, president of the *New Orleans Times-Picayune* and a staunch opponent of news broadcasting, that it was the duty of newspapers to get breaking news like election results to the people as fast as possible, regardless of the means. "My view," Pulitzer stated, was that "the public on election night looks to the newspapers to inform it promptly as to what happened on election day." Moreover, Pulitzer claimed, the public "particularly looks to newspapers like the *Post-Dispatch* which operate radio stations to give it this information by radio," as it was news that Pulitzer believed his audience members felt they could trust. Newspapers simply could not compete with radio when it came to providing spot news reports of ongoing events, Pulitzer claimed, as their extras would be so "hastily prepared and incomplete" compared to radio broadcasts that they would only succeed in lowering the "prestige of the newspaper as a chronicle of information which the public desires and which it thinks it is entitled to hear at the earliest possible moment." Radio was here to stay as a medium for reporting the news, and trying to constrain this after the public was aware of it was for Pulitzer a futile exercise. Essentially, Pulitzer told Nicholson, "we are confronted by a condition and not a theory, and as the radio beats the newspaper extra in speed, accuracy, and public convenience, the newspaper had better utilize the radio and not permit someone else to make use of it and beat the newspaper." One of Pulitzer's executives, A. G. Lincoln, took this position a step farther, stating that he believed that "if news must be broadcast it should be broadcast by newspaper-owned stations."[15]

These sorts of attitudes circulated widely among other publishers during the period around the Biltmore Agreement. F. A. Miller, the president and editor of the *South Bend Tribune* and owner of stations WSBT and WSAM, protested to E. H. Harris, an Indiana newspaper publisher and chairman of the ANPA's radio committee, that the pact impeded newspapers like his that owned radio stations. Miller claimed that the plan was "painfully unjust" and argued that he "did not think newspapers which had had the vision to realize the importance of radio, and had invested in radio facilities, should be penalized for their foresightedness." WGN manager W. E. Macfarlane felt the same way, telling *Tribune* publisher Robert McCormick that the "regulations on broadcasting of news are going to cramp our individuality considerably," and complaining that WGN would have to broadcast news "prepared by somebody else" instead of from "our newspaper." McCormick agreed, and for those in the newspaper industry that had a station of their own, the Biltmore Agreement seemed to be punishment for having been strategic. In the face of the dissatisfaction of publishers like Joseph Pulitzer, F. A. Miller, and Robert McCormick with the Biltmore Agreement, newspapers and radio stations could never be separated with any degree of precision or stability, and the agreement ultimately never gained enough newspaper support to succeed.[16]

The Biltmore Agreement was also subject to harsh public criticism from observers who found it profoundly misguided. Volney Hurd of the *Christian Science Monitor* remarked that it was an example of a "fast machine slowing down to permit a slower machine to keep up with it, in fact, ahead of it." Senator Clarence Dill, one of the principal architects of the Radio Act of 1927 and the Communications Act of 1934, blasted the Biltmore Agreement as a "failure" in a speech to the National Association of Broadcasters in 1934. Radio listeners, Dill declared, were "disgusted with it. Most stations refuse to use it. Many newspapers say it is unsatisfactory." Ultimately, he claimed, the agreement "satisfies nobody because it flies in the face of progress."[17] Within a year of Dill's speech, the Biltmore Agreement had "gone down the chute," as journalist Isabelle Keating put it, and publishers and broadcasters across the country openly ignored it. As journalist T. R. Carskadon wrote, publishers had long "fought the bad fight, using boycotts, reprisals, intimidation, ridicule and injunctions in a relentless effort to make radio shut its many-tubed mouth, but the end is a failure." Though the Press-Radio Bureau existed for three more years as an ineffective and widely derided organization, it was ultimately far less important than another form of ongoing press-radio cooperation: newspapers purchasing or starting their own radio stations.[18]

Adapting New Media

For many newspapers, the Press-Radio War was little more than a temporary irritant, and their activities before, during, and after the episode reflected a group that was more concerned with finding ways to work with rather than against radio. In many cases, people with newspaper backgrounds actually became leaders in the radio industry, including William S. Hedges, the manager of the *Chicago Daily News* station WMAQ, who in 1928 and 1929 served two terms as president of the NAB. Hedges remained so enthusiastic about broadcasting that he built an experimental television transmitter in the *Daily News* building in 1930 to begin work in that even newer medium. Demonstrations of the benefits of newspaper-radio partnerships came with increasing frequency in the 1930s and suggested a much more significant trend in press-radio relations than some of the more bitter public aspects of the 1930s press-radio debate. Despite lingering complaints from a handful of anti-radio publishers, many in the newspaper industry saw radio as partner rather than foe in the 1930s.[19]

This cooperative relationship manifested itself in several ways as newspaper-broadcasters began developing strategies to effectively operate as a special and influential class of owners. One of the most significant forms of collective action came in negotiations with the American Society of Composers, Authors, and Publishers (ASCAP) over royalties paid for music broadcast on the air. Founded in 1914, ASCAP by the mid-1920s had negotiated agreements with motion picture producers and owners of public commercial establishments such as hotels and restaurants to collect licensing fees for the use of music written by its members. In 1922, the organization began demanding royalty payments from radio stations that played member artists' music on the air. Broadcasters, many of whom had yet to become profitable, chafed at the demands, believing that playing the music was actually free promotion for the artists. Many also worried that they would lose their audiences without playing music. According to one 1926 study, 98 percent of stations surveyed claimed that "music was their most popular kind of programming." Seeking to please their audiences without incurring extra costs, some stations refused to negotiate with ASCAP but were soon faced with copyright infringement suits from the organization. In response to the lawsuits and the possibility of greater expenses for playing music, a number of stations began organizing collectively to bargain with ASCAP and formed the National Association of Broadcasters, with William S. Hedges as their leader. The NAB and ASCAP worked out a compromise under which stations would pay variable fees based how much ASCAP music they aired, but tensions between the two organizations persisted throughout the 1920s, and many station owners remained anxious that in the future they would have to make increasingly expensive licensing payments to continue playing music under ASCAP's control. These fears proved true and in 1932, seeking additional revenue during the Great Depression, ASCAP began demanding a fixed portion of stations' revenues regardless of how much ASCAP music was aired, in effect dramatically altering its fee structure and substantially raising costs for stations playing members' music.[20]

Hoping to negotiate another compromise at a moment when the American economy was spiraling downward, H. Dean Fitzer, manager of the *Kansas City Star* station WDAF, met with ASCAP representatives in September to lobby for newspapers to get discounted licensing fees since they devoted so much coverage to artists in their pages. Fitzer argued that this was in effect additional free promotion for the music, something that newspapers should be rewarded for in return. Newspapers, Fitzer claimed, "contributed very definitely to the exploitation and sale of copyrighted music through the publishing of innumerable articles, large and small, about songs and their composers." Fitzer found ASCAP receptive to his plan and convened a meeting of representatives from eighteen newspapers that owned radio stations in Chicago on 19 October 1932 to discuss the ASCAP matter and other issues confronting them. The meeting included representatives from both large urban papers (*Milwaukee Journal, Chicago Herald Examiner, Cleveland Plain Dealer,* and *Dallas Times Herald*) and small regional papers (*Drover's Daily Journal, Janesville Gazette, Racine Journal News,* and *Harrisburg Telegram*), who agreed to establish a special trade group to bargain with ASCAP to secure a reduction in fees. The bargaining was successful, and newspaper-owned stations secured a deal to pay, as William S. Hedges reported, only two-thirds of the fees paid by stations not owned by newspapers. The negotiations in the ASCAP matter gave newspaper-owned stations substantially cheaper fees to play copyrighted music on their stations, and the financial benefits of the arrangement demonstrated to owners that they represented a separate and powerful class. To critics, it seemed like anticompetitive behavior, and the agreement earned a stern rebuke from Senator Clarence Dill, who claimed that the newspaper-owned stations now represented "special favorites of this monopolistic music organization." Dill's comments did little to deter industry representatives from pursuing additional benefits from cooperation, and in 1935 newspaper-broadcasters officially formed a trade group within the National Association of Broadcasters.[21]

As newspaper broadcasters created cooperative institutional arrangements, many also touted the benefits of joint media ownership to other publishers. At the 1933 ANPA annual meeting, Charles Webb, president of the *Asheville Citizen-Times* and owner of a radio station, stated that he believed that newspapers should "use radio to their own advantage. I know that we have done it. I know that my papers have obtained additional advertising by reason of the fact that we own and operate a radio station." Webb claimed that his paper had "increased our circulation by exploiting our newspapers over the radio," and his experience had led him to the conclusion that radio, "instead of being an enemy of newspapers, has even been a friend of newspapers." Other papers made similarly positive statements about the benefits that their newspapers had accrued from radio. Frank Jaffe of the *Des Moines Register & Tribune* claimed that the paper's circulation increased after it began broadcasting, and the paper's management believed that radio had proven itself to be "one of the best means of reaching large numbers of non-readers." The same was true in Roseburg, Oregon, as the *News-Review* found that its station KRNR (the last three call letters stood for *Roseburg News-Review*) helped increase business. Publisher Harris Ellsworth remarked that, "from the very moment we began using a consistent plan of circulation promotion on KRNR, and without using any other type of selling or promotion, our circulation began to climb."[22]

This was the case in larger cities as well, as the *Portland Oregonian, Detroit News, Milwaukee Journal, Atlanta Journal,* and *Kansas City Star* all touted the gains that they had made in circulation and advertising revenues through the use of radio. In 1935, *Dallas News* vice president Ted Dealey wrote in *Editor & Publisher* describing the paper's success with WFAA, the station that it had begun operating in 1922. Dealey claimed that his paper had long used radio as a promotional tool, and he believed that there was nothing "more natural for a forward-looking paper than to take advantage of this new method of communication and to add to its circle of readers a supplementary audience of listeners." Radio had proven financially successful for the *News,* Dealey concluded, and he claimed that "a newspaper and a radio station *can* work together so cooperatively that it seems, at least to the publisher having his own station, nothing short of strange to look upon radio as the bitter rival of the newspaper in the advertising field." Recent declines in newspaper advertising revenue, Dealey stated, were simply "an outgrowth of the depression," and he believed publisher hostility to radio been energy misspent.[23]

These attitudes translated not only into public relations campaigns but also into business strategies to develop powerful regional and national media corporations. William Randolph Hearst, for example, had begun assembling his radio empire in the mid-1920s with the purchase of station WISN in Milwaukee in 1925. Hearst later personally assigned Emile Gough, a career newspaperman, to build up the company's radio business. If radio was properly exploited, Hearst told Gough in April 1930, it would "mean much for the entertainment of our readers, and much directly for the circulation of our newspapers" since it was "one of the great opportunities for reaching the public, pleasing the public, and promoting our publications . . . .In fact, I DO NOT KNOW OF ANYTHING ELSE THAT OFFERS EQUAL OPPORTU- NITIES." In October 1930, Hearst stated emphatically that, "in my opinion every newspaper in our service ought to own at least a controlling interest in a radio station," and he believed that these stations should "develop the most popular possible broadcasting personalities" and create programming "that will be of vital interest to the public, and consequently of great advantage to the paper."[24]

Hearst maintained an active involvement with radio while personally directing his executives in many facets of the company's broadcasting, and his company's success with radio soon inspired high-level discussions about the possibility of purchasing the Columbia Broadcasting System. Though this never came to fruition, Hearst did acquire several more radio stations around the country throughout the 1930s and continued to remain enthu- siastic about the possibilities of using radio to augment his newspaper hold- ings. As he told Gough in 1933, the company had "not yet scratched the surface of possibilities in the use of radio as an instrument to build circula- tion and prestige. Radio can be used for more than just general promotional service—it can be made to intensify interest in the newspaper itself—and ingenuity should constantly be exercised to find ways of accomplishing this." Hearst also remained enthusiastic about the possibilities of cooperat- ing with the major networks and continued to cultivate relationships with CBS and NBC.[25]

Hearst was one of many publishers who worked closely with NBC and used the relationship with the country's leading radio network to profitable ends. As NBC executive Albert R. Williamson remarked, the benefit of own- ing a radio station was "something that every up and coming newspaper man who really knows his stuff knows." Publishers fearing radio simply did not see the future of the media in front of them, Williamson argued. The "smart newspaper man," Williamson claimed, had not ignored radio or engaged in needless competition with it, but rather was in the process of "cashing in on it, both as a circulation builder from the news standpoint and greater advertis- ing for the business office." This strategy worked well for NBC in the 1930s, and the network cooperated with publishers throughout the Press-Radio War. In 1935, Merlin Aylesworth stated that NBC had enjoyed a "pleasant" relationship with publishers like Hearst, and he saw this as a way to create long-term harmony with newspapers. Aylesworth remarked that he had "always favored ownership of radio stations by newspapers" in cases where NBC did not own the stations themselves. "It is only because of the ownership of radio stations by newspapers and the attitude of the whole Hearst Organization toward radio broadcasting," Aylesworth asserted, "that we have been able to work out our problems with the Press."[26]

This partnership between Hearst and NBC worked so well that Aylesworth began setting up affiliations with NBC-owned stations and newspapers in their home cities. Aylesworth asked publisher Roy Howard to assist the company in obtaining newspaper affiliation for NBC-owned stations in Pittsburgh and Cleveland. NBC also established a partnership with the stations owned by the California-based McClatchy newspaper chain in 1936. The McClatchy stations, KFBK (Sacramento), KMJ (Fresno), KWG (Stockton), and KERN (Bakersfield) became, as NBC executive Lenox Lohr described them, "great NBC boosters—over their stations as well as in their newspapers, where nearly a page is devoted in each issue to NBC pictures and news." The network cultivated relationships with key newspaper stations across the country and found "staunch allies" in newspaper-radio owners at the *Buffalo Evening News*, *Detroit News*, *Kansas City Star*, and *Milwaukee Journal*. NBC executive Niles Trammel summed up NBC's attitude in writing to J. S. McCarrens, vice president and general manager of the *Cleveland Plain Dealer*, that "Men such as you and organizations such as yours are the kind of men and the kind of organizations we like to do business with."[27]

WGN, the station owned by the *Chicago Tribune*, was one of the most important stations in the country in the 1930s. The station had a 50,000–watt clear-channel license and could be heard all over the United States. WGN's attorney, Louis Caldwell, had helped develop many of the federal laws governing radio while working as the Federal Radio Commission's first general counsel. When Caldwell went back to private practice, he had an office in his firm's suite on the ninth floor of the National Press Building in Washington, D.C.; the offices of the FRC were on the seventh floor. In mid-1933, the *Tribune* embarked on a more ambitious radio plan to set up its own network. The company had been dissatisfied with WGN's prior affiliations with NBC and CBS, and in August 1933 the *Tribune* began drawing up a list of stations that it wanted to affiliate with on its own terms. Executives envisioned the network operating not as a central hub like NBC or CBS, where it would have exclusive right to parts of the broadcast schedules of its affiliates, but instead like the Associated Press (AP), of which

Figure 7. "NBC Salutes the Newspaper." NBC advertisement, *Editor & Publisher* 68 (27 July 1935): 34–35. Courtesy of NBC Universal, Inc.

NBC SALUTES THE NEWSPAPER

THE IDEALS, AIMS AND ACCOMPLISHMENTS OF NEWSPAPERS AND RADIO ARE ESSENTIALLY ALIKE * AS MAJOR MEANS OF NATIONAL COMMUNICATION, THEY JOIN FORCES MANY TIMES TO TRANSMIT NEWS OF VITAL SIGNIFICANCE * AS ADVERTISING MEDIA, THEY ARE MOST FRUITFUL OF RESULT WHEN WORKING TOGETHER * IN FACT, FROM EVERY ANGLE—NEWS, ADVERTISING, EDUCATION, ENTERTAINMENT—THE PRESS AND THE MICROPHONE COMPLEMENT EACH OTHER * AND SO THE NATIONAL BROADCASTING COMPANY, IN BEHALF OF RADIO, SALUTES THE NEWSPAPER, AND OFFERS CONTINUED COOPERATION IN SERVING THE INTERESTS OF THE SUPPORTERS OF BOTH —THE PEOPLE OF AMERICA.

NATIONAL BROADCASTING COMPANY · INC

A RADIO CORPORATION OF AMERICA SUBSIDIARY

NEW YORK · CHICAGO · SAN FRANCISCO

The National Broadcasting Company reiterates, for 1935, this greeting which appeared in Editor & Publisher's Golden Jubilee Issue of July 21st, 1934 — adding to these sentiments the conviction that newspaper-radio relationships have since progressed and improved, fostered by frank and open discussion of mutual problems. There are today thirty-one newspaper owned or affiliated radio stations associated with the NBC Networks.

Figure 7. "NBC Salutes the Newspaper." NBC advertisement, *Editor & Publisher* 68 (27 July 1935): 34–35. Courtesy of NBC Universal, Inc.

the *Tribune* was an influential member, and leave stations free to choose from programming developed by member stations. WGN manager W. E. Macfarlane described the system in its planning stages as "mutual chain broadcasting," and the name stuck. The Mutual Broadcasting System was formed in September 1934 as a partnership between the Tribune Company and Bamberger/R.H. Macy & Company (the New York department store), the first affiliates being WOR (Newark, New Jersey), WXYZ (Detroit, Michigan), and WLW (Cincinnati, Ohio). The network expanded throughout the 1930s, as thirteen stations affiliated with New England's Colonial Network and ten stations affiliated with California's Don Lee network began broadcasting Mutual programming in 1936, as did a twenty-three-station Texas network in 1938.[28]

At the highest levels of America's leading media corporations in the 1930s, cooperation overshadowed conflict as the dominant mood of the newspaper-radio relationship. As Merlin Aylesworth told the company's board, despite all of the "intense" feelings expressed by many "smaller newspaper publishers who had become convinced that radio broadcasting was taking away advertising and also furnishing news through the air which might soon destroy the small newspaper and eventually the larger newspapers of the country," there was a much more important conciliatory line opened by the "newspapers owning radio stations." Aylesworth was not surprised that this was how the relationship had developed, as he pointed out that key figures within the NBC organization were "always convinced that the newspaper-owned station was the best operated radio station other than those we could own and manage. Our judgment has proven correct, for our only unsatisfactory station relations exist with the stations not owned by newspapers who want more money from the National Broadcasting Company while the newspaper-owned station, because of the very nature of the business of the newspaper, has a better understanding of our mutual problems." In July 1935, NBC expressed this support publicly by placing a two-page advertisement in *Editor & Publisher*. On the left page, a stylized line drawing showed a radio tower perched atop a printing press, the tower sending radio waves in all directions, while the press churned out newspapers. The picture presented a clear message of harmony, something the text on the facing page amplified. From "every angle," the advertisement asserted, "the press and the microphone complement each other." In corporate structures and in visual representation, the newspaper was the foundation of radio broadcasting.[29]

The NBC advertisement, placed in the most important newspaper trade journal, was one of the strongest public signals that cooperation between press and radio was the industry norm by the mid-1930s. Similarly, *Broadcasting* noted that newspapers had placed themselves "among the most zealous seekers after new broadcasting facilities," and *Editor & Publisher* noted in late 1935 that it was becoming difficult to keep an accurate tally of how many papers owned stations because newspapers were "jockeying for a place in the radio sun" with such vigor that any list would be "accurate and complete for only a few days at the most." Indeed, between 1934 and 1936, some fifty-four new newspaper-owned stations began broadcasting, an average of about one every two weeks (see Appendix).[30]

The Scripps-Howard chain was part of this trend, as the company purchased its first station, WCPO, in Cincinnati in 1935. *Broadcasting* reported that the company had "decided to enter the broadcasting field in a comprehensive way" and that the company's ultimate objective was to buy a station in every city that it published a newspaper. This move, which *Broadcasting* described as a "decision to invade broadcasting," was something that the magazine believed was "motivated largely by" United Press president Karl Bickel, the longtime proponent of newspaper-radio cooperation who had written *New Empires* in 1930 to celebrate press-radio cooperation. Bickel became the head of the Scripps-Howard broadcasting subsidiary and described its strategy as a plan that "simply demonstrates an increasingly strong conviction on our part of the developing opportunity for the use of radio in connection with the newspaper." *Broadcasting* editorialized that the Scripps-Howard move, along with similar ones by Hearst, McClatchy, and other chains into radio, showed that "the oft-cited 'war with the press' can really be called a myth." After years of "antagonism" that "some short-sighted publishers have felt toward radio," these "idle and sometimes stupid" efforts were coming to a stop. Radio was widely acknowledged to be an "important public service and business institution *per se* as well as a splendid hand-maiden for . . . publishing businesses." Scripps-Howard expanded its broadcast holdings, purchasing the *Memphis Commercial Appeal* in October 1936, in the process acquiring radio station WMC. Ultimately, the Scripps-Howard creation of an integrated and profitable multimedia corporation was part of a broad and growing movement around the country. With Karl Bickel's help, the company had, like many others, ignored intermedia competition in favor of creating, as Bickel called them, new empires.[31]

Rethinking Media Competition in the 1930s

Ultimately, competition defined and shaped the American media in the 1930s, but the most important line of conflict was not *between* press and radio. Instead, it was competition among newspapers *over* the spoils offered by radio. As *Business Week* remarked in 1932, it was "only the singularly naïve onlooker who imagines it to be a fight between newspapers and radio." The "public expects a grudge fight between natural rivals for a big purse, but insiders know better. It's really newspaper vs. newspaper." Building on foundations they had set in the 1920s, newspapers in the 1930s firmly established themselves as some of the most influential and powerful entities in broadcasting, in the process making the most significant conflicts in the 1930s media not skirmishes between representatives of antagonistic newspaper and radio corporations over advertising dollars and public influence but rather clashes among specific newspapers over the issue of broadcasting. Competition, in other words, was not between corporations representing distinct mediums, but rather was marked by corporations competing in the *media* using both print and radio to try to gain supremacy in the business of providing information to the public.[32]

Some of this competition was, as *Business Week* suggested, motivated by basic commercial concerns, and many publishers kept close watch on their print rivals' strategies in broadcasting. William Randolph Hearst, for example, remarked in October 1930 that "we should have our radio people on all papers watch closely any radio development on any competitor, and make sure that no other newspaper gets ahead of us and also to make sure that our newspapers are informed of the activities of our competitor in every locality." Hearst's activities in radio elicited a quick reaction from his rival Frank Gannett in Albany, New York. Between the two companies, Hearst and Gannett owned all three of the local newspapers, with Hearst owning the *Times-Union* and Gannett the *Knickerbocker Press* and the *Evening News*. Gannett had expressed a mild interest in obtaining or affiliating with a radio station in Albany starting in 1929, and when he learned in November 1930 that Hearst was pursuing a station in the city, his desire to broadcast took on a new level of urgency. Gannett wrote personally to FRC commissioner Charles M. Saltzman asking for help in obtaining a license. "As Albany is the state capital," Gannett wrote, "much news originates there of national interest and we feel that this station should be properly handled by reputable newspapers if such news is to be transmitted by radio." Given his papers' "deep interest in Albany, we are in a position particularly to represent the public," Gannett claimed. Gannett also wrote in more frank terms to George Akerson, Herbert Hoover's press secretary, stating that he wanted the station so that, he told Akerson, he would have a way "to block Hearst in his efforts to control the station at this important news center." Gannett hoped that the White House might inform the FRC of "how important it is to have us control this situation, rather than to have it in [Hearst's] hands." Gannett succeeded in getting a station in Albany, and remained in regular contact with federal officials to get preferential treatment for it and his other stations against competitors, noting that all of them were "friends of the administration."[33]

Gannett's willingness to use political connections to advance his interests in radio against newspaper competitors points to the other main line of conflict in the 1930s media beyond the Press-Radio War: partisan politics. Unlike newspaper publishing, the physical finitude of the radio spectrum limited the number of stations that could be on the air, and in some cases this created competition between editorially partisan newspapers to become broadcasters. Needing a license from the federal government to get on the airwaves, aspiring broadcasters like Frank Gannett sought to use their influence with elected officials to help them in this process. In New York and across the country, newspapers came to see radio as an element of a battle not only over circulation and profits, but also over political power.

In a matter beginning in 1925, the *Madison Capital Times*, the paper in the Wisconsin state capital representing the progressive wing of the Republican Party, began broadcasting with station WIBA, thus injecting a new element of competition into an already contentious Wisconsin media market. Robert La Follette, the leader of the progressive coalition, had since 1909 published *La Follette's Weekly Magazine* to maintain a regular and favorable media presence in the state. In 1917, La Follette's relationship with some of the state's newspapers worsened after he filed a libel lawsuit against the conservative *Wisconsin State Journal* over critical remarks that the paper had made about his antiwar stance. Though the suit settled in 1918, members of La Follette's organization decided to take further action. William T. Evjue, the *State Journal*'s business manager, resigned over the publication of the editorials that led to La Follette's libel suit. Evjue was also a member of the progressive Republican coalition elected to the State Assembly, and with the help of La Follette's law partner and other associates, raised the necessary capital to start publishing the *Madison Capital Times* in September 1917. The paper struggled financially at the beginning but was held afloat by contributions from partisan supporters. As Robert La Follette's son Philip (district attorney of Dane County, where Madison was located, from 1925 to 1927) noted in his autobiography, "we at long last had one daily that told the Progressive story." Since the rest of the state's press was, as Philip La Follette claimed, "unanimously and bitterly against us," the *Capital Times*' editorial support "was manna from heaven." With vigorous editorial support from the paper, Robert La Follette carried the state of Wisconsin as a third-party presidential candidate in 1924.[34]

This kind of partisanship continued over WIBA, the radio station that the paper began operating in the 1920s. As Philip La Follette noted in 1928, WIBA was the only station "in the entire country which is owned and operated by individuals interested in and friendly to the progressive movement," and he believed it to be the radio representative of the dominant politics of the region. La Follette claimed that Wisconsin was an "overwhelmingly progressive state, and . . . the leader in the movement which represents far in excess of five million American citizens. This great mass of people," he stated, now had a station "operated and maintained by an institution friendly to their views."[35]

In 1930, Philip La Follette drew upon this media support when he began what was to be a successful campaign for governor of Wisconsin. His political and media rivals took note, and that same year, the *Capital Times*' competitor, the *Wisconsin State Journal*, purchased station WISJ from Beloit College and applied to the FRC for a new frequency and higher wattage as it sought to remake the station into a commercial outlet. The *Capital Times* immediately tried to block the *State Journal*'s move into radio, and representatives claimed that allowing the *State Journal* to do this would "very materially depreciate our franchise and its value to the people of that community," since there was not enough advertising money in Madison to support two commercial stations. *Capital Times* supporters claimed that conservative interests already controlled the vast majority of Wisconsin's media despite representing a minority of the population, and they implored the FRC to protect their station's viability. State Senator Glenn Roberts, Philip La Follette's former assistant district attorney and a close ally, claimed in an FRC hearing that the *Milwaukee Journal* station WTMJ was politically conservative, as were newspaper-owned stations in Janesville, La Crosse, and Superior. WIBA, Roberts argued, was the only radio station in Wisconsin that was "owned and controlled by interests which are in accord with the majority political view" of the state's people, and he believed that it thus should not have its financial stability impaired by the new *State Journal* station.[36]

For Glenn Roberts and Philip La Follette, the *Madison Capital Times*'s WIBA was a station in need of protecting because it represented their political party and ideology, something its detractors noted was ironic given the progressives' traditional antimonopoly position. Elisha Hanson, the *State Journal*'s attorney and later one of the most prominent media lawyers in the country, looked critically at WIBA's rhetoric, arguing that he thought it was a "most unusual thing for anyone connected with a La Follette organization in Wisconsin to come before any agency of the federal government and insist upon the upholding of the right of monopoly." Hanson, however, could not convince the FRC to grant WISJ the new and more powerful license that it desired, leaving supporters of the *State Journal* to believe that they were impeded in their ability to use broadcasting as a political tool.[37]

Executives at the *Wisconsin State Journal* were outraged that the paper was having such difficulty obtaining a better station license and pleaded for patronage from the White House to help with its application. A. M. Brayton, the paper's editor and publisher, angrily remarked to Herbert Hoover's secretary Walter Newton that he had spent significant time and money trying to get a broadcast license in the interest of helping his conservative allies in the Republican party and that he resented not receiving adequate support in return from Washington. His paper, Brayton argued, "had not gone into broadcasting as a business venture, nor even willingly. We had seen control of the air in Wisconsin going to the Democrats and the radical Republicans," and he felt that "with the coming influence of radio, we were permanently surrendering this state to radicals who are revolutionary and destructive." Brayton wanted a station in the state capital to represent his political interests, and he was concerned that "the enemy should be armed" instead with the radio license. "The fact," Brayton argued, "is that the commission has armed our opponents from helmet to spur, and given us an empty gun," and he claimed that "we shall be slaughtered during the campaign so far as the air is concerned." He had wanted to broadcast "because we believe in the continuance and improvement of America's democratic status, as against any of the revolutionary cure-alls with which the country is threatened," and he was outraged that he was not getting help from the White House to "meet the Soviet crowd in Wisconsin." Brayton, in other words, did not feel threatened by radio in and of itself, but rather by a radio station owned by his political rival.[38]

This fight continued in Wisconsin afterward as the state proved to be a particularly volatile region for partisan newspapers competing to become broadcasters. In Racine, a city some one hundred miles from Madison, the

Times Call took up the campaign that the *State Journal* had begun, applying for a license in 1931 with the hope of gaining regional political influence. State Senator Walter S. Goodland lobbied aggressively for the paper to
Republican National Committee chairman George Vits, claiming that "conservatives in Wisconsin are very weak in active radio support" and hoping
to have the station interject itself "actively into the next campaign." As A. M.
Brayton had, Vits took the matter personally to the White House, noting that
"it would help us a great deal" if the *Times Call* could get a license. Herbert
Hoover himself kept tabs on the matter, directing subordinates to assist his
political allies obtain radio licenses.[39]

Conservative publishers around the state echoed these pleas. In Milwaukee, Julius Liebman, the vice president and editor of the *Milwaukee Sentinel*,
lobbied the White House for assistance with having his transmitter power
increased so that he could reach more Wisconsin listeners. Noting that his
station, WISN, strongly supported President Hoover, Liebman told Walter
Newton that it was clear "how important it is to have a station in this part of
the country with greater power than we now possess." Stephen Bolles, the editor of the *Janesville Gazette*, made a similar request for assistance in getting
more power. "As it is now," Bolles wrote to Walter Newton, his station WCLO
could "not reach more than one-half the circulation of the *Gazette* in this territory, and you are thoroughly familiar with the fact that this newspaper has
a powerful influence in that territory. We would like to have the radio station
and the newspaper coordinate."[40]

Newspaper politics in Wisconsin remained highly charged during the
1932 elections. While campaigning for reelection as governor in 1932, Philip
La Follette had a speech interrupted by John Chapple, the editor of the *Ash-
land Daily Press* and himself an anti-La Follette candidate for U.S. Senate.
Chapple was so disruptive that he was forcibly ejected from the event. From
the state capital, *State Journal* editor and publisher A. M. Brayton continued to lobby the White House for assistance in getting a higher-power radio
license, noting that, "In the political fight to come, we are handicapped by
a lack of power." Brayton claimed that there was a "wonderfully productive
Republican territory" near Madison that he could not reach with his current
license. "We try to make our broadcasting constructive," Brayton claimed,
in order to promote the "soundness of the Republican administration, and
generally of the Republican doctrine." His current license, however, left him
unable to be as influential as he would like to be, and he claimed that this
meant that he and his fellow Republican partisans were "losing almost half

the state, for want of power." The *Capital Times* had more influence, Brayton argued, and given the looming election and Hoover's increasing unpopularity, this was politically problematic. Brayton pleaded to press secretary Walter Newton "confidentially" that, if there was "anything you can do to urge this thing along, I hope you'll find the time. There are only forty-eight states. This one will be close but it's a decided possibility." Brayton's pleas were not heeded, and the candidate he wanted to assist—the unpopular Herbert Hoover—lost the election to Franklin Roosevelt.[41]

Ultimately, these Wisconsin newspapers were not competing against radio, but rather were competing through and over radio. Such competition among newspapers over the control and use of radio was replicated throughout the country throughout the 1930s as many publishers ignored the anti-radio sentiments of those motivating the Press-Radio War. The Depression decade posed many challenges to newspapers, and expansion into radio helped many navigate these challenging circumstances. Whether motivated by the desire to use radio to a commercial or political advantage, as newspapers around the United States became broadcasters in increasing numbers in the 1930s, they created new media institutions with unprecedented power in the public sphere and over American politics and society. After 1932, the clash between these powerful multimedia corporations and the federal government would become a defining conflict in American politics in the New Deal era. The New Deal took national the kinds of conflicts ongoing in Wisconsin, in the process complicating the relationship between press, radio, and politics.

Chapter 3

Reshaping the Public Sphere: The New Deal and Media Concentration

Franklin Delano Roosevelt's election in 1932 marked a turning point not only in American politics but also in the American media. Over the previous twelve years, newspaper corporations had become increasingly active in the radio industry, so much so that people like Karl Bickel and H. O. Davis could call them "empires" as both praise and condemnation. Strategic publishers had created multimedia corporations profiting from the sale of printed newspapers and radio advertisements. These multimedia corporations had also come to have a great deal of political significance, as the struggles over radio licensing in Wisconsin demonstrated. Having a favorable newspaper and radio station, the La Follette organization showed, allowed a party or political organization to maintain a machine-like presence in a particular region. In the 1930s, Franklin Roosevelt's administration adapted this to national politics, as officials within the New Deal worked closely with press and radio in efforts to influence public perception of the administration. At the same time, they also clashed with multimedia corporations whose owners were critical of the New Deal. These cooperative and competitive activities reshaped the public sphere in the 1930s.

Media-based public relations campaigns were central to the style of governance developed by Roosevelt's New Deal administration. After Roosevelt's inauguration in 1933, federal officials employed new and aggressive strategies to communicate with the anxious Depression-era public, hoping in this way to differentiate themselves from the Hoover administration, which many

Americans believed was unresponsive to their concerns about the country's economy. In the process, the New Deal dramatically altered the state's influence over the circulation of public information in the United States. As Elisha Hanson, the attorney for the American Newspaper Publishers Association, remarked in 1935, the New Deal represented a fundamental shift in American governance not only in terms of the volume and type of legislation enacted but also in terms of the ways that the state communicated with the public about that legislation. The New Deal, Hanson argued, "brought with it so many changes in policies as well as in attitudes that a depression-weary public has had difficulty in keeping up with them. Not the least of the changes in attitude was that in respect of keeping the public informed of the acts, proposals, and policies of the Administration."[1]

The federal government under Roosevelt developed a variety of novel strategies to carry out this program, Hanson asserted, as it established "publicity divisions in departments and agencies which had not had them theretofore," expanded "offices of information already in existence," hired "more newspaper men to write news for the Government than were employed by the newspapers and press associations," retained "advertising agencies skilled in handling promotional copy to advise it in the selling of its program," and had officials on the radio, including FDR himself, speaking constantly and directly to the American people. "By these and various other methods," Hanson claimed, New Deal officials created an unprecedented program for the state to inform the people about its activities.[2]

Many Americans responded enthusiastically to these information campaigns, which imparted to them the sense that the federal government was working to ameliorate the ills of the ongoing Great Depression. In the 1930s, the Office of Education, the most active federal agency producing radio content, routinely received hundreds of thousands of letters per year, and in 1940 Americans wrote almost one million letters to the agency. President Franklin Roosevelt's popular "Fireside Chats" on the radio elicited dramatically more correspondence from the public than any president before him. During the Depression, Roosevelt received more than three times the amount of annual correspondence that Abraham Lincoln had during the Civil War or Woodrow Wilson had during World War I, and in December 1933 the White House mailroom had to start a night shift for the first time in order to handle all the mail it was receiving.[3] Media representatives like Elisha Hanson were troubled by the New Deal's increased production of public information, which he termed "official propaganda." Hanson believed that the state was bypassing the press's monitoring function through the creation of its own channels of information distribution. "For the first time in their history," Hanson argued, "the American people have seen their Government turning to propaganda in myriad forms to win their favor and keep their support." Though Hanson's argument was hyperbolic, what he did point to was the unmistakable fact that officials within the New Deal were much more active than their predecessors in the production and circulation of public information about the state's activities.[4]

One of the lasting effects of the New Deal was the transformation of the ways that Americans were reminded on a daily basis about their government's role in shaping the world around them. In some cases these reminders came in the physical forms of the dams, roads, and electrical power systems built through massive public works programs like the Tennessee Valley Authority and policies like the Rural Electrification Act, and in other instances through the creation and distribution of Works Progress Administration art and cultural projects. Quite often, it was the result of government representatives communicating directly with the American people through coordinated public relations campaigns. During the 1930s, the American public sphere was filled increasingly with ideas coming directly from state actors.[5]

The shaping of public knowledge under the New Deal did not stop with the circulation of information, however, as the state also intervened in the economics of information production through increasing regulation of the business practices of private media corporations. While the state produced more information, it also challenged private power in the media and tried to reshape the media's institutional structure. During the New Deal period, corporations controlling the press and radio held tremendous power over Americans' daily understandings of politics, and the two media became connected in two particularly significant ways: President Roosevelt's public popularity was buttressed by his use of radio, which allowed him to circumvent hostile newspaper coverage and editorials; and newspapers throughout the period were acquiring radio stations in increasing numbers and creating powerful multimedia conglomerates.

Throughout FDR's tenure in office and especially after Roosevelt's reelection in 1936, federal officials sought ways to control these newspaper-radio combinations. For the New Dealers, such efforts were ways to rescue FDR's preferred medium from the clutches of hostile newspaper publishers. As Secretary of the Interior Harold Ickes argued, radio and newspapers "should, and must, remain distinct and separate. Each has its own function to perform," and he advocated the passage of laws "forbidding the ownership of radio stations by newspapers." This, he claimed, was the only way to ensure that the American media could provide the best possible service to the American public. "Democracy and freedom will best be served by competition between the newspaper and the radio, the one serving as a check on the other." For publishers, this line of thinking represented an antidemocratic grasp for power and an attempt to stifle a free press in America. As the *New York Herald Tribune* editorialized in 1936, the "whole record of the New Deal has been hostile to a free press and free speech."[6]

To observers on both sides of the issue, New Deal media policy represented a changing understanding of the relationship between the state and the media during a period when the institutions of the public sphere were undergoing dramatic transformations. These projects were carried out in Congress, at the Federal Communications Commission, and through the actions of President Roosevelt himself, and they represented some of the most significant projects undertaken by the New Deal. As private corporations developed new powers of circulating public knowledge during the Great Depression, the state sought countervailing public power in the same arena.

Regulating Multimedia Concentration

During Roosevelt's first term, Congress passed the Communications Act of 1934, thus establishing the Federal Communications Commission as the successor agency to the Federal Radio Commission. Though the 1934 Act was historically part of the New Deal, substantively it bore little relation to other New Deal policy. While the Communications Act did centralize federal control over communications to a greater degree by bringing telephonic and broadcast regulation together in one agency, many of the key provisions regulating radio were taken verbatim from the Radio Act of 1927, which had been signed into law by the Republican Calvin Coolidge. Though influential congressman wanted more provisions encouraging media diversity included, the Communications Act of 1934 passed despite criticism of its moderate tone and stimulated immediate action from opponents of media concentration.[7]

To many critics, the pattern of early FCC decisions tended toward serving broadcasting corporations rather than the public interest. In Congress, the two most important exponents of reformist media policies were Senators Clarence Dill and Burton Wheeler, both of whom expressed strong opposition to media concentration in the period surrounding the passage of the

Communications Act of 1934. Dill, whom *Broadcasting* called "unquestionably . . . the most influential voice in federal radio control of any figure in public life," began criticizing newspaper ownership of radio almost immediately after Franklin Roosevelt's election. In November 1932, Dill gave publishers what *Editor & Publisher* described as a "blunt piece of advice" when he claimed that there was "already a growing sentiment in the country that newspapers should not be permitted to own radio stations." Dill warned that there would be "reason for legislation that will prohibit the newspapers from owning and operating radio stations" if newspapers seemed to be engaging in what could be construed as monopolistic behavior.[8]

When Dill retired from the Senate in early 1935, Burton Wheeler continued to push for a more aggressive broadcast policy. Wheeler had some "very friendly" conversations with Franklin Roosevelt about newspaper ownership of radio, finding the president to be "opposed" to it. Wheeler subsequently commissioned S. Howard Evans of the Payne Fund, a prominent media reform group, to prepare a report on the state of American broadcasting. In April 1935, Evans responded with the *Report on Radio Broadcasting*, a detailed critique of commercial radio. The report asserted that there was "almost unanimous agreement among students of its structure that broadcasting should have a New Deal. The glaring flaws in the present system of commercial competition must be eliminated." The report offered several specific policy recommendations for reforming commercial broadcasting, including authorizing the FCC to undertake a complete and systematic reallocation of broadcasting facilities in order to curtail the power of clear-channel stations and allow educational and nonprofit broadcasters a greater presence on the airwaves, and suggesting that the Commission enact a prohibition of newspaper ownership of radio stations. If newspapers were allowed to continue to own radio stations, Evans argued, this would create a serious impediment to a vibrant, competitive media. Because the number of stations was limited by the physical properties of the radio spectrum, Evans argued, "Clearly all newspapers cannot own radio stations." Those that had been "fortunate enough to receive radio facilities" now had a "tremendous advantage over their fellow competitors in the newspaper field." This, Evans argued, might wreak havoc on the newspaper industry by driving competing papers out of business and thus give the radio-owning newspapers even more power. The only possible solution, as Evans saw it, was to bar newspapers from owning radio stations altogether. Evans's report was received favorably in key quarters of the administration. FCC chairman George Henry Payne told an audience at Cornell University that the report was "one of the ablest documents that I have read on the present problems and perplexities of the entire broadcasting situation."[9]

Following the circulation of Evans's report, Burton Wheeler accrued additional congressional support from opponents of media consolidation. Representative Emanuel Celler of Brooklyn claimed that newspapers should "stick to their own knitting" and be prevented by federal law from owning radio stations. Senator Matthew Neely, a Democrat from West Virginia, stated that "permitting newspapers to obtain a monopoly" of local media by owning both the local newspaper and radio station was a "policy which I think is reprehensible." Representative Joseph Monaghan, a Montana Democrat, denounced newspaper ownership of radio in August 1935 as an effort by "big business" to "control and mold public opinion in order that they may add to the millions that they now possess." Monaghan charged that there was a far-reaching conspiracy between newspapers and radio stations to gain control of the American media. The "Radio Trust," he asserted, had "entered into a gentlemen's agreement with certain newspaper interests," creating a concentration of control of the media he claimed was "unwise" and "unsound." Look at places like Shreveport, Louisiana, Monaghan claimed, or Wilmington, Delaware, or Lancaster, Pennsylvania, where all local media were under common control. "What chance has the honest, unbiased, and independent press of the country when it is forced into competition with a newspaper which also controls a radio station?" Monaghan believed that it was "high time that something is done by the Congress . . . to prevent or lessen this far-reaching evil." By combining some of the antimonopoly impulses of the New Deal with more specific criticisms of the media, many in Congress began to support curbs on media consolidation and newspaper ownership of radio.[10]

For the most part, these congressional critics were frustrated by the pattern of decision making at the newly created FCC. The number of newspaper-owned stations rose dramatically in the FCC's early years, going from 90 (15 percent of the total) in 1934 to 201 (29 percent of the total) by 1938 (see Appendix). In many of the cases involving applications for radio stations by newspapers, critics believed, the FCC too often showed a preference for newspaper applicants at the expense of others who might create more diversity in local media ownership.[11]

The first instance where the FCC explicitly addressed the newspaper issue in an application proceeding came in 1935, when the *Brooklyn Daily Eagle* applied for a new license on a frequency already shared by four other broadcasters, each of whom had a pending application. The Commission denied three of the four renewal applications after deciding that the stations were poorly managed and delivering low-quality programming, then it renewed the license of station WBBC and gave the *Daily Eagle* a new license to share time on the same frequency. If radio frequencies were unlimited, the FCC asserted, the other three stations might be able to continue broadcasting. Since frequencies instead were scarce, however, the Commission was forced to decide who would be allowed to broadcast. "The abstract right of all persons to engage in the business of broadcasting is not absolute," the Commission stated, "but exists only if their operation will serve public interest, convenience, and necessity." Commissioner Irvin Stewart, a Texas Democrat, was dissatisfied with the *Daily Eagle* obtaining a license and dissented from the majority opinion. "It is not clear," Stewart asserted, "that consideration was given to the matter of the public interest involved in the granting of a broadcast station license to an applicant controlled by a newspaper." Newspapers and radio stations were the "two principal sources of current public opinion and enlightenment," Stewart stated, and the "two principal media of local advertising and two of the principal media of national advertising in any community." Stewart felt that allowing the two media to fall "under the same control inevitably presents a problem of major moment which should be squarely faced by the Commission," and he believed that this had not been done in this case.[12]

In subsequent cases, the FCC did begin to consider the problem of newspaper ownership in greater detail. Unfortunately for Commissioner Stewart, however, this consideration did not lead to a policy promoting diversity of ownership. Soon after the Brooklyn case, the Commission was faced with another comparative hearing involving a newspaper, this time in Mason City, Iowa. One of the applicants, the Mason City Globe-Gazette Company, published the only newspaper in the city of 23,000 people. Listeners in Mason City could receive broadcasts from a handful of stations in the surrounding region, but the city lacked a local station providing clear service at all hours of the day. The *Globe-Gazette* had been editorializing about the lack of quality local radio service for several years, charging that the offerings available to Mason City represented a "disregard of listeners' rights," and the paper eventually decided to rectify the situation itself. Lee Loomis, the publisher of the *Globe-Gazette*, argued that the paper already had the "organized news-gathering facilities" and infrastructure to operate a high-quality radio station. More important, it had the "knowledge of what the people of our community want, gathered through years of serving them as a newspaper." This, Loomis argued, would help the paper serve Mason City "better than someone who had to acquire that knowledge after they started to operate."[13]

The *Globe-Gazette* radio application was challenged by Charles Wilkinson, a local citizen claiming that a *Globe-Gazette* radio station would give the paper "complete, absolute and exclusive control of the dissemination of news and public expressions" in Mason City. Wilkinson claimed that the paper already had an overly commercial policy "of conducting a newspaper with maximum advertising," and he claimed that if it got a broadcasting station, it would "stifle the life of the community" by continuing to put concerns about profits ahead of concerns about the public good. Two additional parties filed applications for the frequency as well, but the FCC ultimately gave the *Globe-Gazette* the license. Charles Wilkinson's arguments in favor of diverse local media ownership were not persuasive enough to convince the Commission that a *Globe-Gazette* station would be harmful to the Mason City area. The other two applicants, the Commission found, were "backed largely" by out-of-town interests. Given the choice it had, the FCC stated, the *Globe-Gazette* was the most qualified potential broadcaster. The Commission decided that the newspaper's personnel and facilities would be beneficial to the station and, more important, that a *Globe-Gazette* station would be "under the control and direction of local people with local interests." The Commission saw no reason why the diversity issue should be the primary ground for the decision and, when given a choice between a local newspaper applicant and a nonlocal, non-newspaper applicant, it chose the former.[14]

Two cases in 1937 showed the FCC continuing to struggle with similar issues in ongoing proceedings, one again in Iowa and the other in Texas. Recognizing that media outlets were limited and the market for information controlled by a small number of firms, the FCC sought a way to most effectively allocate radio licenses in different communities. In one of these 1937 cases, the *El Paso Times* application for a broadcasting license was challenged by Tri-State Broadcasting Company, the owner of the only two currently operating stations in the city. A *Times* station, Tri-State argued, would "result in destructive competition and loss of revenue" to its stations and "consequent deterioration of program service now available to the listening public of El Paso." Tri-State argued that there were "insufficient new sources of revenue available from broadcast sponsorship," and further alleged that the radio station would contribute to media consolidation in El Paso. Though it owned radio stations already, Tri-State claimed, it aimed to provide an alternative to the *El Paso Times* and to contribute a wider range of perspectives to local residents. The *Times* station, in contrast, was "designed to serve as an adjunct to the applicant's newspaper and not as an independent informative and entertaining medium." After a hearing, the Commission awarded the paper a license over Tri-State's protests.[15]

As in the proceeding involving the *Brooklyn Daily Eagle*, Commissioner Irvin Stewart dissented to the granting of a broadcasting license to a newspaper. Stewart pointed out that those who followed the radio industry were "aware of the exceeding rapidity with which broadcast stations are passing into newspaper control." This trend was undesirable, Stewart argued, and he believed that the Commission needed to take steps to prevent newspapers from owning radio stations in communities like El Paso that had fewer media outlets. The American public needed ways of getting information "independent of the newspaper," Stewart argued, and he believed that as long as newspapers and radio were "separately controlled, the listener may receive the full benefit of both" and be able to "decide for himself what is really happening." With both media under common ownership, access to this diversity of perspectives was limited. "To some," Stewart concluded, "this solicitude for channels of information independent of each other may seem a counsel of confusion; to me, it is a principal hope of democracy." Though not invoking Oliver Wendell Holmes's *Abrams* dissent directly, Stewart invoked it in spirit by advocating for a vigorous competition among ideas offered from as many perspectives as possible. When he considered the application of the *El Paso Times* in this light, Stewart felt that the Commission should deny it in order to encourage ownership diversity. Stewart's dissent, while unsuccessful in swaying the majority, was called an "outburst" by *Broadcasting* and greeted with consternation throughout the trade press.[16] Stewart continued to press for the Commission to devote more attention to the problem of newspaper ownership of radio, writing in a subsequent law review article that the "cry of monopoly of news and information is being heard to some extent. I think we shall hear more of it." With diverse ownership of newspapers and radio, Stewart argued, "one can be checked against another" and he disagreed with the prevailing sense that the matter of joint ownership "has no element of public interest."[17]

The Commission's second controversial decision in 1937 came in the *Sanders Brothers* case, a matter involving two applications for radio licenses in Dubuque, Iowa. One applicant, Sanders Brothers Radio, wanted to move its existing WKBB across the Mississippi River from East Dubuque, Illinois, to Dubuque, Iowa, in order to build a new transmitter that would allow the station to increase the reach of its signal. The other applicant, the *Dubuque Telegraph Herald*, wanted a license to build a new station in Dubuque. Sanders Brothers Radio alleged that granting a new license to the *Telegraph Herald* would cause financial distress to their station, claiming that there was not enough advertising revenue in the area to support another station. The company also claimed that the *Telegraph Herald* had demonstrated long-term editorial hostility toward WKBB, as station president William Klauer stated that the paper had "never printed a line about WKBB in its columns." After a hearing, the FCC approved both applications, and Sanders Brothers appealed the FCC's decision in federal court.[18]

The *Telegraph Herald* defended its proposed station as providing service to the Dubuque area that WKBB was neglecting, and they charged WKBB with skimping on educational programming and ignoring significant issues related to the agricultural industries in the area. In contrast, the *Telegraph Herald* portrayed itself as a public-spirited company with deep historical ties to Dubuque. "The fact that" it was "still flourishing after a period of 100 years' service to the community is indicative of its appreciation of that which the community most desires as well as that which is best for the community." The Court was not persuaded by these arguments and ruled in favor of Sanders Brothers, charging that the FCC did not conduct a proper economic assessment of the economic feasibility of having two stations in the Dubuque media market, and it sent the matter back to the Commission for review.[19]

Before conducting a new hearing, the FCC appealed this decision to the Supreme Court and in the process unintentionally established a precedent that limited its own ability to regulate newspaper-radio combinations in the years to come. On appeal, the Commission argued that Sanders Brothers had misconstrued its broadcasting license as being "exclusive" and "absolute," and the Commission asserted that its function as an agency was to promote competition among broadcasters by giving more licenses to use available frequencies. Moreover, the FCC argued, the "very foundation of the radio broadcast industry" under the Communications Act of 1934 was the idea that competition between multiple radio stations was beneficial to the public. It was up to individual radio stations to "attract and hold a listening audience" that would bring in advertising revenue to support them. The FCC cited case law dating back to the 1837 *Charles River Bridge* decision to the effect that having a public license or franchise conferred no legal right to object to the authorization of a "competitive enterprise, no matter how severe the economic injury resulting from competition may be."[20]

The Supreme Court reversed the appellate decision and found in favor of the FCC, asserting that "resulting economic injury to a rival station is not, in and of itself," a factor the FCC had to consider in granting licenses. The Court supported the license grant to the *Telegraph Herald* and took the position that the "field of broadcasting is one of free competition" and ruled that it was not the FCC's responsibility to "regulate the business of the licensee." Ultimately, the Court found, radio broadcasting was "open to anyone, provided there be an available frequency over which he can broadcast without interference to others," and so long as the applicant "shows his competency, the adequacy of his equipment, and financial ability to make good use of the assigned channel." The Court went on to make an explicit statement that the overriding goal of the FCC was to ensure that the consumer had the widest array of choices on the radio, stating that "Plainly it is not the purpose of the Act to protect a licensee against competition but to protect the public." After the resolution of the court case, both Sanders Brothers and the *Telegraph Herald* were given radio licenses, as the FCC had originally decided. In defending its authority to promote competition in local radio markets, the FCC at the same time undercut its future ability to promote a more broadly competitive media marketplace by arguing that a newspaper broadcaster could contribute to rather than constrain competition in a local market. Essentially, the Commission had won its case by arguing that newspaper owners were satisfactory and even desirable applicants for broadcast licenses, and publishers never tired of citing the case whenever the FCC tried to deny one of their license applications.[21]

As the *Sanders Brothers* case worked its way through the court system in 1937 and 1938, media industry insiders remained uneasy that the FCC might take a more assertive stance against cross ownership. Trade journal *Broadcasting* noted that it was "glaringly apparent that just about the knottiest job" the FCC had to do was to create a policy regulating newspaper ownership of radio, and it saw signs that this policy might soon take on a more reformist character. FCC staffers had been looking more critically at newspapers' applications to broadcast, the magazine claimed, and commissioners had shown noticeable "zeal" as they questioned newspaper applicants during oral arguments. The magazine concluded that it was "difficult for us to believe that these new newspaper comers into the radio fold are being prepared, like lambs, for a slaughter," yet it cautioned that "these are days of queer political developments, and it is a foolish owner or stockholder in a radio station, who happens also to own or have an interest in a newspaper, who can sit back calmly and think the issue has been solved."[22]

Broadcasting and Reform in Media Policy

Franklin Roosevelt opened his first term in office with a burst of energy and his relationship with the media was particularly important in establishing the tone for his administration, especially as he replaced Herbert Hoover, who had become aloof toward and often withdrawn from reporters during his last year in office. Given little information from Hoover as the Depression deepened, many in the Washington press corps had become restless and bitter while covering the White House. After his inauguration, Roosevelt immediately began holding regular press conferences and displaying a new openness and accessibility to the media, something that quickly earned the respect of Washington reporters. In fact, after his first White House press conference, reporters gave Roosevelt a standing ovation, the first time that the press corps had done that to any president.[23]

Despite this auspicious beginning, Roosevelt's amicable relationship with the newspaper press did not survive his first term in office. Roosevelt proved to be personally highly sensitive to press criticism, and this sensitivity quickly turned to antipathy and resentment. Attempts by the administration to regulate the wages and hours of newspaper workers through provisions in the National Industrial Recovery Act (NIRA) of 1933 created animosity between FDR and newspaper publishers, some of whom charged Roosevelt with targeting their business practices out of political spite over their news coverage.[24] After extensive press criticism of the Social Security Act of 1935, the relationship between FDR and the press became bitter, personal, and eventually openly antagonistic. FDR retaliated against the press by accusing specific editors and publishers of undermining his programs through biased and often patently false coverage. Publishers responded in kind during the 1936 presidential election. William Randolph Hearst used his chain of newspapers to vigorously support the Republican Alf Landon's campaign, and the *Chicago Tribune*'s Robert McCormick became so adamantly opposed to Roosevelt that he provided office space in the Tribune Tower for one hundred Landon campaign workers. In subsidizing their expenses along with those of a nationwide grassroots movement of what one historian describes as "as many as 50,000 citizen activists," McCormick became one of the most significant financial supporters of Landon's ultimately unsuccessful campaign. Landon's running mate was Frank Knox, the publisher of the *Chicago Daily News*, making the 1936 election in some respects a direct clash between Franklin Roosevelt and the newspaper press.

After winning the election, Roosevelt expressed outward disdain for the press with increasing frequency and vigor.[25]

Newspaper publishers became perhaps FDR's most vociferous group of enemies. Historian Graham White points out that Roosevelt "reserved for American newspaper owners . . . [an] active and implacable hostility." He believed them to be "unfitted by background or training for their task" and felt that they "lacked journalistic talent . . . and had little grasp of their wider public responsibilities." White offers the provocative argument that Roosevelt dramatically overstated the level of animosity between himself and the press, concluding that Roosevelt "persistently exaggerated the extent of press opposition which he faced and the extent to which the calculated, proprietor-inspired distortion of news occurred." In other words, Roosevelt conflated opposition from publishers and criticism on the editorial page with opposition from "the press" more generally, a claim White finds at odds with the generally fair coverage that he received in news reports. As White sees it, Roosevelt, "actually welcomed" editorial opposition since positioning the press as an enemy gave him an opportunity to present himself as more of a populist.[26]

Whether or not Roosevelt overstated press opposition to the New Deal, the president's ire at the press reached even greater heights after the 1936 election. After defeating what could reasonably be described as a Republican newspaper ticket, Roosevelt sought reprisal against publishers. "It is not the editors" who were the problem, Roosevelt told reporters at a press conference. "Hell, most of the editors have got families," he claimed. "They cannot lose their jobs. They have to write what the owner tells them to." In 1936, many commentators noted that the press's standing was damaged by the election and that Roosevelt's win was a "serious blow to the prestige of many important newspaper publishers." Indeed, the *New Republic* noted that the press "lost" the election, and press critic George Seldes called the election a "repudiation of the press" and noted that the result was "a symptom of the universal suspicion and growing anger of the public" at newspapers.[27]

By the start of Roosevelt's second term, rumors abounded in Washington that the president wanted to exert more control over radio as a way of working around a hostile press. Behind the scenes, FDR helped political allies obtain station licenses and on several occasions had surrogates suggest to FCC commissioners that they should deny broadcast license applications from newspapers that had been particularly adversarial toward the New Deal. Concern about this private maneuvering became more widespread among newspaper publishers after 1936. The *Los Angeles Times* editorialized, "Under the present laws . . . radio is the serf of the administration," and throughout Roosevelt's second term there were persistent claims being made in Washington and in press circles that one had to be friendly to the administration to get a license for a radio station. Newspapers grew even more concerned that Roosevelt might soon tackle existing radio ownership by newspapers, especially anti-New Deal papers.[28]

Though FCC policy up to 1936 was rarely threatening to newspaper-broadcasters, trade groups soon began mounting campaigns against policies that they believed were forthcoming. The ANPA and the trade journal *Editor & Publisher* regularly argued that the FCC's regulatory control over radio made it a tool of Franklin Roosevelt and the Democratic Party. At the 1936 ANPA annual meeting, the Association's Radio Committee claimed that, because broadcasters were subject to regular license renewals, "a station is not likely to jeopardize its license by offending this political body. It is for these reasons that radio offers a convenient vehicle for control by a political party." The press, on the other hand, was protected by the First Amendment and thus "freed not only of licensing" but of "any governmental control whatever." As authoritarian leaders in Europe used government-owned radio systems for propaganda purposes, publishers and broadcasters in the United States began to draw parallels to what they saw as Roosevelt's domination of the American media. The Radio Committee even invoked the specters of fascism and authoritarianism in suggesting that political developments across the Atlantic showed how easily the "temptation to use this medium of communication for propaganda purposes" could manifest itself. "In several European countries . . . radio has been used by the party in power to destroy the confidence of the public in the press. The final result of it in those countries has been the suppression of the press and the destruction of the newspapers."[29]

Apprehension about a policy change on media ownership soon became more acute as some New Dealers began to push for legislation threatening a separation of press and radio. In July 1937, Wallace White submitted a Senate resolution demanding a "thorough and complete investigation of the broadcasting industry" and of the "acts, rules, regulations, and policies" that governed it. White listed thirty specific issues that the investigation should cover, including virtually all policies relating to broadcast ownership. Most troubling to publishers, White proposed to investigate the "extent" and "effect . . . upon the public interest" of newspaper-radio ownership while calling newspaper involvement in radio the "greatest danger to a free press in the

United States." Ultimately, White claimed, his concerns were rooted in apprehension about the "monopoly of the transmission of information and news and opinion to the American people. I happen to be one of those who do not want to see such a monopoly developed here in the United States."[30]

A similar bill was proposed in the House later that year, and the rhetoric of many representatives was less measured than Senator White's. Representative William McFarlane, a Texas Democrat, called media owners "dictators" and claimed that there were fewer than three hundred Americans who had "an absolute monopoly in the molding of public opinion through undisputed control of radio stations, newspapers, and motion pictures." McFarlane railed against the "radio monopolies" composed of broadcasters and equipment manufacturers, and he had even harsher words for newspapers that owned radio stations. "Is that monopoly," he wondered. "Is that dictatorship?" McFarlane echoed these remarks the following month by charging that "radio control of newspapers is a widespread evil," and alleging that both newspapers and radio stations were controlled by the "same crowd that controls almost everything that is worthwhile—the banking interests of Wall Street."[31]

Publisher and broadcaster anxiety about potential legislation reached a fever pitch in 1937 after Montana Senator Burton Wheeler began consulting with FCC staffers about the possibility of creating regulations against cross ownership. Wheeler told the newspaper and radio trade press that "Something ought to be done to prevent the newspapers from owning broadcasting stations or monopolizing them." Wheeler was unsure if he would seek this legislation in Congress or ask the FCC to do it, but he was clear that "something should be done either in a legislative or regulatory way about newspaper ownership of broadcasting stations." In January 1937, Wheeler made inquiries to FCC chairman Anning Prall indicating a mounting interest in the problem of concentrated media ownership. Wheeler asked Prall to consider what could be done about the growing size of media enterprises like William Randolph Hearst's and whether or not the FCC believed it could reasonably deny newspaper applications for radio licenses.[32]

Hampson Gary, the FCC's general counsel and a former commissioner, responded to Wheeler in a detailed memo stating that he believed the FCC had both the obligation to consider the "business connections of the applicant" and the power to deny applications from newspapers if it found that a newspaper applicant would in fact not serve the public interest. The Commission did not, however, have the authority to make an independent and unilateral decision to ban all newspapers from broadcasting, given the powers specifically delegated to it by Congress under the Communications Act of 1934. But if Congress were to pass such a policy, Gary concluded, it would withstand constitutional challenges. Not surprisingly, Gary's memo caused a great deal of consternation in media industry circles. *Variety* claimed that the memo "threatened" a "shotgun divorce" of newspaper-radio enterprises and reported that "secret huddles" between industry figures and friendly legislators were taking place all over Washington to formulate a "battle plan to meet the anti-radio animus" of Wheeler and his congressional allies. The trade press speculated that the memo and the proposed legislation were motivated primarily by partisan politics. *Broadcasting* editor Sol Taishoff thought that the fact that an "estimated 85% of the daily newspaper circulation of the country is said to have opposed Mr. Roosevelt during the last presidential campaign," was largely responsible for "administration sentiment against newspaper 'domination' of radio." It was a "tempest of major proportions," the magazine claimed, and "its inception is largely political" and based on an "overpowering desire to prevent publishers from dominating the 'editorial policies' of radio stations as they do those of their newspapers."[33]

Roosevelt's ill-fated plan to reform the Supreme Court in early 1937 stoked publishers' criticisms that he was abusing his executive authority, that he cared little about separation of powers, and that he was essentially a dictator in disguise. Roosevelt had become increasingly irate at the Court, which continued to strike down key New Deal programs, including perhaps the centerpiece of the entire enterprise, the NIRA. On 5 February 1937, Roosevelt proposed legislation that would allow him to make an additional appointment to the Court in any instance when an acting justice did not retire within six months of turning seventy years of age. The bill was specifically designed to allow Roosevelt to appoint new judges to balance the older judges whom he believed were anti-New Deal, and it would have granted him the authority to add six new justices to the Court. The plan was widely attacked by FDR's critics, and even some of his allies considered the proposal to be profoundly misguided. With widespread popular support, Congress defeated the plan in July 1937, providing a stinging rebuke to Roosevelt and the New Deal.[34]

An unintended consequence of the Court-packing plan was a slowing of the momentum in Congress on the newspaper-radio ownership issue. Burton Wheeler, one of Roosevelt's key congressional allies on media reform, was also a passionate advocate for an independent judiciary and became the leader of the Senate opposition to the Court-packing plan. This dramatically curtailed the time and attention that Wheeler devoted to the newspaper-radio issue. As *Broadcasting* noted, the Supreme Court battle had taken a "virtual monopoly on congressional activity" and had "overshadowed completely" Wheeler's activities on broadcast reform. The magazine noted that Wheeler "himself has admitted that he will be unable to devote any time to the matter until the Supreme Court issue is out of the way." The situation stayed this way throughout the Court-packing fight, and *Broadcasting* commented that "the antagonism now prevailing between President Roosevelt and Senator Wheeler" kept Wheeler from taking any action on a matter on which he had been quite actively involved.[35]

The Court-packing plan further provoked anti-New Deal forces to attack Roosevelt's attempts to regulate the media. Fred Crawford, a Republican Representative from Michigan, drew connections between the two policies when he remarked that 1937 "will go down in history as a year of tampering with the Federal Court system" and warned that still more dangerous and antidemocratic policies were forthcoming from the Roosevelt administration. "We are about to enter a new year and harbingers of a drive against another cherished liberty of the Republic may be seen lurking on the horizon," Crawford claimed. "I refer to the freedom of the press. Recent slaps at the press both directly and indirectly by the present administration impels me to draw attention to this matter today." Crawford drew connections between the Court-packing plan and Roosevelt's anti-newspaper statements, and he urged his fellow congressmen to be alert. "Curb on a free press will not come through these open and readily distinguishable sources," Crawford stated. "By bringing these citations to your attention I would not imply that it is the time to shout 'Wolf, wolf.' Yet who 12 months ago would have given serious thought to the idea that the administration had in mind in tampering with the Supreme Court? An administration bold enough to attempt to subordinate an independent judiciary may be considered likewise bold enough to attempt to curb a free press." Crawford had some reasons to be suspicious as, in December 1937, Vice President John Garner, acting as Roosevelt's "emissary," according to one report, had begun privately "feeling out members of the Senate" about the possibilities of an "Administration-sponsored measure being introduced in January" about newspaper-radio ownership.[36]

Some of Crawford's fears were also motivated by concerns over House Resolution 3892, the most aggressive congressional effort to date to address cross ownership. The bill, introduced by Iowa Democrat Otha Wearin the week following the circulation of Hampson Gary's controversial memorandum in January 1937, proposed amending the Communications Act to stipulate that it was "against public interest to permit the creation or the continuance of monopolies in the distribution of general information, news, and editorial comment," and to ban "any combination resulting in unified control of newspapers, magazines, or other printed publications, with radio broadcasting." The law would apply to all future licenses as well as all present licenses "immediately upon termination" of their term. Wearin's bill accrued some support in both the House and the Senate. Senator Sherman Minton, a Democrat from Indiana and later a Truman-appointed Supreme Court justice, remarked that he thought the bill was "probably more justified, now that we find that the press is trying to strangle the radio."[37]

Soon after the introduction of H.R. 3892, the journal *Public Opinion Quarterly* published a debate on newspaper-radio ownership between Wearin and Alfred Kirchhofer, the managing editor of the *Buffalo Evening News* and executive director of WBEN and WEBR, the two stations owned by the paper. Wearin claimed that, since newspapers and radio stations were the "two major agencies of disseminating public opinion," he believed that it "would be an unfortunate thing for the American people . . . to be handicapped through having" the ownership of them "in the control of a single individual or organization." The federal government, Wearin argued, had the duty to "guarantee the average individual safety from the danger of monopolistic control of public opinion." Monopoly in general was harmful to the public, Wearin argued, but of "all the monopolies the world has ever known none could be as bad as a monopoly of public opinion in the hands of any existing agency of news dissemination." The only way to fix the problem, he claimed, was "complete divorcement" of newspapers and radio stations.[38]

Alfred Kirchhofer responded to Wearin that newspapers were not only good candidates for radio broadcasting, but also that they were in fact the best candidates. Having newspapers operate radio stations was a "better guarantee of free speech and fair discussion over the radio" than having anyone else do it. Newspapers, Kirchhofer claimed, had "popularized radio as they never have aided any other invention," and to force them to abandon broadcasting "would destroy the tradition, experience, and leadership" that they had brought to it. Kirchhofer also warned that Wearin's proposal might lead to all sorts of unintended consequences, as the bill left open the possibility of a "future policy that might bar labor groups, church groups, even educational interests from radio operation." Moreover, Kirchhofer argued, newspapers were part of a "tradition of free speech and accurate reporting which, no matter how easy it may seem to replace, is an inheritance that should be protected and maintained for the public interest and the preservation of our political unity."[39]

Newspapers owning stations always kept close watch on legislative developments, but H.R. 3892 and the circulation of the Gary memorandum brought about new levels of concern, as it was the most direct federal challenge to their businesses that they had encountered. *Chicago Tribune* attorney Louis Caldwell responded to the proposed legislation almost immediately and drafted a detailed summary of the situation that he sent to WGN manager W. E. Macfarlane, who agreed that H.R. 3892 was "going to be very serious." Despite concern at high levels of leading media corporations throughout 1937 and 1938, congressional allies ultimately mollified fears about the proposed legislation. As Charles Halleck, a Republican Representative from Indiana and member of the House Committee on Interstate and Foreign Commerce, reported to *Tribune* executives, Wearin's requests for a hearing on H.R. 3892 were successfully stalled in committee by opponents of the bill like himself.[40]

Despite some of the severe floor proclamations on the consequences of increasing media consolidation and radio ownership by newspapers, none of the bills in Congress ever garnered enough bipartisan support to pass, and similar bills stalled in both houses in 1939 as well. Though legislatively unsuccessful, the consistent agitation by reform-minded congressmen was successful in keeping many media industry figures in a constant state of unease. Fearful that Congress might essentially outlaw profitable elements of their businesses, newspaper-radio owners lobbied legislative allies and foes alike to combat any legislation, and this struggle over broadcast regulation essentially held the entire matter in a state of suspended tension. All the while, though, newspapers continued in even greater numbers to apply to the FCC for radio licenses.[41]

Publisher fears that the FCC might adopt policies against them were realized in 1938 during a case involving competing applications for the same frequency in Port Huron, Michigan. One of the applicants was a company owned by a father and son, Harmon and Herman Stevens. Herman was an attorney and long-time resident of Port Huron, while Harmon had taken an interest in broadcasting while a student at Michigan State University. The other applicant for the license was William Ottoway, the president and business manager of the *Port Huron Times Herald*, the city's only newspaper. Though Port Huron residents could receive broadcasts from WWJ and WJR in Detroit, the city had no local station, a situation bemoaned by Mayor George Harvey.

"At the present time there is no local radio station in Port Huron," Harvey told the FCC, and this meant that there were "no radio facilities available to help the city officials to directly contact the people." Though Port Huron did have a local newspaper, Harvey felt that radio was a "more effective means of explaining problems than the printed page, because the voice is more effective than the printed word." William Ottoway argued that he was the best candidate to provide this service to Port Huron, citing his journalism education and his several years of work experience at the *Detroit News*, the owner of station WWJ.[42]

When the FCC handed down its decision, it ruled for the first time that newspaper ownership of a radio station might be harmful to a community, and it awarded the license to the Stevenses over William Ottoway. The Commission ruled that it was ultimately unclear how Ottoway "would disassociate himself from the newspaper in the operation of the station." Ultimately, the Commission believed, giving the license to the Stevenses would "better serve public interest, convenience, and necessity in that there will be added to the Port Huron area a medium for the dissemination of news and information to the public which will be independent of and afford a degree of competition to other such media in that area." The Port Huron case was the first instance in which the FCC applied the diversification principle to deny a license to a newspaper, and publishers began to pay even closer attention to what the Commission was doing in developing a policy. Though *Port Huron* was a single case based on a small city, the precedent that it set seemed to many publishers like it could be a major turning point.[43]

Toward a New Deal Policy on Media Ownership

As the FCC and Congress considered whether to enact legal separation between newspapers and radio throughout 1937 and 1938, the cooperative relationship between the two media continued to harmonize, especially after what became known as the Munich Crisis of September 1938, the combined newspaper and radio coverage of which became one of the most significant moments in American media history. Prior to 1938, there had been a great deal of news and information on the radio, as commentators like Walter Winchell and Boake Carter attracted large audiences throughout the 1930s with their interpretations of current events, and most stations provided short spot news announcements throughout the day. The year 1938 was pivotal for radio news, however, as NBC and CBS deployed capital and correspondents to Europe and provided regular eyewitness accounts· of the growing tensions on the continent. In the months after Adolf Hitler took over Austria in March 1938, Germany made increasingly aggressive moves toward occupying Czechoslovakia as well and, with war on the continent suddenly looming, American radio broadcasters began delivering constant coverage of the events. For eighteen days stretching from 12 to 29 September, radio reporters and commentators such as Edward R. Murrow, William Shirer, and H. V. Kaltenborn narrated to rapt audiences the ongoing events leading to the conference in Munich where European leaders allowed Germany to take over Czechoslovakia's Sudetenland.[44]

James Rorty, a frequent critic of commercial radio broadcasting, lauded the American press and radio for their coverage of the Munich Crisis while criticizing British and French radio for their "relatively timid, unenterprising, and heavily censored" programming and claiming that "Nazi broadcasting stations were used continuously to implement the Führer's hypocritical banditry." American broadcasters, on the other hand, gave what Rorty described as exemplary public service, delivering a "day-by-day performance . . . that can only be described as magnificent," in the process ushering in a whole new era of news reporting. "For the first time," Rorty claimed, "history has been made in the hearing of its pawns. Radio has given them not only the words but also the voices of the protagonists. Hitler, Benes, Chamberlain, Daladier, Mussolini. The radio has our ears." Combined with subsequent and more analytical newspaper coverage, this gave American listeners unprecedented access to ongoing events. "American newspaper correspondents were almost continuously on the air, speaking from European capitals," Rorty stated, and newspapers, "an hour or two later gave the eye a chance to read and digest what the ear had heard; gave us the shaded maps that the radio can't give us." This was the "big chance" for American broadcasters to "prove the validity of the 'American system' of advertising-supported, privately owned broadcasting," and Rorty saw them taking full advantage of it. Radio had come into its own, Rorty felt, and it was "scarcely too much to say that the future of civilization will be determined to a considerable degree by who rules radio and how." Newspapers saw their circulations increase rapidly throughout the crisis, suggesting to many in the business that radio "served to stimulate rather than limit newspaper sales." Munich meant that the last lingering hostilities between press and radio in the early 1930s had drawn to a close, not just for this reason, Rorty claimed, but because of the fact that "the newspaper business is rapidly 'joining' the radio business." Rorty was not sure, however, that this was necessarily desirable. "This trend, of course, suggests other problems affecting the public interest of a democracy."[45]

The tremendous public interest in the unfolding events in Europe definitively demonstrated to publishers and broadcasters the great benefits of cooperation. High levels of public interest not only kept listeners glued to radio stations for updates but also made them buy newspapers for more comprehensive coverage and analysis of the events. The news coverage that this united media produced was, as the ANPA claimed, "without precedent in national and world history." Journalist Leland Stowe wrote that "radio had the whole world by the ears" and that "For the first time in our lives we have all taken part in a world crisis." Radio, he claimed, had done a wonderful job, and it "must be evident to any newspaperman who has eyes to see (and ears to hear!) that radio news-casting has won its spurs, and has become a vital adjunct to the daily press."[46] After Munich, Joseph Pulitzer stated, "the American newspaper has given way to the radio as THE medium for informing the public as to spot news," and he believed that there was no reason for publishers to remain hostile to radio as a purveyor of news.[47]

At its 1938 annual meeting, the ANPA devoted considerable attention to growing tensions in Europe, suggesting that "events of the past year all over the world . . . emphasize the significance of Radio as a social phenomenon which a vigilant press cannot ignore." The ANPA presented government control of radio in America as a possible first step in a move toward government control of the press, and it argued that their campaign for a "free" radio was the front line of defense against authoritarianism taking root in the United States. The task facing newspapers, the ANPA asserted, was to get past the "friendly competition between the newspapers and the broadcasters," and to "guard against any encroachment upon American democracy by the Federal government with Radio as an instrument of political power." The solution was for newspapers to work together and create a "constant and effective opposition to all tendencies toward the misuse of Radio, especially by any dominant political interest."[48]

Secretary of the Interior Harold Ickes, a close Roosevelt ally and active critic of the press, launched a counterattack for the administration when he debated publisher Frank Gannett on 12 January 1939 on the national NBC program *America's Town Meeting of the Air*. Ickes blasted newspapers for having "financial and economic tie-ups" that put them in the "shackles . . . of private interests." Gannett responded bluntly that Ickes was only protesting because many newspapers had opposed New Deal policies such as the attempt to reorganize the Supreme Court. The debate struck a chord with listeners, as NBC reported that it received more letters after that broadcast than any other *Town Meeting* program that year. It also struck a chord with publishers, several of whom attacked Ickes as "pompous" and compared his statements to "some of the outbursts of the German Minister of Propaganda."[49]

Ickes and Gannett continued attacking each other after the debate, and their clash represented one of the high points in the level of animosity between the New Deal and the press. Gannett issued a point-by-point refutation of Ickes's *Town Meeting* arguments in early February 1939, and his opposition to the secretary drew support from other influential publishers. S. S. McClure, for example, the founder of *McClure's* magazine, wrote to Gannett that his campaign against the New Deal was "second in importance to nothing since the work of the men who made the Constitution and wrote the Federalist Papers." Frank Gannett remained one of Roosevelt's most vocal critics throughout 1939. In a mass mailing, Gannett claimed that readers would be "amazed by the revelation of dictatorial powers now held by the President and his successors" over the American media. Gannett fumed that, at a time when Americans were "deciding issues which place in the balance the lives and happiness of millions of American citizens, the President under the Communications Act of 1934 may, if he chooses, prevent all adverse criticism of the course he desires to take. And, on the other hand, he may saturate the public mind exclusively with those particular arguments or facts that support his administration." Gannett went so far as to raise the specter of European-style media suppression emerging in the United States through Roosevelt's influence over radio licensing. Ultimately, Gannett claimed, "the powers conferred on the President by the Communications Act of 1934 are the same powers with which Adolf Hitler is keeping the German people in the dark. They are the powers that Stalin and Mussolini exercise over the radio in Russia and Italy."[50]

Harold Ickes continued his feud with Gannett in a speech before the National Lawyers Guild, stating that he felt it was a "pity" that many newspapers "persist in representing a class interest, a money interest, instead of the public interest" at the same time that they regularly "color news, distort news, suppress news and invent 'news' in favor of those with whom they are allied financially and socially, and with whose objectives they are in sympathy."[51] Ickes hammered away at newspapers with such vigor that *Editor & Publisher* called his campaign a "private war" against the press.[52] His most sustained attack came in the publication of a 1939 monograph entitled *America's House of Lords: An Inquiry into the Freedom of the Press*, in which Ickes expounded upon his argument that "American journalism is not merely a Big Business, it is a semi-monopolistic one." Noting that many publishers had purchased radio stations, Ickes urged that the two be separated. If radio was to "survive as an independent instrument of communication," Ickes argued, "it must not become a handmaiden of the press."[53]

Franklin Roosevelt by this point had become so outraged at newspaper coverage of his presidency that he conducted a staged and transcribed "interview" with Lowell Mellett, the executive director of the National Emergency Council, and sent copies to stations around the country. In the piece, Roosevelt criticized anti-New Deal newspapers and presented radio as the only way that he could adequately inform the public of what his administration was doing. "It should be possible," he remarked, to use radio to "correct the kind of misinformation that is sometimes given currency for one reason or another." In parts of the country, Roosevelt stated, "it is the unhappy fact that only through the radio is it possible to overtake loudly proclaimed untruths or greatly exaggerated half truths." *Broadcasting* claimed that FDR's statements were the public expression of what had "long been an open secret in Washington," and a clear sign that figures inside the administration were looking to radio "more and more" to present their views to the public independent of the newspaper press. This same animus against "editorial opposition to the Administration and purported coloring of news," the magazine noted, was animating the "crusade for divorcement of newspapers from broadcast station ownership." By 1939, these two fronts on which Roosevelt and New Dealers were working to reshape the public sphere were converging. In April 1939, *Broadcasting* cited sources inside the Roosevelt administration hinting at an impending investigation on newspaper ownership of radio. Citing recent reports that Roosevelt "again has commented privately on the growing tendency of newspapers to absorb stations," the magazine feared that a legislative push was imminent.[54]

This convergence continued at the FCC, where the changing roster of commissioners began to shift policy in a more assertive direction. *Time* featured Commissioner Frank McNinch on its cover in May 1938, remarking that McNinch brought a "sharp regulatory attitude" to the FCC. More importantly, newly appointed chairman James Lawrence Fly, a close ally of President Roosevelt, sought to shape the spirit of commissioner Irvin Stewart's dissents into a policy prohibiting newspaper ownership. This process began soon after the Port Huron case in a 1939 proceeding in which the Martinsville Broadcasting Company applied for a license to construct a station in Martinsville, Virginia. The company was owned by Jonas Weiland, the owner of a radio station in North Carolina, and William Barnes, the publisher of the local *Martinsville Daily Bulletin*. The competing applicant, the Patrick Henry Broadcasting Company, had an eclectic assembly of stockholders that included a laundry business owner, the president of the Virginia Underwear Corporation, the director of First National Bank of Martinsville, and the head of the local school board. The FCC was not persuaded that this group had the necessary technical qualifications to own a radio station and decided that, even though there was no other radio station in Martinsville, the newspaper should get the license. Fly dissented from the decision, arguing that it was "inconsistent with that of the Commission in *Port Huron Broadcasting*." Fly was aware that *Port Huron* was not "intended to be applied generally to all newspaper applicants" but he argued that it did merit consideration in cases where a newspaper-owned station "would tend toward creating a local monopoly in the channels for the public expression of opinion and in the dissemination of news and information," as he believed the situation in Martinsville did. Later, as FCC chairman and with McNinch's support, Fly aggressively continued to push the Commission to continue in this direction.[55]

As Franklin Roosevelt's second term came to a close, debates over the broadcasting industry were shaped by increasing animosity from the president, growing regulatory activism at the FCC, and close cooperation between many broadcasters and publishers. By 1940, a showdown between the federal government and the media over the issue of newspaper-radio ownership had become unavoidable. According to some estimates, during Roosevelt's third presidential campaign, the percentage of American newspapers that endorsed him on their editorial pages was less than half the percentage of Americans that voted for him. In 1932, Roosevelt had received 57 percent of the popular vote, and 41 percent of American daily newspapers supported him. In 1936, Roosevelt garnered 60 percent of the popular vote while his editorial support slipped to 37 percent. In 1940, Roosevelt received 55 percent of the votes with the support of only 25 percent of American dailies. To Roosevelt, this declining editorial support motivated his increasing ire at newspaper publishers as a group.[56]

At the same time, the media trade press was encouraging newspapers to pursue radio licenses on AM and on the new FM band, and this troubled governmental opponents of media concentration, many of whom thought that FM would offer a way around the problem. With influential publisher-broadcasters like Walter Damm of the *Milwaukee Journal* and WTMJ promoting FM as "the way for many more papers to build and operate radio stations" and encouraging newspapers to apply for licenses, and with newspapers and radio putting on an invigorated post-Munich united front, many in the administration felt that there was an urgent need for a new policy. *Broadcasting* reported that, as of May 1940, the "signs of growing friendship and cooperation between radio and the press continue to multiply, and they are all to the good." The magazine noted that, "far from carping and criticizing as they formerly did," the ANPA "simply took radio for granted" at their recent annual convention. Believing that it could wait no longer to prevent this cross-media ownership from developing into a full media monopoly, the FCC under James Lawrence Fly began a major investigation of the issue in 1941.[57]

Chapter 4

Reform Liberalism and the Media:
The Federal Communications Commission's
Newspaper-Radio Investigation

The problem of corporate power was among the greatest concerns for New Dealers as they sought to end the Great Depression. During Franklin Roosevelt's first term, the National Industrial Recovery Act proved to be an unsuccessful and ultimately unconstitutional way to reform the economy through cooperative management by government and industry.[1] Early in Roosevelt's second term, the economy slid into a recession that New Dealers blamed on corporate opposition to their policies. Resentful monopolists, many believed, were deliberately sabotaging the New Deal, and historian Ellis Hawley remarks that "theory that capital was on a sitdown strike was soon to become the official version of the recession." Starting in late 1937, New Dealers responded with an aggressive and coordinated campaign against corporations that they believed were monopolists in a variety of industries.[2]

New Deal agitation against monopoly manifested itself in several significant plans for reform. In early 1938, at Franklin Roosevelt's urging, Congress authorized the formation of the Temporary National Economic Committee, thus initiating a massive and comprehensive investigation into the problem of monopoly in the United States. Thurman Arnold took over the Justice Department's Antitrust Division in March 1938, revitalizing an agency that soon began an aggressive and unprecedented campaign against monopoly in a wide range of industries. As an antimonopolist, Arnold was not philosophically opposed to large corporations, but instead had the overarching goal of making sure that corporate concentration did not have adverse effects on consumer prices. The philosophical opposition to corporate size was, however, represented with increasing prominence in the New Deal by a vocal and influential group who were proponents of the ideas of Louis Brandeis. For these New Dealers, corporate size was a problem with ramifications far beyond issues of consumer prices. It was, as Alan Brinkley describes this mode of thinking, "not economic; it was social, cultural, even moral. 'Bigness' was a threat not just to prosperity but, more important, to freedom." For the Brandeisians in the New Deal, the promotion of economic justice meant that corporate size had to be reduced and economic power dispersed. If this spirit "could be summed up in one word," Ellis Hawley remarks, "that word would probably be 'decentralization.' Centralized wealth, centralized control, and centralized location," many New Dealers believed, "were all complementary, all aspects of a broad general trend that should be reversed."[3]

Throughout the late 1930s and early 1940s, these various strands of New Deal antimonopoly sentiment generated attempts to regulate large and powerful media corporations. On one front, in 1938 Thurman Arnold's Department of Justice filed a suit against eight of the major motion picture corporations, charging them with monopolizing the motion picture industry in the United States through control of both film production and the distribution and exhibition network. The Justice Department had been investigating the motion picture industry for the previous two years, and in the 1938 case sought to divorce the film production business from that of distribution and exhibition. In effect, the Justice Department claimed, the marketplace for cinema was restricted because of anticompetitive behavior by the dominant firms, as independent exhibitors were denied access to major motion pictures to show in their theaters and independent film producers were denied venues to show their works. This proceeding, which eventually became popularly called the Paramount Case, finally reached the Supreme Court in 1948, which upheld most of the Justice Department's case.[4]

On another front, the Justice Department in August 1942 filed a suit against the Associated Press for allegedly violating the Sherman Antitrust Act by refusing to allow *Chicago Sun* publisher Marshall Field III, a Roosevelt ally, to obtain membership in the AP for his new paper. Field wanted the *Sun* to provide an alternative to the conservative *Chicago Tribune*, through which publisher Robert McCormick had long been active in AP leadership circles and played a prominent role in blocking Field's membership application. The Justice Department won the case, which was eventually upheld by the Supreme Court in 1945. Justice Hugo Black ruled that there was nothing unconstitutional about the government regulating publishers' business practices. "Member publishers of AP are engaged in business for profit exactly as are other business men who sell food, steel, aluminum, or anything else people need or want," Black wrote. "All alike are covered by the Sherman Act. The fact that the publisher handles news while others handle food does not . . . afford the publisher a peculiar constitutional sanctuary in which he can with impunity violate laws regulating his business practices." Black also extended Oliver Wendell Holmes's *Abrams* reading of the Constitution in writing that it "rests on the assumption that the widest possible dissemination of information from diverse and antagonistic sources is essential to the welfare of the public."[5]

Under James Lawrence Fly, the Federal Communications Commission brought an activist New Deal perspective to the regulation of broadcasting, and the agency developed a firm commitment to the Brandeisian idea of decentralization. From 1938 to 1941, the FCC conducted an investigation of chain broadcasting, the ultimate finding of which was that the National Broadcasting Company's ownership of two of the four major networks (NBC-Red and NBC-Blue) gave the company too much power in the radio industry. In the *Report on Chain Broadcasting*, the FCC's summary and decision in the investigation, the Commission asserted that the creation of "fair competition" in radio was "contingent upon ending the abuses inherent in dual network operation," and it ordered NBC broken up as a "necessary and proper means of reestablishing that fair competition." A competitive radio market, the FCC asserted, demanded a diverse group of "individual station licensees" to select what would be "put on the air and what . . . will not." In language drawn directly from Brandeisian antimonopolists, the FCC stated that, for the American system of broadcasting to work, this power of selection needed to be dispersed among as many people and stations as possible. "Decentralization of this power is the best protection against its abuse," the FCC concluded.[6]

At the same time that it was investigating concentrated control of network broadcasting on the AM band, the FCC also confronted the rapid concentration of ownership on the new FM band. Many heralded FM as the future of radio broadcasting, extolling its superior sound quality and touting it as a solution to the problem of ownership diversity on the air. The new band promised to open up spectrum space for hundreds of new stations across the country, and the FCC was determined to encourage diversity of ownership on it. Fly told an audience at the 1940 National Independent Broadcasters convention that there would be "no vested interests in FM. Radio needs new blood and a broadened base. FM must be free to move forward and not forced to drag the anchor of a heavy investment in the present type of broadcasting." Against Fly's wishes, the opposite trend characterized FM's development as newspapers applied for over 30 percent of the first wave of commercial FM licenses. This expanded on their already sizable stake in AM, where they owned roughly 30 percent of AM stations by the end of the 1930s (see Appendix). With competition in the newspaper industry also declining (the percentage of U.S. cities with competing daily papers shrank from 45 to 24 between 1920 and 1940), Fly steered the FCC toward a policy that was increasingly aggressive about policing concentrated media ownership.[7]

In late 1940, Fly's concerns about media consolidation converged with New Deal antimonopoly sentiment in a broad sense and more specifically with the ire that President Franklin Roosevelt felt toward many American newspapers. Roosevelt, who owed a significant portion of his popularity to his success in speaking directly to the American people over the radio, decided to hit back at this declining newspaper support by attacking publishers over the issue of radio ownership. The issue had become, as FCC Commissioner Paul Porter recalled, a "fetish of FDR's, and he was constantly putting the blow torch" on Fly to do something about it. On 3 December 1940, shortly after winning his second reelection, Roosevelt sent Fly a memorandum with a single sentence: "Will you let me know when you propose to have a hearing on newspaper ownership of radio stations." Fly responded eagerly by initiating an investigation into the issue, in the process generating one of the most significant inquiries to date into the basic structures of ownership in the American media, and opening up the possibility of major structural changes to media ownership laws.[8]

With Fly's leadership, the FCC began an investigation that convened wide-ranging hearings attempting to demonstrate that newspaper-radio combinations were undesirable in several significant ways. The Commission wanted to show that newspaper ownership of radio was a more dangerous concentration of corporate power than existed in other industries, as the commodity at hand was information, the very stuff of American culture and democracy. The Commission also wanted to show that joint media enterprises were constraining the marketplace of ideas and limiting the number and range of voices that could become part of public discourse. Ultimately, the FCC in 1941 wanted to show that virtually everything about the newspaper-radio combination was bad for the media and a serious threat to the foundations of American democracy, and its practical aims were to create policies that would prevent multimedia monopolies. In the early 1940s, the FCC drew upon some of the most activist ideas and antimonopoly philosophies of the New Deal as it strove to reform the basic structures of the American media.

James Lawrence Fly and the Antimonopolist FCC

James Lawrence Fly became chairman of the FCC in September 1939, an event that historian Susan Brinson describes as the moment when "the New Deal came to the Commission."[9] A native Texan, Fly had been a student of Felix Frankfurter's at Harvard Law School before joining the Antitrust Division of the Justice Department in 1929. By the mid-1930s, Fly had established himself as an antitrust crusader, and in 1937 he became the general counsel of the Tennessee Valley Authority. Throughout the 1930s, Fly was steadfast in his desire to use the federal government as a countervailing force to private power regardless of the industry involved, and when he joined the FCC in 1939, Fly brought a deep commitment to promoting diversity of ownership among the corporations shaping the public sphere.[10]

Fly's colleague Marcus Cohn recalled that Fly "adored Roosevelt and adored the New Deal and what the New Deal stood for," and that Fly believed it was "terribly important" that "radio be kept independent of the newspapers." Fly feared that there would not be a "viable, dynamic, democratic process in America if the ownership of the broadcasting medium at that time . . . ended up in the hands of the newspapers." Fly quickly influenced the overall direction and perception of the FCC, and in just several months made the FCC into an entity that *Collier's* reported was believed to be "Public Enemy No. 1" by the broadcasting industry. Former National Recovery Administration head Hugh Johnson also remarked that Fly was the "cockiest . . . New Deal wight who ever figuratively and gleefully cut a tory's throat or scuttled an economic royalist's ship." Fly's activism drew heated criticism from media corporations, and he was a lightning rod for attacks from them in the late 1930s and early 1940s.[11]

In early 1941, the FCC completed the Chain Broadcasting Investigation and, with the broadcasting industry thus already outraged about the new network regulations, Fly began the push toward the investigation of news-paper ownership of radio stations that Roosevelt wanted.[12] Fly consulted the other members of the commission and found both support and dissent, the latter coming especially aggressively from commissioners T. A. M. Craven and Norman Case, who Fly cautioned Franklin Roosevelt would "endeavor to embarrass us at every turn." Fly remained committed to the investigation, telling Roosevelt that he was "in wholehearted agreement that the problem of newspaper ownership of radio stations should be given a thorough airing so that the desirability of having as many *independent* channels of information and communication as possible may be brought home to the public," and he succeeded in initiating an investigation by a one vote margin among FCC commissioners.[13]

The FCC's investigation began on 21 March 1941 with the release of Order No. 79, which froze all pending FM applications, ordered the construction of currently authorized FM stations halted, and stated that the FCC should offi-cially assess whether policies should be enacted to bar newspapers from own-ing either AM or FM radio stations. Hearings were scheduled for the summer in Washington, and the Commission subpoenaed a variety of industry wit-nesses and academic experts to testify on the subject of cross-ownership.[14]

Industry reaction was immediately fearful and indignant. The trade jour-nal *Broadcasting* mocked the investigation in editorial cartoons and called it an "action obviously calculated to 'get' those publishers certain New Deal-ers don't like." FM Broadcasters, the dominant trade group representing FM station owners, claimed that Order No. 79 was nothing but "discrimination toward newspaper interests" and warned that "No one can minimize the is-sues at stake or the fact that, by this time, a battle of goodly magnitude is brewing."[15] Newspaper publishers were widely critical of the investigation. Privately, *Chicago Tribune* business manager W. E. Macfarlane feared that the investigation might make it "possible to discriminate against the renewals of AM licenses according to the administration's attitude toward various news-paper publishers." This Macfarlane believed, might force the staunchly anti-New Deal *Tribune* to sell its station, WGN. Publicly, trade journal *Editor & Publisher* feared that "numerous people who do not particularly admire the present generation of newspaper publishers will use the Commission's hear-ings as a sounding board for their prejudice."[16]

In late March 1941, more than 150 newspaper and radio executives formed the Newspaper-Radio Committee to respond to the investigation. Mark Ethridge, publisher of the *Louisville Courier-Journal*, was selected

Drawn for BROADCASTING by Sid Hix

*"He Keeps Hanging Around—I Think He's an FCC Man Investigating
Joint Ownership of Newspapers and Radio."*

Figure 8. "He Keeps Hanging Around." Cartoon, *Broadcasting* 20
(28 April 1941): 9.

as the group's chairman. On 14 May, at the annual meeting of the National
Association of Broadcasters in St. Louis, Ethridge gave a rousing speech attacking James Fly with the FCC chairman sitting nearby. Since Fly joined
the Commission, Ethridge argued, the FCC had "gone beyond any powers
conferred in the law and . . . has been prejudiced and frequently punitive."
Ethridge finished his speech to raucous cheers from the assembled broadcasters, leaving Fly visibly outraged.[17]

The protests only emboldened Fly to make the FCC's investigation more
aggressive. On 8 July 1941, the Commission expanded the scope of its inquiry
when it issued Order No. 79–A, which presented an even broader investigation of the basic structures of ownership of the broadcasting industry. The
Commission announced that it would now "from time to time direct" investigations on all manner of issues related to the ownership of radio stations,
and that it would investigate whether newspaper ownership of radio tended
to "prejudice the free and fair presentation of public issues and information
over the air" or "restrict or distort the broadcasting of news, or to limit the
sources of news to the public."[18]

The FCC followed this new order by sending questionnaires to newspapers that owned radio stations asking them to provide information about the relationship between their various media properties. Newspapers were incensed by the inquiry, as *Editor & Publisher* remarked that the FCC was not just "seeking facts," but was "looking for data that can be used for hypodermic cross-examination of newspaper people in the forthcoming hearings." Many publishers expressed "deep resentment" at the questionnaire and claimed that FCC staffers were "descend[ing] upon stations, networks and press associations to comb through their files" to "procure grist for the inquiry." *Broadcasting* claimed that investigators were "swooping down upon broadcast stations, networks and press associations and figuratively flipping their lapels to reveal shiny badges, then ransacking files, personal and otherwise, to sift out the 'dirt.' All this in preparation for a 'trial' before the same FCC . . . .This isn't censorship. It's something worse—intimidation." The magazine kept a steady

Drawn for BROADCASTING by Sid Hix

It's a Commission Investigator. He Thinks There's a Secret Panel Into a Newspaper Building Next Door!"

Figure 9. "It's a Commission Investigator." Cartoon, *Broadcasting* 21 (21 July 1941): 7.

stream of criticism directed at the investigation in reports and editorial cartoons, at one point going so far as to call these field investigators "radio's
Gestapo, begot by the FCC!"[19]

The newspaper industry also pursued legal efforts to stop the hearings
by arguing that they were beyond the scope of the FCC's administrative authority. The American Newspaper Publishers Association filed a petition
asking the FCC to terminate the proceedings on the grounds that the FCC
was "without authority to conduct a general inquiry into the newspaper
publishing business." Elisha Hanson, the ANPA's lead attorney, claimed that
the investigation was unconstitutional, thus striking a constant theme that
publishers and broadcasters would invoke throughout the investigation: the
FCC simply had no authority to regulate the conduct of newspaper corporations, even if those corporations were among the most powerful groups in
the broadcasting industry. The FCC denied the petition, arguing that it had
carefully considered the matter, and that it seemed "inconceivable to us that
an argument could be seriously advanced against the inherent power of any
administrative agency . . . to conduct general hearings of the type involved
here." Hearings like the Newspaper-Radio Investigation were in fact among
the "principal reasons for the establishment of administrative agencies" in
the first place. The FCC stated that it had always been making qualitative
choices between different kinds of applicants, that it had considered this issue
of newspaper ownership in a number of previous cases, and that it would
continue to do so in the future.[20]

One particularly aggressive publisher, James Stahlman of the *Nashville
Banner*, went beyond criticizing the hearings and refused to take part in them
at all. Stahlman, a staunch anti-New Dealer whose paper had long been editorializing against the FCC, filed suit in federal court to challenge the subpoena
the FCC had served him on the grounds that the FCC had no jurisdiction to
conduct the investigation.[21] Press critic George Seldes described Stahlman as
the most "vocal upholder of what is known as 'freedom of the press' in ownership circles," and the ANPA was pleased to have Stahlman, a former president
of the organization, lead the legal challenge. In court filings, Stahlman presented some seventeen grounds upon which the court could halt the FCC's
investigation, the most serious of which was that the Commission was hiding
an attack on the American press within an investigation into radio ownership. For Stahlman, the "matters contained in Order No.79–A . . . show on
their face that the Commission is asserting power to command . . . nothing
more or less than a bill of particulars in respect of the newspaper publishing

business." Stahlman's motives may have been principled, but they were also certainly practical, as his newspaper had a pending application for a radio station and he did not want the FCC's investigation to prevent the *Banner* from entering broadcasting.[22]

With Stahlman's court challenge pending, the FCC made is final preparations for the hearings, and the Commission would ultimately spend seventeen days between July and December 1941 questioning some forty-three witnesses about various aspects of the relationship between newspapers and radio stations, and presenting a variety of its own findings. The FCC granted permission to the ANPA both to call witnesses of its own and to cross-examine witnesses called by the FCC.

On 23 July 1941, James Lawrence Fly opened the FCC's hearings in the auditorium of the National Archives Building in Washington, D.C., in front of a large audience that included more than fifty editors and publishers. Fly's introductory statement was immediately interrupted by ANPA attorneys registering their disapproval of the proceedings. Attorney Thomas Thatcher lambasted the entire proceeding as a "hydra-headed, double-headed investigation" that the FCC had no authority to be conducting. Elisha Hanson charged that the entire investigation was designed to allow the federal government the unprecedented ability to investigate and regulate the nation's press. The investigation, Hanson asserted, was "nothing more than an impertinent effort" by the government to "inquire into the newspaper publishing business . . . the editorial policies of newspapers . . . [and] the news policies of newspapers." The ANPA's strategy enjoyed a wide public presence through press coverage, as the *New York Times* editorialized on the hearing's opening day that it "must be gravely questioned whether the FCC even has the legal authority to make the kind of blanket disqualification of a whole group of station licensees that it is considering."[23]

Fly's FCC ignored both procedural and public opposition to the hearings and began taking testimony from witnesses including broadcast executives, newspaper publishers and editors, elected officials, and representatives from organized labor discussing their views on the consequences of media consolidation. Allan S. Haywood, a national officer of the Congress of Industrial Organizations (CIO), made a particularly forceful argument about the negative effects that newspaper ownership of radio had for the presentation of diverse issues and viewpoints at both the national and local levels. To Haywood, many newspapers consistently demonstrated that the antilabor biases that they exhibited in print influenced the kind of content that they allowed onto their radio stations. These antilabor views and conduct were especially prevalent, Haywood argued, among larger and more heavily capitalized papers. It was "notorious," Haywood asserted, "that the daily press is by and large a big business institution," and the CIO thus had "looked with great hope to the development of radio as a medium through which it might find fairer treatment and greater opportunity for expression than it was accorded in the press." What the CIO found, to its dismay, was more of the same bias on the radio, and it was "disappointed to observe the encroachments in the radio field of the same kind of big business controls that have affected the press" and troubled by the fact that the "same kind of considerations of not offending big advertisers or potential sponsors" had "militated against granting labor the freedom of expression and sympathetic consideration to which it is entitled." It was up to the FCC to act immediately, Haywood argued, and if media consolidation continued and newspapers obtained more radio stations, the CIO would have "every reason to believe that democracy has been asleep at the switch" and that the "constitutional rights of freedom of speech and press have been placed at the mercy of a wealthy minority interest."[24]

To support his case, Haywood presented several examples of specific local discrimination against the CIO by newspaper-owned stations. Haywood claimed that in Detroit, a center of labor activism and in 1941 perhaps the key industrial city in the United States, the *Detroit News* station WWJ had been preventing the CIO from getting time on the air to discuss its ongoing activities. The union had often sought airtime in the city because of the vast numbers of members living there and, though it had "frequently obtained time from the other Detroit stations which are not newspaper-owned," it had "despite many requests . . . been able to obtain only one period in the past two years from station WWJ." Haywood discussed a similar situation in New York and asserted that the Transport Workers of America had been denied airtime on WINS, a station owned by William Randolph Hearst. Like most New York papers, Haywood argued, Hearst's had been "editorially hostile" to the union, which sought radio time to "offset the misleading propaganda." Despite a number of attempts to get on WINS in April and May 1941, the union was rebuffed every time. The CIO had a similar experience with WISN, another Hearst-owned station in Milwaukee, when it wanted to purchase time to broadcast in June 1941, to answer the "anti-CIO propaganda" it believed the station broadcast consistently. The station refused, though the CIO eventually "obtained time on station WEMP, which is not owned by any newspaper." Haywood urged the FCC to use a "less restricted interpretation of the spirit and intent of the Federal Communications Act" to protect freedom of expression and to promote a diversity of perspectives on the air by forcing a separation of newspapers and radio stations. If the Commission did not, Haywood argued, commonly owned newspapers and radio stations could continue presenting biased coverage of some of the most important issues of the day and could selectively avoid presenting coverage of certain issues or groups they disliked.[25]

The FCC solicited testimony from a variety of witnesses and, though the antimonopolist James Fly would have preferred that all testimony was as critical as Allan Haywood's, much of the record is ultimately equivocal. Some supported the sentiments that Haywood expressed, for example, John Rivers, the manager and president of station WCSC in Charleston, South Carolina, who claimed that the newspaper-owned station in his city was using aggressive and possibly illegal tactics to try to drive him off the air. Conversely, other witnesses like *Kansas City Star* managing editor Roy Roberts and a series of representatives from the Hearst Corporation presented their multimedia corporations as intelligent business enterprises committed to public service. Despite probing and often hostile questions from FCC attorneys, witnesses from media corporations that the FCC had called generated little evidence suggesting that newspaper ownership of radio was the sort of widespread problem that critics and New Dealers perceived it to be. Though the FCC's empirical case proved less robust than James Lawrence Fly might have wanted, however, the Commission was much more successful in introducing critical perspectives on media ownership from a series of academic experts that it called. The ANPA's strongest witnesses proved to be drawn from the academic ranks as well, and the most profound parts of the FCC's hearings soon became debates about the history of press freedom and the limits of state authority over the media.

Academic Experts, the History of Press Freedom, and the Limits of Administrative Authority

In order to consider the threats posed by newspaper ownership of radio, the FCC called a series of witnesses to offer learned perspectives about the past, present, and future of media ownership. The FCC hoped that these witnesses might demonstrate the gravity of the issue motivating the hearings and offer support for what were sure to be controversial regulations. The FCC's chosen expert witnesses included several of America's eminent scholars of the press and civil liberties: Elmo Roper, a professor of journalism at Columbia University and director of *Fortune*'s public opinion survey; Mitchell Charnley, a journalism professor at the University of Minnesota; sociologist Alfred McClung Lee, author of a leading monograph on the history of the American newspaper; lawyer and civil libertarian Morris Ernst; law professor Zechariah Chafee; and political scientist Carl Friedrich. The ANPA countered with its own group of experts and intellectuals by calling upon Ralph Casey, director of the University of Minnesota journalism school; Fred Siebert, director of the University of Illinois journalism school; journalism historian Frank Luther Mott; sociologist Paul Lazarsfeld, director of the Office of Radio Research; Arthur Garfield Hays, senior counsel for the American Civil Liberties Union; and law professor Roscoe Pound. Ultimately, this collection of experts and intellectuals significantly expanded the scope of the FCC's inquiry by convening a philosophically diverse group to discuss the direction of FCC policy. More important, this expert testimony ultimately structured the range of policy outcomes the FCC had to choose from at the end of its investigation.

By the 1940s, technical and academic experts were regular participants in a variety of policymaking procedures. In many hearings on radio broadcasting the federal government relied on expert opinion from engineers to craft policy for spectrum allocation. In the Newspaper-Radio Investigation, the desire for expert opinion expanded beyond the purely technical. The FCC invited historians, political scientists, journalism professors, and legal scholars to help them explain the social and political aspects of media concentration, in the process stimulating a theoretical debate about how media ownership related to democracy in the United States.[26]

These intellectuals and expert authorities were the most important witnesses of the entire hearings and, taken together, their testimony constituted an extended conversation about the history of the American press and the effect of radio on it, and also about the possibility of an administrative solution to the problem of media consolidation. The expert authorities were all very conscious of the fact that what they were talking about were explicitly historical questions: was the newspaper-radio combination the natural culmination of the noble history of the American press, or was it a dangerous new development with dire consequences for media, society, and politics? And what role did the FCC as an administrative agency have to play in regulating it? Questions by both the FCC and the ANPA directed the witnesses toward these lines of inquiry, and attempted to not only discuss the ways that newspaper ownership of radio worked in practice but also to consider what joint ownership meant in historical, philosophical, and political contexts. The issues at hand extended beyond statistics, interest group politics, and local case studies, and became instead normative considerations of government, rights, and the relationship between media and democracy. Historical interpretation became expert opinion in the context of one of the most significant public policy debates of the period.

To some academic experts, the most significant problems with the contemporary media stemmed from transformations in the economics of the newspaper business. In historical perspective, some believed that the vibrant circulation of ideas generated by competing newspapers had given way in the mid-twentieth century to a press dominated by fewer and more heavily capitalized corporations that were too often insulated from new competition by high financial barriers to entry to their industry. As sociologist Alfred McClung Lee, a New York University professor and author of the 1937 book *The Daily Newspaper in America*, testified in July 1941, the United States "has had for many generations the press with the greatest freedom of any country in the world." In contemporary America, however, he saw "significant changes—changes of broad social significance" that demanded that Americans look critically at the conduct and ownership structures of the press. During the colonial and revolutionary period, Lee argued, "papers were relatively small, easy to start and sufficiently numerous to represent conflicting points of view." The early American press, Lee suggested, was a vibrantly competitive press, and the economics of the business allowed this, as financial barriers to entry were low. The opposite was true for the contemporary press, Lee argued, and he believed that many publishers hypocritically portrayed themselves as heirs to an independent colonial press as their businesses worked in practice as monopolies. Publishers like William Randolph Hearst and Robert McCormick, Lee argued, claimed to uphold the "dicta of Jefferson and his fellow patriots on freedom of the press, without admitting . . . that they modified drastically the intent of such statements." The contemporary press was a heavily capitalized and increasingly concentrated industry and, outside of a few metropolitan centers, most readers had only one local paper and thus did not have access to competing editorial viewpoints. "In less than 100 cities," Lee claimed, "does freedom of the press bear some resemblance to the competitive press freedom which the founding fathers wanted to achieve by the First Amendment to the Federal Constitution." This, Lee concluded, was a system in need of improvement.[27]

Carl Friedrich, a professor of Government at Harvard and director of the University's Radio Broadcasting Research Project, emphasized similar historical changes in the economics of the news business. As Friedrich saw it, "in the days of Benjamin Franklin, it was very easy to start a paper if you had a point of view which you thought was not adequately represented in the existing papers." In the mid-twentieth century, Friedrich claimed, it was much more difficult financially to start a newspaper. The newspaper had "become increasingly an enterprise, a production enterprise similar to other highly mechanized industries," and in order to get into business one had to "have a very much larger amount of capital than you used to." These economic conditions, Friedrich argued, had dramatically reduced the number of viewpoints that Americans were capable of getting through the media, and he wanted a media marketplace that had more competition. "My general inclination," Friedrich argued, "is to say, the more diversity, the better," and he suggested that "it would be a more . . . democratic set-up, to have radio stations separate from the newspapers." For Friedrich, monopoly in general "always interferes with the workings of democracy," and this problem was even more acute in the "opinion industry." Americans needed choices in all markets, Friedrich believed, and in the media this meant choices between competing points of view. Citizens were more capable of making good decisions if they were able to consider diverse perspectives, and Friedrich believed that this necessitated the decentralization of media ownership. Democracy was best served, Friedrich ultimately asserted, by the promotion of the widest distribution of viewpoints, and he concluded that the "average man in the street, the common man in whom I believe," would be "best enabled to exercise his civic function in a democracy if he gets the presentation of facts from as many different sources as possible."[28]

While agreeing in substance with Carl Friedrich and Alfred McClung Lee, legal scholar Morris Ernst offered a much more critical assessment of the American media and suggested much more radical moves for the FCC. Ernst was in many ways the FCC star witness, the one who voiced the most assertive version of the policies that James Fly and Franklin Roosevelt wanted to enact. At the time of the FCC hearings, Ernst was in the middle of a wide-ranging career that had earned him a reputation as one of America's foremost civil libertarians. Ernst served as counsel to the ACLU and had written the forward to the first American edition of James Joyce's *Ulysses* published in the United States after the ban on the work was lifted. The ability to publish the work domestically, Ernst wrote in 1934, was a sign that "the new deal in the law of letters is here."[29] Ernst also had provided legal counsel to the CIO and to numerous newspaper, magazine, and book publishers, and was politically connected in elite circles in New York. Ernst had been an acquaintance of Franklin Roosevelt's dating back to FDR's days as the state's governor, and his friendship with the president drew closer in the early 1940s. A lengthy profile of Ernst in *Life* in 1944 reported that Ernst had become such a regular partner and confidant of the president that many saw him filling the "role of 'fixer,' 'operator,' [and] confidential odd-jobber . . . for his good friend Franklin Roosevelt." Some suggested that his successes in this role had made him "today one of the President's favorites." Before the FCC's investigation began, Ernst had encouraged Roosevelt to take action barring newspapers from radio ownership, and he made public statements to this effect in February 1941. His testimony before the FCC in October 1941 reflected both his loyalty to and intellectual sympathies with the president, and also his commitment to using an activist state to promote a more diverse and democratic media in the United States.[30]

Ernst argued that the questions about media ownership before the FCC were of signal importance for safeguarding democracy in America. The "problem before the Commission," Ernst stated, was "the most important problem facing the American people with regard to our way of life." It was, he claimed, the "question of the bottle-necks going into the marketplace of thought," something he called the "most terrifying of the American problems." Like Lee and Friedrich, Ernst urged the FCC to think about newspapers, radio, and the Constitution in historical perspective. The "right of a free press in 1787 is a very different thing than in 1941," Ernst argued. He was dismayed at how commercial newspapers had become over time, and he did not want to see this business ethic imported into radio. "Historically," Ernst stated, "I have looked at the record of what the newspapers" had done "out of profit motives," and what he found was "sort of a frightening record."[31]

Ernst's understanding of the problems created by concentrated media ownership was influenced significantly by Louis Brandeis, from whom he borrowed his staunch opposition to large corporations. The 1944 *Life* profile noted that Ernst had "adopted, whole hog, Brandeis' economic philosophy whereby most of the flaws in our industrial and financial setup are laid to business bigness." Reducing corporate size and expanding the number of participants in the marketplace were thus Ernst's primary economic policy goals, and in 1940 he published *Too Big*, a monograph dedicated to Brandeis and devoted to explicating Ernst's argument that "One of the great threats to our present democracy is the increasing size of business units." In 1941, Ernst used his testimony to apply his perspective on monopoly to newspapers and radio. "It is bad enough for insurance companies, utilities and banks who can dominate the economic tangible things," Ernst argued, "but that doesn't worry me at all in comparison to having fewer and fewer people having control over the marketplace of thought." The country could not "maintain democracy and the Bill of Rights with this concentration continuing, particularly in dominating the ideas of the nation," Ernst argued, and he implored the FCC to correct the problem.[32]

In order to do this, Ernst believed, the only possible solution was an absolute separation between newspapers and radio stations. Even though this might involve the closure of well-operated stations, Ernst asserted that he would "go the whole hog on the thing." Ernst was unrelenting on this point, telling the Commission, "I would exclude all newspapers. Of course I would." Since, he pointed out, "nobody desires that all of the permits be given to the newspapers," the only question remaining was "at what point should we be frightened, at what point should it be stopped." There was no easy answer to this question, he cautioned, and "there can be honest differences of opinion as to just where is the frightening point." Ernst asserted that he was already past that point himself. "I am frightened when I see one," Ernst stated, "because I want the greatest possible variety of prejudices into that marketplace whether I agree with them or not." The central issue of the FCC's investigation was for Ernst ultimately a decision about the fate of the Bill of Rights and of the Constitution, and he believed that if the FCC declined to act, the consequences might be catastrophic. "I think the Bill of Rights is in danger," Ernst concluded, "if you allow your press to continue to hold your radio and to continue to own more and more of it."[33]

In response to these arguments in favor of banning newspapers from owning radio stations, the ANPA selected a series of its own expert witnesses to present the industry's perspective. Not surprisingly, witnesses chosen by the ANPA rejected most of the arguments put forth by the FCC's experts about both the current state of the media and the historical trajectory of media ownership. For the ANPA and its experts, the primary goals were twofold. First, they wanted to challenge the idea that joint media ownership contributed adversely to the quality and diversity of information available to the public. And second, they strove to present an alternative explanation of the history of the American press that challenged the interpretations that the FCC witnesses offered. If Alfred McClung Lee, Carl Friedrich, and Morris Ernst wanted to create a diverse marketplace of ideas by decentralizing media ownership, the ANPA experts argued instead for the need to protect the rights of all participants, regardless whether they were individuals or multimedia corporations, to freely offer ideas into that marketplace. Laws preventing this, they claimed, only did harm to the overall integrity of the public sphere. What history should teach contemporary Americans to fear was not media corporations, the ANPA and its experts argued, but rather an overreaching state.

To support its first argument about the quality of newspaper-owned radio stations, the ANPA called on Paul Lazarsfeld, a sociology professor at Columbia University, director of the Office of Radio Research, and one of the country's leading authorities on radio broadcasting. After immigrating to the United States from Austria in the 1930s, Lazarsfeld was instrumental in developing models for understanding radio's effects that went beyond the then-influential technological determinist model of psychologists Hadley Cantril and Gordon Allport.[34] In June 1941, Lazarsfeld conducted for the ANPA a quantitative analysis of the program logs of fifty newspaper-owned stations and fifty non-newspaper-owned stations in order to ascertain whether there were any differences in programming between the two groups of stations. In private correspondence, Lazarsfeld expressed sympathy with the general movement to improve radio and stated that "nothing would hurt me more than to be considered an 'industry man.'" What he concluded from his research, however, was largely supportive of the existing industrial structure of the media. Ultimately, as he testified before the FCC in January 1942, "you find, by and large, that the two samples of stations don't show much of a difference" in the kinds of programs aired. Lazarsfeld's conclusions were based on tabulations of the amount of time that stations devoted to various types of programming, and his interpretation that stations were about the same regardless of ownership had to do with the amount of the broadcast day devoted to certain categories of programming, not with the actual content of those programs nor the perceptions of local audiences.[35]

After this tabulation, Lazarsfeld concluded that what was broadcast on radio had less to do with whether a particular station was owned by a newspaper or not but instead with the commitment of the owner to provide quality programming. A newspaper publisher, Lazarsfeld believed, might be just as likely to be a good broadcaster as any other type of owner. As an avowed proponent of newspapers, Lazarsfeld also saw radio as a means for them to stay commercially viable and socially influential. It would be a "real cultural danger," Lazarsfeld stated, if newspaper reading was "displaced by mere listening to the radio," and he believed that a "wisely guided combination of radio and newspapers might be a desirable technological advance."[36]

Privately, Lazarsfeld claimed that he was highly skeptical that diverse media ownership had a direct relationship with the quality of public information. After giving "considerable thought to the role of competition in the much-quoted marketplace of ideas," Lazarsfeld remarked, he concluded that, "In a monetary society the free competition of ideas does not necessarily lead to the selection of the best of them." For Lazarsfeld, the clash of ideas in a metaphorical marketplace that had seemed to Morris Ernst (and Oliver Wendell Holmes before him) to be competition in the service of democracy seemed to be only competition for the sake of competition. Success in this competition did not prove merit, as Lazarsfeld saw it, but only popularity. Lazarsfeld also privately revealed that his views on the subject had to do with the fact that he did not have the personal background of the American critics who he believed made a fetish of markets and competition. His philosophy was "closely linked with my European background. I really do not share the belief in free competition which seems so paramount among American liberals," and thus he thus did not believe that numerical diversity of media owners directly correlated with the quality of the media. Publicly, the Newspaper-Radio Committee touted Lazarsfeld's statements before the FCC as the "cold, formal testimony of a professional social scientist and statistician," and claimed that they definitively gave the "answer to the questions, some concrete and some nebulous, as to whether a newspaper-owned station is any worse—or any better—than a radio station not in any manner affiliated with a newspaper."[37]

Paul Lazarsfeld's testimony provided an interpretation of the current media marketplace that was amenable to the ANPA's antiregulatory argument. In order to present an argument about the broader significance of the hearings, the ANPA also attempted to combat the FCC witnesses' interpretations of media history. In employing this dual strategy, the ANPA attempted to demonstrate how high its members believed the stakes of the hearings to be. This was not a simple matter of debating a regulatory standard, ANPA witnesses claimed, but was a discussion about a significant rupture in the history of the American media and a potential blow against press freedom. Attorney Louis Caldwell handpicked several witnesses to challenge what he thought were "very questionable statements of historical fact" from some FCC's witnesses, in particular Morris Ernst. For the ANPA's experts, the history of the press was a triumphalist narrative, and all presented the newspaper as a long-term agent of improvement in American life. One of the most important aspects of press history, the ANPA argued, was the newspaper's independence from government control, and representatives used this historical interpretation to argue that an administrative attempt to prevent newspapers from owning radio stations would violate the First Amendment and would start the country down a dangerous path.[38]

The ANPA's two primary exponents of newspaper boosterism were Ralph Casey, a former journalist at the *Seattle Post-Intelligencer* and in 1942 the director of the University of Minnesota School of Journalism, and Frank Luther Mott, the author of several major works on journalism history, including the 1939 Pulitzer Prize winning *A History of American Magazines*. As an administrator at Minnesota, Casey had developed innovative practices in journalism education that had made him a leading national figure in the profession, and in his role as an editor at *Journalism Quarterly* he also exerted a strong influence on academic research in the field of journalism history. Before the FCC in 1942, his testimony was a celebratory account of the press stressing the ways that newspapers had been instrumental in radio's development. It "certainly should be borne in mind that the pioneers in the broadcasting of news were newspaper owned stations," Casey argued, as newspapers imported an air of credibility into radio that the new medium desperately needed. For Casey, journalists had through professional training and experience become "aware of what is uppermost in the public consciousness," and were adept at finding ways to present that to the public. They also brought a "sense of public responsibility" to broadcasting that was a "distinct service to radio in the early days." It was the actions of publishers and journalists that ultimately "saved radio from falling solely into mere showmanship." Ultimately, Casey saw the contemporary state of radio as nothing but a positive confirmation of the presence of newspapers, and he saw no reason whatsoever that a newspaper should be kept from owning a radio station.[39]

In a similar vein, Frank Luther Mott rejected the arguments offered by Morris Ernst and Carl Friedrich that the quality of the press had deteriorated since the colonial period, and instead advocated a Whiggish approach to media history. At the time of the FCC's hearings, Mott was among the most influential journalism historians in the United States, and his 1941 book *American Journalism* became the standard text in the field into the 1970s.[40] In the book, Mott narrated the story of American journalism as a steady process of improvement led by committed publishers and professionals, and he advanced these arguments in his testimony to the FCC as well. Colonial newspapers, Mott pointed out, looked "disconcertingly small to a modern reader" and did not contain a "great deal" of information. During the late eighteenth century, Mott claimed, the American newspaper had become primarily a partisan organ, and by the mid-nineteenth century, many cities were "loaded up with too many newspapers," many of which were of questionable quality. The contemporary newspaper industry was more consolidated, Mott allowed, but he believed that the increasing capitalization and circulation of larger newspapers helped them produce a better product. Lesser papers went out of business, Mott argued, and it seemed "very apparent that consolidations have in a great many cities given those cities better newspapers." Mott portrayed the rise of radio as just another episode in the development of the American media, and suggested that preventing newspapers from owning radio stations "would be an arbitrary diversion of the natural and historic course of newspaper development. And that development has always followed the lines of new technologies and new challenges."[41]

As Casey and Mott celebrated the press for its contributions to American life, other ANPA witnesses emphasized the fact that these contributions were based on newspapers' freedom from state encroachment. The most vocal exponents of this libertarian argument about media history and law were Arthur Garfield Hays, a founder of the ACLU in 1920 and in 1942 its director and senior counsel, and Harvard Law School professor Roscoe Pound, who together brought to the investigation a strident First Amendment defense of newspapers' right to own radio stations. For both men, opposition to the Newspaper-Radio Investigation was based on a simultaneous commitment to protecting individual liberties, especially the right of free expression, and opposition to the growth of the American state in an era of totalitarianism around the world.[42]

For Hays, the fundamental rule of free speech law was to "stick very definitely to the question of rights as opposed to opportunities." This absolutist defense of civil liberties was a central theme in Hays's career as a lawyer. It animated his defense work in the trials of John Scopes and Nicola Sacco and Bartolomeo Vanzetti in the 1920s, and it sparked his opposition to what he believed were ill-conceived and even dangerous new regulations on media ownership sought by the FCC.[43] This was the core issue in the FCC's investigation, Hays claimed, and he had no sympathy with the argument that a ban on newspapers owning radio stations was a necessary and proper way to promote democracy in the media. Newspapers should have the same rights as churches, universities, or any other institutions to broadcast, and a law against them might soon encroach upon other areas of expression. Hays argued that once this sort of regulation started, there was no telling where it might lead, and it would be the "first step away from what seems to me to be sound democratic principles and is a great danger to free speech." Hays presented the issue at hand as something that was not just a "narrow" legal matter, but rather as something that was in fact a significant constitutional question. "I think it involves the Bill of Rights," Hays stated flatly. "I think this will be the first step where the Government has tried to bring about economically equal opportunities, regardless of what that may do to the rights of people," and this, he argued, was a "pretty dangerous precedent, because whenever governments in the past have done that," the result was "fixed rigid rules and a very dangerous control." If the state asserted authority here, Hays argued, it would be a radical advancement of public power, and regardless of whether or not this "change will be for the public good," this kind of regulation had "always been the basis of government interfering in private matters, and has been the basis of Fascism or Communism, or any other rigid governmental system."[44]

Hays's testimony was a direct rebuttal of his ACLU colleague Morris Ernst, who had argued that the FCC should bar newspapers from owning radio stations so as to encourage diversity on the airwaves. For Ernst, regulation in the public interest demanded that the FCC place limits on media ownership. Hays, in contrast, saw regulation in the public interest as a matter of simply granting broadcast licenses in a manner that avoided frequency interference. Hays was clear that this conception of the FCC mission did not "mean to say that diversity of view and expression of different opinions is not a good thing," but he felt that "you can't bring that about by passing rules that certain groups shouldn't own stations." The potential for unhinged and unchecked government regulation loomed throughout Hays's testimony, and he ultimately concluded that "democracy is much safer if the government leaves its hands off."[45]

One week after Hays testified, Roscoe Pound took the stand to offer a lengthy and occasionally rambling disquisition on the history of the press and the Bill of Rights that wove its way through three hundred years of Anglo-American history. Like Hays, Pound strongly and explicitly disagreed with Morris Ernst's understanding of media history and prescriptions for FCC action. "It is a great mistake," Pound began, to assume "that the Bill of Rights is something that we can talk about from the date of the Federal Constitution." One must go back further, Pound argued, to the experience of the American colonists throughout the seventeenth and eighteenth centuries, in order to understand how the dissatisfaction with English laws relating to freedom of expression inspired the First Amendment. In particular, Pound claimed, the First Amendment was designed to check the arbitrary and overreaching policing of speech and expression that colonists had experienced under British rule, and he believed that the FCC would be engaging in a similar kind of suppression if it barred newspapers from broadcasting. Ultimately, Pound suggested, current laws protecting free speech had deep historical roots in attempts to prevent the government from stifling free expression, and he urged policymakers to understand the stakes of their decision.[46]

In addition to this historical argument, Pound was particularly vigorous in his criticisms of what he saw as the FCC's abuse of administrative authority. An advocate of administrative governance in the Progressive Era, Pound had by the 1930s repudiated this position in favor of viewing administrative authority as tending toward undemocratic ends. Pound's FCC testimony was in many ways an application of an argument that he had developed in the 1930s against James Landis, his Harvard Law School colleague and a former Securities and Exchange Commission chairman. Landis had had been instrumental in drafting the Securities Exchange Act of 1934 and the Public Utility Holding Company Act of 1935, and remained throughout the 1930s a proponent of administrative regulation as the best solution to the problem of governance in an advanced industrial capitalist society. After leaving the SEC, Landis in 1938 published *The Administrative Process*, a strident defense of expert-staffed commissions in which Landis called administrative law "in essence, our generation's answer to the inadequacy of the judicial and legislative process." The book was, as historian Thomas McCraw describes it, the "clearest individual expression" of the "single overarching idea" connecting all branches of New Deal thought: the idea that "economic regulation by expert commissions would bring just results."[47]

Roscoe Pound proved to be one of the strongest opponents of this theory of governance. In 1938, Pound directed a blistering critique of the New Deal's expansion of administrative authority while the chairman of the American Bar Association's Special Committee on Administrative Law, and he continued this line of attack in his testimony before the FCC in 1942. Pound saw lurking in the FCC's desire to ban newspapers from owning radio stations the possibility of conferring to an administrative body the authority to run roughshod over the First Amendment. European governments had taken such steps, Pound said, and "the result has been autocracies everywhere in every important country."

The thing to be feared, Pound argued, was not a media concentrated under private ownership but a media subject to onerous state regulations. Like Frank Luther Mott, Pound also subscribed to a theory of press regulation holding that one law in the present might lead to a host of unintended and potentially antidemocratic consequences in the future. "Suppose you start with the proposition that nobody can own a broadcasting station and a newspaper at the same time," Pound stated. "Well, then, the next proposition is that it is a great abuse to have absentee ownership of newspapers," and then perhaps the idea that it was a "great abuse to have chain newspapers." Once the government embarked on this line of lawmaking, "where is the line going to be drawn?" Whatever specific policy outcome, Pound saw it as frighteningly undemocratic.[48]

In the context of World War II, Pound expressed deep suspicion of governmental authority, arguing that "the tendency of those who have power is to reach out for more power. That is exactly the purpose of the Bill of Rights, to check that zeal for power on the part of humans, it is part of the psychology of the human race." Like Hays, Pound strenuously advocated a libertarian conception of free speech rights and argued that the idea that the state should take a stronger role in regulating the public sphere was "absolute nonsense. It is refuted by all history on this subject. What has happened in Continental Europe? All the agencies of news gathering steadily got under the control of government. The governments reached out more and more until they got complete control. What is the answer? You have got autocratic governments." With radio, Pound argued, the government had done its regulatory duty once it had set up an adequate administrative body to efficiently allocate station licenses. Having done this, Pound concluded, "you have gone about as far as you need to go, and certainly as far as you constitutionally ought to go."[49]

Roscoe Pound's antistatist defense of individual liberties provided the final substantive contribution to the FCC's hearings, which formally concluded the following week when James Stahlman testified after a federal appeals court rejected his suit claiming that the FCC did not have the legal authority to conduct its investigation. Though the FCC had expended considerable effort to bring Stahlman to the stand, his testimony was cursory and ultimately contributed little to the record that the Commission could use to buttress a case that newspaper-radio combinations were having adverse effects on their communities. In February 1942, having heard from a variety of witnesses and generated a spirited conversation about the American media, the FCC was left with the difficult task of deciding what course of action it could take.

Toward a Flexible Standard

As of early 1942, the FCC's investigation had done little to suggest concretely how federal policy on media ownership might develop. Newspaper corporations remained in a state of perpetual unease about what might happen to their radio businesses. For proponents of media reform, the content of the FCC's investigation was ultimately rather frustrating. Though witnesses such as Carl Friedrich, Morris Ernst, and the CIO's Allan Haywood provided testimony supporting a ban on newspaper ownership of radio, contrary perspectives from Arthur Garfield Hays and Roscoe Pound complicated the issue significantly and made a simple and aggressive course of action tough to pursue. Given this record to work with, reformists on the FCC also found that the broader context of the investigation changed in some significant ways as witness testimony was concluding. The Commission received lukewarm public support from the ACLU and the federal court deciding James Stahlman's case, issues that paled in comparison to the hostility that some members of Congress began directing at the FCC. And, perhaps most significantly, the United States entered World War II, an event that transformed domestic reform efforts on virtually every front.

The Japanese attack on American forces at Pearl Harbor took place on 7 December 1941, right in the middle of the hearings. With the United States immediately drawn into war, ANPA representatives asked the FCC to postpone or adjourn the proceedings. In one such petition, the ANPA's Harold Hough argued that the FCC was hindering the American press and radio from properly supporting the war effort and that continuing the hearings would only serve to "create a diversion of the energies of all parties concerned from the necessary and essential activities of war-time." Hough argued that many broadcasters and publishers had been consistent opponents of the New Deal but had "in many cases set aside personal preferences and convenience in order to serve the war-time effort." Despite Hough's pleas and in the face of multiple other public and private entreaties, the FCC refused to stop the investigation. Ultimately, all of the expert witnesses selected by the ANPA provided their testimony after Pearl Harbor.[50]

The federal appellate court decision in James Stahlman's case also created problems for the FCC's investigation. Though the court upheld the legality of the investigation, other aspects of the decision tempered reformist enthusiasm. The court took care in its decision to add specific limitations to the scope of the investigation, adding that the FCC should not construe the judgment against Stahlman as encouragement to engage in an open-ended inquiry of the newspaper business. Even more damaging to the FCC's case was the court's assertion in dicta that it would not uphold a prohibition on newspaper ownership of radio if that were the ultimate result of the investigation, as it would give the Commission broad and unconstitutional power to control channels of expression. *Broadcasting* called the decision a "thumping opinion" that could "only be interpreted as a repudiation of the FCC," claims that were a bit hyperbolic and premature. ANPA attorney Louis Caldwell reported soon after the ruling that it was "clear from remarks made by some of the members of the FCC and its staff that little or no attention will be paid to the recent decision," and he fully expected the hearings to continue. Moreover, the D.C. Court of Appeals and the Supreme Court were in 1942 and 1943 issuing a series of rulings on the Chain Broadcasting Hearings, all of which were in the FCC's favor, and neither court was hesitant during this period about backing up the Commission's authority to conduct investigations and strongly regulate media ownership.[51]

The FCC was also challenged by a variety of public relations campaigns defending the rights of newspapers to broadcast. As the ANPA's expert witnesses began testifying, the Newspaper-Radio Committee published and distributed that testimony in pamphlet form. In 1942, the ANPA produced a larger bound volume entitled *Freedom of the Press: What It Is, How It Was Obtained, How It Can Be Retained*, containing excerpts from the testimony of a number of its key witnesses and promoting the ANPA's case as a crusade for free speech rights. The ANPA argued that the FCC's investigation raised "questions of deep importance to a Democratic Nation, such as the protection of our Bill of Rights and the preservation of newspapers and radios as a safety valve for the uncontrolled and free source of information for the growth of independent public opinion." The fight against the FCC had prompted "advocates of free speech and civil liberties" to testify "for the purpose of helping to preserve the 'freedom' guaranteed by the Constitution and Bill of Rights."[52]

The FCC's response to all of this criticism and opposition was to just continue taking testimony and then, upon completing that task, simply to do nothing. This strategy was in many respects the most effective move that the Commission could make at that point. Instead of issuing a ruling or trying to bring the matter to a quick conclusion, the FCC kept the investigation open, a move that kept all newspaper applications in the pending file for an indefinite term and did not foreclose any future action. This decision kept publishers anxious throughout 1942 and 1943, something that may have been small comfort to Franklin Roosevelt and James Fly. As George Biggers of the *Atlanta Journal* and station WSB confessed to George Burbach of the *St. Louis Post-Dispatch* and station KSD, "We have been loath to do anything that would give the FCC any legitimate reason to get after us because we are a newspaper-owned radio station."[53]

Publisher anxiety increased further in May 1943 when the Supreme Court upheld the findings and legality of the *Report on Chain Broadcasting*, a decision that forced NBC to sell the Blue network.[54] Justice Felix Frankfurter, writing for the majority, rejected NBC's arguments that the FCC was abridging the network's First Amendment rights and defended the Commission's actions on the grounds that, "unlike other modes of expression, radio inherently is not available to all. That is its unique characteristic, and that is why, unlike other modes of expression, it is subject to government regulation." Frankfurter's opinion upheld a vigorous definition of the FCC's regulatory powers, and critics were afraid that the FCC might apply this activist regulatory model to its consideration of newspaper ownership of radio. *Broadcasting* editorialized that the decision "went all out, covering by implication" a host of other matters, including newspaper ownership. "The newspapers definitely are in line for regulation of this character," the magazine feared. "The question of newspaper ownership of stations is inextricably interwoven in the Frankfurter opinion," and regulations on ownership could now "be accomplished by adopting the language of the Frankfurter formula."[55]

Debates about the implications and possible outcomes of the FCC's investigation also created spirited discussions within the ACLU throughout 1942 as the organization sought to balance the positions of two of its most prominent members, Arthur Garfield Hays and Morris Ernst, each of whom offered dramatically different views in their testimony before the FCC. ACLU member Lewis Mumford, who in the early 1930s believed that "the dangers of radio . . . seem greater than the benefits," strongly supported keeping media ownership diverse. Allowing the radio industry to benefit from association with newspapers made Mumford uneasy, and he asserted that he was "heartily in favor" of a policy that would limit cross ownership. Prominent print journalist H. L. Mencken expressed similar support for FCC action, suggesting that "ownership of radio stations by newspapers should be discouraged," and stating that he could discern "no reason whatsoever why the owner of a newspaper should want to operate a radio also. Such dual enterprises, I am convinced, are bound to do damage to both halves." Drama critic Walter Prichard Eaton was less sure about the need for a new FCC policy on media ownership, which he felt would only lead to harm against the press. "To discriminate against newspapers as radio owners," Eaton argued, "treating them differently from other owners, is not, it seems to me, to encourage freedom of speech and the press, but still further to hamstring the greatest and hitherto most powerful organ of free speech, our newspapers. I am definitely against it."[56]

After considering these perspectives, the ACLU in March 1942 released an official policy statement taking a moderate stance on the issue. While allowing that, "under certain circumstances," especially instances where there was only one newspaper and radio station in a given city, newspaper ownership could be considered a significant factor in deciding whom to grant a radio license, the furthest that the ACLU would go was to suggest that "Extreme care should be taken by the F.C.C. in each case to see that as a practical matter no monopoly in the presentation of news and opinion is created." An absolute ban on newspaper ownership of radio was, the ACLU concluded, "without merit" as a policy choice.[57]

In addition to this public opposition, the FCC was also constrained by congressional action, some of which became vigorous and even malicious. Some congressional vigor stemmed from the politics that historian Barry Karl argues were characteristic of the "Third New Deal" after 1937. For much of Roosevelt's second term and into his third, the tenor of American political life shifted in some significant ways as FDR created a stronger role for the executive branch. Starting in the late 1930s, Karl argues, relations between the executive and the legislature "established a pattern of adversary politics that made Congress responsible for negotiating the local and regional adjustments to the national politics the president was advocating." In some cases, congressmen stoked fears of government action by promoting the idea that federal bureaucrats under Roosevelt's charge were acting in dangerous and often shadowy ways to erode American freedoms. Members of Congress from Roosevelt's own party began to contest many New Deal policies in these terms, and opposition from southern Democrats became particularly active.[58]

This oppositional tone in Congress shaped members' responses to radio regulation in the early 1940s and structured potential policy outcomes. In the context of the FCC's Chain Broadcasting and Newspaper-Radio Investigations, many in Congress voiced increasingly strident criticisms that the Commission was overextending its authority and some, like Louisiana Representative Jared Sanders, began trying to legislatively limit that authority.

Harold Hough, Thomas Thatcher, and Sydney Kaye of the ANPA's Newspa-per-Radio Committee testified at congressional hearings in 1942 that the FCC was abusing its authority by conducting its newspaper investigation. Hough testified it had "never occurred to us that we had any different rights than any other citizens. This is the first time in history that a distinction has been created about us because of our occupation." Press representatives remained regulars at congressional hearings on the FCC and sought to persuade Con-gress to rein in a Commission that they claimed was abusive and capricious. At a Senate hearing in late 1943, Hough proposed that the Communications Act should be amended "so that it will be perfectly clear beyond any doubt that the Federal Communications Commission has no power whatsoever to discriminate against newspaper ownerships." Hough was exasperated with being "segregated into a special class along with aliens and convicted crimi-nals and told that we, as a group, are not fit to engage in radio."[59]

The most serious and acrimonious congressional challenge against the FCC was led by Representative Eugene Cox of Georgia. Cox was one of a number of the anti-New Deal Southern Democrats that rose to power in Congress in the early 1940s. Cox allied himself with Martin Dies, the chair-man of the House Committee on Un-American Activities, and began attack-ing Fly and the FCC. Dies had been clamoring about what he claimed was communist influence within the FCC since the early stages of the Newspa-per-Radio Investigation and had called a number of Commission staffers to respond to his allegations. Dies was all too happy to have Cox expand this red-baiting program into a more general attack on the FCC. In January 1943, Cox called the FCC the "nastiest nest of rats in the country," alleged that Fly had "Communist affiliations," and charged the FCC with acting like the "Gestapo" through its investigations. Cox subsequently convinced the House of Representatives to pass by an overwhelming margin a measure authorizing an investigation of the FCC. *Broadcasting* called the resolution the "climax" of opposition to Fly's actions as FCC chairman, remarking that all of Fly's activ-ism had finally "caught up with the Commission." Fly attacked the hearings and claimed that Eugene Cox was working with "the radio monopoly and Wall Street interests" to undermine the commission. "The aim," Fly charged, "has obviously been to wreck the commission, the only agency representing the public in this important field, to set up monopolistic control by commer-cial interests and to establish actual and coercive surveillance of the nation's most significant mechanism of free speech." Even Louis Caldwell, certainly no friend of the FCC, agreed with Fly, commenting that the charges against the FCC "as a whole are not well founded" and were "designed primarily to eliminate Chairman Fly from the Commission and to nullify the powers exercised by the Commission during his administration."[60]

The five-member Select Committee to Investigate the Federal Communications Commission convened its first session in July 1943, enumerating some twenty-four charges against the agency. Select Committee general counsel Eugene Garey claimed that Fly's FCC had consistently abused its licensing authority and "purposefully terrorized" the radio industry. Garey charged that Fly had demonstrated a "lust for power" and turned the FCC into his own personal platform to attack those who dared stand up to him or the New Deal.[61]

The motivation for Cox's investigation was partly political, as Cox was a die-hard anti-New Dealer committed to the notion that centralized federal power was eroding individual rights and freedoms. Cox's hostility toward the FCC was also personal, as Cox was enraged at the FCC's investigation of his work for the *Albany Herald*, a paper in his home district in Georgia. Cox had been instrumental in helping the paper obtain a license for its radio station WALB in 1941, and the FCC later learned that Cox had been paid $2,500 for "services rendered" during the licensing process. Accepting such a payment constituted a criminal offense, and when the FCC began inquiring into the matter, Cox began denouncing the FCC and calling for his own investigation of the Commission. After getting approval to form the Select Committee, Cox convinced House Speaker Sam Rayburn to appoint him chairman of it. In May 1943, two months before the hearings began, the FCC asked the Justice Department and Speaker Rayburn to remove Cox as the chairman of the Committee, citing the payment that Cox had received from the *Albany Herald*.[62]

When neither party responded to the FCC's requests, commissioner Clifford Durr, an ally of James Fly, went public with the WALB evidence. Durr took copies of the checks that Cox had received from WALB to Eugene Meyer, the publisher of the *Washington Post*, which attacked the hearings the next day in a front page story and repeatedly in editorials over the following weeks. Cox never denied taking the payment but claimed that the money "had been contributed to local charities," and he fumed that "personal attacks . . . had diverted public attention from the real issues involved in the investigation." Nevertheless, Cox decided to resign from the Committee to free it from, as he put it, "any possible embarrassment of my personal problems or controversies."[63]

Select Committee hearings continued into 1944 with Clarence Lea, a Democrat from California, taking over as chairman, but the momentum was spent. In March 1944, the Select Committee's final report absolved the FCC of most of charges against it, finding that the hearings were marked by "exaggerated statements" and "reckless charges" from Cox, and blaming "innumerable bitter conflicts based largely on personal interests and animosities" for "obscur[ing] the constructive problems . . . which were the matters of most concern to legitimate investigation." The Select Committee found that the FCC had not been abusing its licensing power, as Cox charged, but it did want Congress to make "clear-cut expression" delimiting the FCC's authority on the newspaper issue, which it felt "should not exclude" publishers from "owning and operating a radio station."[64]

Though Fly remained FCC chairman, and though the Commission pressed on with the newspaper ownership issue, the cumulative pressure of the congressional attacks curbed the FCC's reform drive on the matter. In mid-1943, *Broadcasting* reported that the "view of observers is that the FCC, in light of the legislative tidal wave in Congress against New Deal agencies in general and the FCC in particular, is not disposed to resurrect any controversial issues at this time." By late 1943, these congressional battles had worn Fly down. Pete Shuebruk, an FCC staff attorney, recalled that, "about the end of '43, Fly became convinced that this thing ought to be settled. He got too much. He was getting badgered too much on the Hill . . . whenever he went up there for appropriations or anything else." Fly began privately discussing bringing closure to the investigation, and by December 1943, Louis Caldwell remarked that "Matters are jumping back and forth at a dizzy rate on the newspaper ownership issue," and he predicted an imminent resolution.[65]

As the FCC reviewed the record of its investigation and considered public opinion about the issue in late 1943, the broader contexts of congressional opposition and the ongoing war virtually ensured that whatever rules were enacted would fall short of the kind of strong regulations that Fly had initially hoped for. With the Japanese attack on Pearl Harbor taking place in the middle of the hearings, the needs of war mobilization trumped many of the larger policy aims. Harry Plotkin, an FCC staff attorney in the 1940s, recalled later that he was unsure whether the Commission "could have carried [the investigation] through or not if the war had not come." Once the war started, however, there was little that the FCC could do. As Plotkin saw it, "the war killed it anyway . . . the war just got in the way, you know."[66]

As the FCC began the process of drafting a formal resolution to the investigation, the Commission considered both the strong antimonopoly position of Morris Ernst and the libertarian and antiregulatory positions of Arthur Garfield Hays and Roscoe Pound. Ultimately, however, it eschewed these more extreme positions and found a compromise position in the testimony of Zechariah Chafee, a professor at Harvard Law School and at the time perhaps the foremost American legal authority on free speech law.[67] Chafee had become a leading scholar of civil liberties in the period immediately after World War I after the publication of two widely influential articles in the *Harvard Law Review* and the book *Freedom of Speech*. In these works, Chafee was critical of wartime restrictions on freedom of speech, favoring instead a more libertarian conception of the First Amendment that protected a wider range of expression and criticism. In his 1919 article, "Freedom of Speech in War Time," Chafee advocated for a wider interpretation of the "clear and present danger" test that Oliver Wendell Holmes had developed earlier that year in upholding the conviction of the socialist Charles Schenck for mailing antiwar leaflets in *Schenck v. United States*. Chafee's article, which appeared in the eight-month interval between *Schenck* and *Abrams*, strongly influenced Holmes's dissent in the latter case, and in many ways initiated the significant 1920s shift in First Amendment jurisprudence toward a more libertarian direction. According to legal historian David Rabban, Holmes "relied heavily on Chafee's article" in his *Abrams* dissent and support of extending First Amendment protection to controversial expression.[68]

In his testimony to the FCC in late 1941, Chafee offered similarly influential views on the history of the American press, the contemporary economic structure of the media, and the necessity of regulations limiting media ownership. As he had helped to shape Oliver Wendell Holmes's understandings of media law two decades earlier, Chafee's pragmatic reasoning proved influential on the FCC in the 1940s as well. Though not as Whiggish as historian Frank Luther Mott, Chafee believed that the contemporary media system was the product of a long process of gradual improvement. The newspapers of the early republic were "little better than scandal sheets and handbills," Chafee argued, and "impartiality was the last thing to be expected from the vituperative party organs of the Jeffersonian and Hamiltonian period." Over time, newspapers had developed much better standards for reporting and a clearer separation of the news and editorial page, though Chafee acknowledged that this was still an ongoing process. "The idea of newspaper impartiality," he argued, "is very recent and is easily smothered by the much longer tradition of taking sides." In contemporary America, radio "had the advantage of making a fresh start . . . .It began without any handicaps of tradition of partisanship." Radio's popular appeal, Chafee argued, stemmed not only from its apparent break with the press, but also from its novel characteristics as a medium. Where a newspaper rarely printed the texts of entire speeches and relied instead on selective and potentially biased reports, radio worked better in the service of the "presentation of varied views" since it had "no editor and no headlines. Every speech is necessarily given in full." Radio, Chafee argued, had thus given rise to a "Popular confidence in the superior fairness and accuracy" of the information it presented.[69]

Despite the fact that Chafee looked to radio as an antidote to press bias, he was hesitant to endorse absolute legal separation between the two media. Chafee's reasoning was partly practical, as he suggested that a blanket rule separating newspapers from radio stations would mean that more than a third of existing American radio stations would have to be sold, including some that were "efficient and prosperous." Barring newspapers from owning radio stations also would not necessarily ensure that radio would become any better, as the presence of advertisers would remain a constant in commercial broadcasting. "The pressure of advertisers," Chafee asserted, "is one of the main causes of newspaper unfairness or bias," and he believed that it was a "mistake to assume, whatever the policy adopted, that the radio can be completely protected from influences that are inclined to warp information and the expression of opinions." Chafee ultimately felt that radio was going to be just as susceptible to advertiser and commercial influence as newspapers were, and this was not something easily eliminated by categorically barring newspapers from broadcasting.[70]

Chafee ultimately encouraged the FCC to handle the issue of cross ownership on a case-by-case basis rather than through blanket exclusion. In this respect, he mixed some of the libertarian sentiments of Arthur Garfield Hays and Roscoe Pound with his own beliefs in the positive effects of state power. Chafee was not a complete absolutist when it came to free speech, suggesting that "speech should be fruitful as well as free," and he wanted policies that would encourage both unrestricted and intelligent expression. In cases where it was clear that denying a newspaper a radio license would in practice promote the circulation of diverse viewpoints, the FCC should do just that, even if that offended libertarians like Hays and Pound. "We should not be content with adjusting the negative forces which restrain liberty," Chafee asserted. "We should also consider the development of positive forces which will encourage and remove the sluggishness of thought into which we all easily lapse even without any prohibitions upon opinion." As Chafee saw it, the FCC might best serve the public interest through a commitment to licensing broadcasters that were best equipped to contribute to the presentation of diverse perspectives over the radio. This group might well include newspapers, but Chafee wanted the FCC to have enough policy flexibility to prevent this if need be. Where his Harvard Law School colleague Roscoe Pound had abandoned his Progressive Era pragmatism in favor of an absolutist defense of individual liberties, Chafee retained a faith in the efficacy of administrative commissions like the FCC to promote social change.[71]

In particular, Chafee believed, the law had to act in a positive way to not only protect rights but expand opportunities to enjoy them. What was the point, Chafee argued by analogy, "of telling an unpopular speaker that he will incur no criminal penalties by a proposed address so long as every hall owner in the city declines to rent him space for his meeting and there are no vacant lots available." Protecting the absolute rights of speakers to speak did not inherently do anything to enable them to do so. Rather, it simply protected them once they did, and this was insufficient. "There should be municipal auditoriums, school-houses out of school hours, church forums, parks in summer, all open to thresh out every question of public importance with just as few restrictions as possible." When he applied this analogy to radio, Chafee concluded that "plainly" it was "desirable that a newspaper and a broadcasting station in the same city should be independently owned. Then the community gets two voices instead of one and obtains all the advantages of diverse points of view. This is particularly true if the city has only one newspaper and one broadcasting station." For Zechariah Chafee, the promotion of media ownership diversity should be a key goal for the FCC, and he encouraged the commission to consider the specific structures of ownership in individual media markets, and to deny newspapers radio licenses in cases where one corporation would attain too much power over the circulation of public information.[72]

This dual commitment to promoting free speech and media diversity that Chafee advocated became the basis for the FCC's final policy statement in the proceeding. FCC commissioner Ray Wakefield incorporated this viewpoint into a draft policy statement for the Commission, which stated that the FCC would "not adopt a categorical rule barring newspaper owners" but rather that it "should consider newspaper ownership as one element of public interest" in granting licenses. James Fly took the recommendations to Franklin Roosevelt in December 1943, stating that this was the "rough contours" of the "maximum that can be achieved at this time," given the current political climate. "The adoption of an arbitrary rule or any rule that will have a telling impact will lead to substantial added criticism of the Commission and, I believe, of the Administration itself." Word began trickling out that the FCC would be issuing a policy statement similar to what Wakefield was suggesting, and broadcasters and publishers found even this flexible standard to be too stringent. *Broadcasting* remarked that the policy would mean that newspapers were to be "tolerated but not necessarily accepted as wholesome or desirable" station owners and that it would discriminate "against a class of Americans who, by heritage, tradition and public service, are well qualified to participate in the development of radio—a projection of journalism." The policy "frowns upon newspaper ownership" and thus was "ever so slightly . . . tantamount ultimately to a ban." Publishers and broadcasters found a key supporter in FCC commissioner T. A. M. Craven, who made it clear to his fellow commissioners that he would vote against the resolution and enter a blistering dissent into the record. Fearing any further battles over the proposed ruling, the FCC, in what *Broadcasting* called a "full-scale reversal," issued a unanimous order with even softer language than before.[73]

The FCC released its final statement in the Newspaper-Radio Investigation on January 18, 1944, asserting it would not "adopt any general rule with respect to newspaper ownership of radio stations," partly because of the testimony presented in the hearing, but also because of "the grave legal and policy questions involved." The Commission did, however, reserve the authority to consider newspaper ownership on a case-by-case basis in future licensing hearings as part of a general promotion of media diversity. "All the Commissioners agree to the general principle that diversification of control of such media is desirable," the FCC wrote. The Commission did not want to prohibit or discourage anyone from applying for a broadcast license, but it did "desire to encourage the maximum number of qualified persons to enter the field of mass communications, and to permit them to use all modern inventions and improvements in the art to insure good public service." The Commission would consider newspaper ownership while assessing whether or not applicants would adequately serve the public interest, and it would deny them in cases where it felt the applicant might contribute to undue media concentration. Newspapers were as qualified as any other applicants were, the FCC stated, but it did not "intend in granting licenses in the public interest to permit concentration of control in the hands of the few to the exclusion of the many who may be equally well qualified to render such public service as is required of a licensee." Though unable to establish an absolute standard, the FCC did set some flexible guidelines on newspaper ownership, and it would continue to use these guidelines to invariably controversial effect after World War II.[74]

Broadcasting called the decision an end to "one of the ugliest episodes in the annals of so-called administrative law," and hailed it as a "signal victory" for commissioner Craven, whom the magazine called "Commander Courageous" for standing up to Fly, who it in turn claimed had "used more intemperate or abusive language in dealing with industry or public" than any "official in our times."[75] Craven downplayed his role in the ruling, saying that, if "anything won the newspaper case it was the newspapers themselves." His actions did not go unrewarded, as Craven quit the FCC several months later to take an executive position with the Cowles Broadcasting Company, a part of a "new dynasty in communications" whose parent company owned newspapers in Des Moines and Minneapolis, five radio stations, and *Look* magazine. With the FCC's investigation of newspapers now closed and with Craven onboard, *Business Week* reported that the company had plans to apply for new FM licenses as well.[76]

Fly tried to save face somewhat after the decision was released. While testifying before Congress in June 1944, Fly remarked that the issue remained a "grave policy" concern. "When you have got 40 percent of your stations owned by newspapers, the whole question of whether or not you will proceed with grants of radio stations to newspapers is a serious question of policy." Unable to get a rule barring newspaper ownership, Fly settled for a general statement that diversification of ownership was desirable, but he refused to capitulate philosophically to his critics in the publishing and broadcasting industries. Fly left the Commission at the end of the year to enter private legal practice.[77]

After all the controversy generated by the Newspaper-Radio Investigation and with the momentum that the FCC had built up with the Chain Broadcasting Investigation, the Commission's final ruling on newspaper ownership stands at best as an ambivalent and at worst as a meek commitment to fundamental reform of the structures of the American media. When the FCC eschewed employing a strongly reformist philosophy with the Radio Act of 1927, it did so at a moment when the path of radio's development was unclear. By 1944, it was clear to the Commission that newspapers and large broadcasting corporations had attained a great deal of power in the radio industry, and that they wanted to continue this in FM radio. At that point, the FCC had

clear policy precedents to draw on to support policies that promoted ownership diversity in broadcasting. With the Radio Act of 1927, communications
giant AT&T was barred from broadcasting in an explicit statement that separated the business of radio station ownership from that of wired telephony,
a provision also included in the Communications Act of 1934. In 1943, the
FCC had succeeded in convincing the Supreme Court that NBC's ownership
of two broadcasting networks was an illegal monopoly position and that the
Commission had the authority to force the company to divest itself of one
of them in order to promote ownership diversity. But in its 1944 ruling on
the Newspaper-Radio Investigation, the FCC ultimately pursued a moderate course amenable to existing media corporations and avoided structural
reforms.

In some respects, the FCC's ruling fits with the historical trajectory of reform liberalism sketched out by historian Alan Brinkley. The New Deal, Brinkley argues, moved from an early phase seeking to reform the basic structures
of the American economy to one that was by the end of World War II "reconciled to the existing structure of the economy and committed to using the
state to compensate for capitalism's inevitable flaws." In 1944, the FCC declined to pursue regulations that would have fundamentally and absolutely
limited the size of multimedia corporations in favor of establishing a flexible
standard that might prevent some of the more egregious examples of consolidation. This standard represented something of an abandonment of reform
liberalism's direct application to the business of broadcasting, and it signaled
a broader shift in future media policy, which would aim more at adjusting
periodic imbalances in media power rather than it would in establishing clear
and positive statements about the need for diversity in media ownership.[78]

At the same time, however, this was not a willing reconciliation for many
New Dealers such as James Fly. The FCC slackened its reform energies not entirely by choice or change in philosophy, but also because it was constrained
by practical and historical circumstances. Though examples of the dangers
of media consolidation were available before 1941, consistent opposition
from newspaper publishers and their advocates in public and official settings,
lukewarm support from the ACLU on media ownership policies, and unrelenting attacks against the Commission from congressional conservatives
ultimately precluded more reformist policy outcomes. Perhaps most important, the United States was approaching the later stages of a war against fascism,
Nazism, and authoritarianism, a war that much of the American media
avidly supported. Stringent government regulation of the media, especially

newspapers, perhaps seemed less defensible in the face of all the patriotic support the media was giving to the war effort.

Given these factors, the Commission ultimately heeded the alarmist and anti-regulatory testimony of Arthur Garfield Hays and Roscoe Pound, the quantitative data presented by Paul Lazarsfeld, and especially the critical yet moderate testimony of Zechariah Chafee, more than that of reformer Morris Ernst. Though the final order stated that the Commission remained committed to the principle that diversification of media ownership was a desirable goal, the FCC may have had in mind Justice Frank Murphy's dissenting opinion in the Supreme Court's decision on the Chain Broadcasting Investigation that "events in Europe" had demonstrated that media laws "should be approached with more than ordinary restraint and caution." Realizing that the newspaper represented a political limit to its administrative authority, the Commission's final ruling simply stated that it could consider newspaper ownership as one factor in licensing hearings, essentially codifying the often frustrating standard it had used throughout the 1930s. In doing so, the FCC's resolution of the Newspaper-Radio Investigation simultaneously created the possibility of postwar media consolidation and left open a space for reformers and opponents to fight against it.[79]

Chapter 5

Media Corporations and the Critical Public: The Struggle over Ownership Diversity in Postwar Broadcasting

In May 1942, Archibald MacLeish, the poet turned director of the government's Office of Facts and Figures, addressed the 20th Annual Convention of the National Association of Broadcasters in Cleveland to plead with broadcasters for their assistance in the war effort. MacLeish stated that Americans "do not need exhortation; they do not need and do not want the promises and threats which the Nazi radios pour upon the German people; they do not need and will not abide the hysteria, the false heroics, the brassy rhetoric of the Italian loud-speakers. They need, and want, and are entitled to have the truth; they need and want and are entitled to know what is expected of them, what they are required to do." It was the task of broadcasters, MacLeish claimed, to rise to the occasion. "You have something to give this war which no other body of men could possibly give it," MacLeish stated. "You have the inventiveness, and the courage and the imagination which have made American radio one of the great forces of enlightenment in the world. We ask you to mobilize these qualities for the winning of this war."[1]

Broadcasters responded eagerly and became active participants in the war effort. Many radio comedies and dramas incorporated war-related themes, broadcasters increased their news coverage of the war and international affairs, and the networks produced a variety of programming to boost domestic morale and sustain support for the war. With key radio industry figures moving into government positions during the war, state and media developed an efficient and effective system to integrate messages supporting the war effort into regular broadcasts. Broadcasters' motivations for cooperating with the government in the war effort were at some level undoubtedly patriotic, but they were also undoubtedly self-serving. Aiding in the war effort was financially beneficial to broadcasters as it allowed them to maintain their existing program schedules as much as possible, thus ensuring that radio continued to generate healthy revenues.[2]

Aiding in the war effort was also legally and politically strategic for broadcasters, as it gave them a chance to challenge government regulation through patriotic participation. As the trade group Broadcasters' Victory Council told its members, the war offered broadcasters an opportunity to "justify our existence and at the same time safeguard our unique privileges of free kilocycles and free speech." At a time when the federal government was conducting major investigations of the structures of the media industries, broadcasters essentially traded good behavior during World War II for what they hoped would be favorable treatment later. Byron Price, the director of censorship for the federal government's wartime Office of Censorship, made this clear in a speech in March 1943. "War is too gigantic a business to be carried on in complete secrecy," Price argued, and if newspapers "were to publish everything they knew, the task of war would be hopeless." Price argued that the media had acted graciously and professionally in complying with the wartime needs of the state, and that this would "stand to their everlasting credit when the books of our war sacrifice are balanced."[3]

Once the war ended, broadcasters and publishers mobilized to balance these books. Across industries, leaders of such organizations as the National Association of Manufacturers and the U.S. Chamber of Commerce began aggressive lobbying and public relations campaigns to promote postwar economic development. Working within a broader context of domestic anticommunism, these groups often incorporated strong antistatist and antiregulatory language as part of their effort to promote their strong pro-business agendas. Media trade groups were active in these ways as well, as National Association of Broadcasters president Justin Miller began deploying the broadcasting industry's accumulated political capital to scale back or eliminate what he thought were onerous regulations and inveighed against government regulation throughout the immediate postwar period.[4]

In June 1947, Miller convened representatives from various media industries at the "All-Media Conference on Freedom of Expression" at NAB headquarters in Washington. The meeting featured a lunchtime visit to the White House and was attended by representatives from the American Book Publishers Council, the American Newspapers Publishers Association, the Motion Picture Association of America, the National Publishers Association, and the Society of Independent Motion Picture Producers. Miller's opening remarks were both a screed against government regulation and a call to arms for media corporations. Miller argued that there was an ongoing campaign against "free communication" being waged in the United States by the government and aided by "college professors . . . blithely urging that government regulate the program content of radio broadcasting." Miller urged the assembled media representatives to stop "taking potshots at each other," as this only worked to create dissent among media allies, "while our common enemies chortle with glee. This is the point at which sophomoric professors, selfish special interests, religious fanatics, power-crazed bureaucrats, and irascible legislators come together on common ground, to emasculate the media of free communication." Miller saw radio regulation as the front line of the battle to protect freedom of expression, and he urged media corporations to "make common cause" against government regulation. "Some have suggested to me," Miller claimed, "that each of the media must fight its own battle." Miller strongly disagreed with this and instead promoted cross-media cooperation. "Whatever is done to weaken the freedom of radio or motion pictures or book publication weakens the position of the press, of newspapers and of periodicals as well."[5]

Miller amplified this argument soon after at an American Society of Newspaper Editors convention, exhorting editors to join with radio in a common cause to fight a unified battle against government regulation. When "the time comes to . . . put rings in editorial noses," Miller cautioned, "the strong-government boys will be concerned with resemblances, not differences." The "precedents and procedures which are being forged for this new, upstart, highly competitive medium" would soon after be used against all media in "increasing attacks on freedom of communication." What was required, Miller argued, was cooperation between press and radio to combat overreaching government officials. "Divided, like the proverbial bundle of sticks, we are ready to be broken singly; first, the new and different media, the young, awkward, brash media; while precedents are built up which can be used against the older ones to break them more easily when they stand alone." Take action now in the fight against media regulation, Miller asserted, or "inexorable logic requires the conclusion that the same thing can be done to the press, newspapers, magazines, books and all the varied forms of printed publications."[6]

What Miller accomplished rhetorically was to blur the lines between press and radio by linking them together as part of a common history, the bedrock of which was the newspaper press. Radio, Miller argued, drew heavily upon the "techniques of news gathering, news analysis, news editorializing, as well as business management, previously developed in the newspaper field." Newspapers also provided the financial backing for hundreds of radio stations in the early years of AM. In post-World War II America, Miller claimed, FM and television were benefiting from the same support, as they were "depending, largely, upon money produced by newspapers." Having established this common history, Miller then gathered newspapers and broadcasting together into the "media," a constellation of different entities whose differences were far less important than their similarities. Technological developments, he claimed, had "brought all the great media into hotchpotch," and there was now "such a close identity of purpose and such an intermixture and amalgam of techniques and procedure among these several media of communication as to make absurd any effort to deny their identity."[7]

Many media companies shared Miller's views and began gearing up for a surge of postwar growth. Newspapers led the way, and with FM radio and television ready for deployment after World War II, a pattern of media consolidation developed quickly. By 1950, newspapers owned 272 of the 768 (35.4 percent) FM stations on the air, and the number of AM stations owned by newspapers increased from 268 to 491 between 1945 and 1950. (The total number of AM stations went from 913 to 2,088, so the percentage of newspaper stations nationally declined from 29.4 to 23.5.) Across the country, newspapers were taking to the postwar airwaves in greater numbers (see Appendix).[8]

One of the clearest indications of the growing harmony between newspapers and radio during World War II was the move into broadcasting by the *New York Times*, perhaps the country's most influential daily newspaper. The *Times*, long ambivalent toward radio, began to consider obtaining a station of its own in late 1943. *Times* publisher Arthur Hays Sulzberger wrote to FM pioneer Edwin Armstrong asking if he "would take time off some day to tell me a little bit about FM and how we could protect ourselves against the future." After some deliberation, the *Times* bought the New York City classical station WQXR in July 1944. The paper instituted a policy rejecting advertising "inconsistent with the acceptability standards of the *New York*

Times," and the station continued to devote the vast majority of the broadcast day to the presentation of classical music. The *Times* and WQXR made a fine partnership in the minds of listeners, one of whom wrote to the station that it was "One of the few things (very few indeed) that gladdens the heart of a returning veteran."[9]

Not all Americans were as sanguine about newspapers purchasing radio stations. Attorney and media reform advocate Morris Ernst remained a vocal critic of media consolidation after the conclusion of the FCC's Newspaper-Radio Investigation in 1944. Ernst was particularly troubled by the numerous cities across the country where the only local newspaper owned the only local radio station. "What price democracy in that area?" Ernst wondered in a 1944 speech. "What chance for diversity of opinion, other than by little pamphlets or speeches on street corners? What chance of driving a mayor out of office if the two main conduits to the minds of the people of the district are owned by the same entity?" In 1946, Ernst published *The First Freedom*, a strident defense of the need for media ownership diversity, in which he charged that the conduct of many newspaper-radio combinations demonstrated that "evil practices have disturbed the market places of thought."[10]

The Commission on the Freedom of the Press, with *Time* publisher Henry Luce's money and University of Chicago president Robert Hutchins's direction, conducted a major investigation of the American media from 1944 to 1946, and found the situation troubling.[11] After extensive study and commentary by leading scholars in a variety of fields (with the glaring absence of anyone from journalism), the Hutchins Commission's 1947 report, *A Free and Responsible Press*, was sharply critical of the conduct of media corporations.[12] The Commission asserted that the "importance of the press to the people" had been increasing throughout the twentieth century, but it also noted that the media's growing concentration had "greatly decreased the proportion of the people who can express their opinions and ideas through the press." While the various media had become more important in the lives of ordinary Americans, the Hutchins Commission found, their capacity to affect the larger structures of control of those media or to make their voices heard through them had declined. Those who owned media corporations, the Hutchins Commission argued, were often derelict in their duties, and *A Free and Responsible Press* cited numerous instances where the "few who are able to use the machinery of the press as an instrument of mass communication have not provided a service adequate to the needs of the society." Particularly troubling to the Hutchins Commission was the "*local* monopoly of local news" in the "hundred small communities" in which the only newspaper and only radio station were under common ownership, a phenomenon that had been a major concern during the FCC's Newspaper-Radio Investigation.[13]

The Hutchins Commission report was the subject of extensive and often critical press coverage, having been widely disseminated in monographic form and published by *Fortune* magazine as a special supplement. Though written in an academic style by a group of America's most prominent intellectuals, the report was not disconnected from the concerns of many Americans outside of the academy. South Carolina resident Furman Lee Cooper wrote to the FCC in September 1945 that he was concerned that "newspapers are taking over their competitor, the radio, just as fast as they can. The *New York Times* bought WQXR (a station for which I had great hopes), the *Washington Post* bought WINX, the *New York Post* bought WLIB, the *Philadelphia Bulletin* bought WPEN, the *Fall River Herald* bought WSAR—to mention just a few transfers made last year." As an ordinary citizen, Cooper remarked, he was concerned about this trend toward consolidation, and he believed that, "when newspaper and radio are on a separate and competing basis, I shall get more of the golden grains of truth than I would get from just one threshing machine, owned entirely by only one of the interests and used, naturally and primarily, for profit to itself and its supporters." Though the authors of *A Free and Responsible Press* might have aspired to shape American thinking about the media, they were making arguments that many Americans already knew all too well and, in many ways, the report might be seen not as much as an influence on the American media but rather as a reflection of widespread public criticism of the American media.[14]

At the end of the FCC's Newspaper-Radio Investigation in 1944, the Commission adopted the "general principle" that diversity of media ownership was a "desirable" goal. Though the FCC did not categorically bar newspapers from owning radio stations, it resolved to "encourage the maximum number of qualified persons to enter the field of mass communications." This flexible standard proved highly controversial as the FCC was confronted with newspaper applications in hundreds of proceedings for new and renewal AM and FM licenses in the immediate post-World War II period. Between 1945 and 1953, as the number of radio stations on the air in the United States more than tripled from 971 to 3,100 (see Appendix), concerns circulated about whether the broadcasters on all of these new stations would fulfill their responsibilities to the public.[15]

In many cases, ordinary Americans became involved in these proceedings both to encourage the FCC to license particular broadcasters and to challenge the applications of newspapers in order to promote media diversity in their communities. The FCC, a lightning rod for criticism before the war, remained one afterward as it tried to develop and apply a coherent policy on media ownership. To observers on all sides, however, coherence was the last thing that FCC policy suggested, as the Commission's decision-making seemed to shift direction arbitrarily. In some cases, the FCC favored non-newspaper applicants in competitive hearings and cited the general diversification principle as justification. In other cases, the Commission granted licenses to newspapers with no mention of the diversification issues involved. Ultimately, few seemed happy with the direction of FCC policy, and publishers, broadcasters, and ordinary Americans all criticized the FCC as the Commission struggled to articulate a policy. At stake in these debates was a definition of diversity as applied to media ownership.[16]

Diversity, Localism, and the Drift of FCC Policy

Though the reform-minded James Lawrence Fly left the FCC in late 1944, the Commission contained at least one vocal proponent of broadcast ownership diversity into the early 1950s. In the immediate postwar period, commissioner Clifford Durr filled this role, and in 1945 Durr outlined what he saw as the two main reasons for limiting newspaper ownership in his dissenting opinion in a licensing case involving a newspaper in Stamford, Connecticut. In the case, local businessman Stephen R. Rintoul sold station WSRR to a company owned by the *Stamford Advocate*, the city's only local daily. The Commission majority, though sensitive to concerns about concentrated ownership, approved the transfer largely because Stamford residents could receive other stations from nearby New York City. Durr found the reasoning dubious in the ways that it dismissed localism as a concern. "It does not seem to me," Durr asserted, "that it is an answer to the problem of the concentration of controls of the media of mass communications in Stamford to say that diversification still exists in New York." There would always be in Stamford "peculiar local problems in which out-of-town radio stations and out-of-town newspapers cannot reasonably be expected to have any great interest." Durr also doubted publisher claims that commonly owned newspapers and radio stations actually would be operated independently, and he found it difficult to believe that an owner could "divide his mind into two separate compartments and compete with his own social, economic, and political philosophies or his own self interest." Ultimately, Durr argued, one would be more likely to discover "schizophrenia in the individual than diversification in the field of informative and cultural fare presented to the public" if one person or corporation was allowed to own both a newspaper and a radio station.[17]

Though Durr's arguments were part of a dissenting opinion in a case where the newspaper ultimately received the license, similar concerns shared by other commissioners soon led to a series of decisions against newspaper owners in licensing hearings. In these cases, the FCC elected to use its flexible diversity standard in an assertive way. In June 1946 in a competitive licensing hearing for a station in Orangeburg, South Carolina, the Commission had to decide between three parties, one of which was the owner of the only local daily newspaper. The Commission ruled that the public in Orangeburg would be best served "by a grant to the applicant which has no connection with . . . other media," and they awarded the license to the Observer Radio Company, a company with no newspaper affiliation. In an October 1946 case in Meadville, Pennsylvania, H. C. Winslow, a local surgeon and entrepreneur, received a radio license after a competitive hearing against the owners of the *Meadville Tribune-Republican* and *Meadville Republican*, the city's only newspapers, despite the fact that Winslow had "no experience in broadcasting." This was, the FCC said, "based upon the Commission's policy of so exercising its licensing power so as to promote where practical, diversification in the controls of the media of mass communications."[18] These sorts of decisions continued throughout the immediate postwar period as the FCC demonstrated an ongoing commitment to diversifying local media ownership by awarding licenses to applicants who had no connection to the newspaper business. Newspapers were denied applications in competitive licensing proceedings in places as geographically diverse as Morganton, North Carolina; Daytona Beach, Florida; Augusta, Georgia; Green Bay, Wisconsin; Sebring, Florida; Sacramento, California; Fort Smith, Arkansas; Danville, Kentucky; Binghamton, New York; New Orleans, Louisiana; and Norman, Oklahoma. In what was perhaps a vindictive decision, the FCC denied the application of the *Nashville Banner*, the paper published by James Stahlman, the FCC's staunchest opponent in the Newspaper-Radio Investigation, in favor of an applicant not affiliated with a newspaper.[19]

In many instances, these decisions were made after citizen opposition to newspaper applicants, and a particularly contentious 1948 proceeding in

northern Ohio demonstrated the strong consideration that the FCC sometimes gave to local opinion about media consolidation. In the case, the FCC
rejected newspaper applications for AM and FM licenses after finding staunch
local opposition to the papers. The *Mansfield News-Journal* and the *Lorain
Journal*, a pair of newspapers under common ownership, each applied for AM
licenses in their respective cities, and the Mansfield paper also applied for an
FM license. The media markets in both cities had little ownership diversity, as
the *News-Journal* and *Journal* were the only local dailies. Lorain had no local
radio station, while Mansfield had only one AM station, WMAN. The *Mansfield News-Journal* had a contentious relationship with WMAN, something
that played a significant role in the hearing and in the FCC's decision. The
Commission received numerous letters and took testimony from Mansfield
merchants stating that they had been barred from purchasing advertising in
the *News-Journal* after they had advertised on the radio. WMAN representatives testified that the *Mansfield News-Journal* had refused to carry its program logs and never gave the station any favorable coverage. Local residents
were similarly critical of the newspaper. As one wrote to the Commission, "I
know fair play when I see it, and I never thought there could be such unfairness as the *News-Journal* practices." As a broadcaster, the paper ultimately
"wouldn't help to build up Mansfield but rather tear down, just as any dictatorial power when it gets everything its own way."[20]

Local elected officials also criticized the *Mansfield News-Journal* for what
they claimed was biased and unfair reporting. Mansfield Mayor William
Locke claimed that the paper "has carried on a long-standing effort to 'cru-
cify' me" because he refused to keep important news releases from WMAN
until after the *News-Journal* appeared on the street. "In my opinion," Locke
concluded, "a city of our size needs one good newspaper and one good radio
station," and they needed to be under separate ownership.[21] Ultimately, the
FCC was persuaded by these criticisms of the *Mansfield News-Journal* and denied its applications for AM and FM licenses. The Commission ruled that the
Mansfield paper had been operated "with a consistent objective of suppress-
ing competition and establishing monopolies in the field of local advertising,"
and it felt that there was nothing in the record to show that the company
would operate its radio station in a more benevolent manner. As the *Lorain
Journal* was owned by the same company, the FCC also had grounds to deny
that paper's AM application.[22]

Though these decisions were often controversial, the FCC found the federal courts willing to support their assertive use of the diversification prin-

ciple in denials of newspapers' applications. One such court case stemmed from a licensing proceeding in Cleveland, Ohio, in 1949 in which the FCC awarded a license to Cleveland Broadcasting, a locally owned company with extensive civic connections but little broadcast experience, over Scripps-Howard Radio, a company with extensive broadcast experience and extensive newspaper holdings, including the *Cleveland Press*. The Commission chose Cleveland Broadcasting because it felt that it would, among other things, "undoubtedly be conducive to a greater diversification of the media of mass communications in the Cleveland area." Scripps-Howard appealed the case in federal court, which affirmed the FCC's decision and found the FCC to be "well within the law when, in choosing between two applications, it attaches significance to the fact that one, in contrast with the other, is dissociated from existing media of mass communication in the area affected." In competitive hearings involving newspaper applicants, the court concluded, the FCC could, "in the interest of competition and consequent diversity . . . let its judgment be influenced favorably toward the applicant whose situation promises to promote diversity."[23]

This line of decisions from 1946 to 1949 showed an FCC pursuing media ownership diversity by denying newspapers' applications to broadcast, and they demonstrated the Commission's willingness to apply some of the reformist ideas from the Newspaper-Radio Investigation. These decisions did not, however, remain the consistent pattern at the FCC. During the same period, the Commission also granted a number of radio licenses to newspapers, creating a sense of drift and incoherence in the policymaking process.

For example, a 1946 case in Raleigh, North Carolina, involved an application by the *News and Observer*, a paper whose ownership group included former secretary of the navy and ambassador to Mexico Josephus Daniels. After working as a journalist as a young man, Daniels became the editor of the *News and Observer* in 1894, and while making the paper into one of the most influential in the state bought an ownership stake in 1905. A leading advocate for military control of radio after World War I, Daniels also implored Franklin Roosevelt to nationalize American radio broadcasting as the federal government was developing the legislation that became the Communications Act of 1934. After these unsuccessful efforts to encourage government control of radio, Daniels had reconciled himself to the existing structure of broadcasting and decided to move his paper onto the airwaves. Daniels testified to the FCC that he "had this feeling . . . that radio complemented the paper, and that the two together would render a more adequate service."

Capitol Broadcasting, owner of an existing station in Raleigh, challenged the *News and Observer* application for the AM license. As owner A. J. Fletcher put it, the paper already was "a second Bible in North Carolina" and was "all-powerful . . . in Raleigh and this area." Allowing the *News and Observer* to have a radio station, Fletcher argued, would grant it an unfair advantage to extend its local and regional influence. "If you turn that crowd loose with radio, where does the public come in?" Fletcher asked. "They do not have a chance for any diversity of expression of opinion or emphasis on news that should be conveyed to them." Over Fletcher's protests, the FCC granted the license to the *News and Observer*.[24]

That same year in Providence, Rhode Island, the Providence Journal Company applied for an FM license and was greeted with widespread public criticism. Ambrose McCoy, the mayor of nearby Pawtucket, wrote to the FCC that the Providence Journal Company was a "rich and powerful corporation" that, despite representing a "very small select group of bankers and big industrialists within our state," had a "virtual monopoly" on news distribution in Rhode Island. Woonsocket mayor Ernest Dupre made a similar charge, saying that he was "completely opposed to the granting of a broadcasting station license" to a corporation that had "restricted free speech" through its biased news coverage. Dupre claimed that the *Providence Journal* had slandered him and ignored the interests of the Rhode Island public, and he implored the FCC to avoid giving it a greater monopoly on the city's media. The *Journal*, Dupre asserted, "cannot be allowed to extend its undemocratic control over any other medium of information." The FCC also received resolutions passed by the Providence City Council and Rhode Island House of Representatives claiming that the *Journal* should not be given a broadcasting license, but the Commission ultimately granted the license to the paper despite these complaints.[25]

In contemporary competitive proceedings in Orlando, Florida; Midland, Michigan; and Grass Valley, California, the FCC similarly chose to award newspapers licenses instead of other non-affiliated corporations. In the Grass Valley case, the FCC granted a license to 49er Broadcasting, a company whose ownership group included the publisher of the only local newspaper, over a competing company owned by three men who did not reside in Grass Valley. The Commission ultimately decided that 49er Broadcasting was clearly "better qualified to gauge and appraise . . . local needs" than the other applicant, and concluded that "this greatly superior knowledge of the community and its listening needs, outweigh the usual considerations of newspaper connections."[26]

These conflicting and often contradictory decisions reflected an FCC struggling to balance the principles of localism and diversity in broadcast licensing. In cases like the one in Grass Valley, California, the FCC ruled that localism superseded diversity as the primary concern, and it was willing to grant local newspapers licenses for radio frequencies over applicants with no connection to the community even if that meant licensing monopolies on local media. In other cases, such as in Mansfield, Ohio, the FCC ruled that the local newspaper should not be given a radio license so as to encourage more diversity of media ownership in the community. Diversity and localism ultimately proved difficult for the FCC to harmonize into an overall policy, as illustrated by two decisions issued on 28 June 1947 with contradictory rulings on the issue of newspaper ownership of radio.

In one case in Sandusky, Ohio, the FCC denied the application of the *Register Star-News*, the only local newspaper, after a competitive hearing. The other applicant for the frequency, Lake Erie Broadcasting, was owned by Lloyd Pixley, a resident of Columbus, Ohio, a city 110 miles away, and part owner of station WCOL there. The two applicants presented the FCC with a familiar choice: a local newspaper touting its long-term ties to the community versus a nonlocal, nonnewspaper applicant. As in other similar cases, opponents of the newspaper portrayed it as biased and incapable of providing adequate service as a broadcaster. Several witnesses for Lake Erie Broadcasting also charged the *Register Star-News* with having a general bias against organized labor. Wilmer Smith, a member of the local painters union, claimed that Sandusky residents could find more and better news about organized labor "from foreign newspapers" than they could in the *Register Star-News*. With other witnesses making similar claims, the FCC decided to award the license to Lake Erie Broadcasting, citing its general desire to, "where practical," promote "diversification in the controls of the media of mass communication."[27]

That same day, the FCC granted a license to a newspaper in Hanford, California, even though the grant created a local media monopoly. Two parties, Fresno Broadcasting and Hanford Publishing, applied for what was to be the first local radio station in Hanford. The former corporation was based in Fresno, a city thirty miles from Hanford, while Hanford Publishing was owned by two local residents and published the *Daily Sentinel* and the *Hanford Morning Journal*, the only daily newspapers in the city. Citing localism instead of diversity as the determining factor, the FCC ultimately granted the license to Hanford Publishing after expressing satisfaction with the company's record of public service.[28]

In the absence of a firm rule prohibiting newspapers from owning radio stations, the FCC often employed the diversification principle to bar newspapers from broadcasting in order to discourage media concentration. In many other cases though, the FCC granted newspapers licenses after judging them to be competent to serve the local community. For many media owners and critics, perhaps the most troubling aspect of FCC rulings on newspaper ownership was this unpredictability, and few were ultimately satisfied with the drift of FCC policy. For every decision that critics of newspaper ownership could praise for limiting ownership consolidation, there seemed to be a contrary decision that authorized a local media monopoly. Publisher-broadcasters who wanted to see some stability in FCC policy were likewise left generally uneasy by a policy that seemed to shift directions arbitrarily, thus leaving their businesses in constant states of flux and uncertainty.

This instability left the Commission open to widespread criticism, and it also left open a space for citizens' movements to invoke the diversification principle to challenge applications from newspapers. Two particularly contentious cases in the immediate post-World War II period illustrated some of the key issues animating both public animosity toward newspaper-radio combinations and public desire to diversify local media ownership.

The first of these cases involved the application of the *New York Daily News* for an FM station in New York City. The application was greeted by widespread public opposition, especially from many in the Jewish community, who charged that the paper had a record of racism and anti-Semitism in its editorials and news coverage. A second major public campaign against a newspaper-radio combination took place in Baltimore and was led by journalists Drew Pearson and Robert Allen, who attempted to obtain the frequency licensed to William Randolph Hearst's WBAL when the license came up for renewal in 1946. Dissatisfied with the service of both WBAL and Hearst's *Baltimore American* and *News-Post*, Pearson and Allen formed the Public Service Radio Corporation and presented a case that they could offer better radio programming to the Baltimore area. Taken together, the two campaigns demonstrated a commitment on the part of diverse groups of Americans to shape their local media. In actions more significant than simply changing the channel or buying different newspapers, these Americans created active, organized opposition to the basic structures of the postwar American media.

Anti-Semitism, Local Activism, and Citizen Opposition to the
New York Daily News

A New York City FM license offered the chance to broadcast to the largest
and perhaps most diverse media market in the United States. The FCC began
accepting applications for the newly available licenses in 1941 before the
wartime freeze on new broadcast licenses went into effect. When the freeze
was lifted, seventeen parties filed applications for the five frequencies that
the Commission allocated for the area. Several of these applications came
from newspaper publishers, including the *New York Post, Newark Evening
News, Newark Star-Ledger, Staten Island Advance,* and *Long Island Star-
Journal.* Most controversially, the News Syndicate Company, publisher of the
New York Daily News, applied for a license.[29]

News Syndicate[30] was a wholly owned subsidiary of the Tribune Company, the publisher of the *Chicago Tribune.* The *Tribune* had earned a national
reputation as a conservative daily, and many New Yorkers believed that this
editorial policy carried over into the *Daily News.* In Philip Roth's 2004 novel
The Plot Against America, the narrator recalls his father reading the paper
in the early 1940s and describes it as a "right-wing New York tabloid that he
unfailingly referred to as a 'rag.'" In one scene, a fictionalized New York City
Mayor Fiorello H. La Guardia refers to *Daily News* writers as "Hitlerites" during a speech. Though Roth's representation of the *Daily News* is fictional, it
does conform to understandings that many New Yorkers actually had of the
paper at the time.[31] From the early stages of the application process, many
New Yorkers were strongly opposed to the idea of the *Daily News* having a
radio station. Alexander Pekelis, an activist with the American Jewish Congress and a professor at the New School for Social Research, wrote in the *New
Republic* in late 1945 that the paper had a history of racial and anti-Semitic
bias and urged "all truth-loving men and women" to boycott the paper. Sentiment against the *Daily News* generated large public protests in New York, as in
January 1946 when more than two thousand people attended a rally at Hunter
College denouncing the *Daily News* as a "discriminatory newspaper."[32]

In the weeks leading up to the FCC hearings on the New York FM
licenses, hundreds of letters, postcards, and petitions poured into the FCC's
offices slamming the *Daily News* and portraying it as a conservatively slanted
paper with dubious journalistic standards. It was, as Anna Mars described it,
an "immoral, filthy, yellow lying sheet. It is a war mongering, race hating un-
American daily newspaper. It has too much power for evil right now." George

Ehrlich wrote that the paper was the "cheapest, yellowest, most vulgar and disrespectful sheet on the journalistic market," and claimed that it had for some time been spreading "intolerance, lies and hate to the point of anarchy against government officials and peoples representatives." Unlike the *Times* or the *Herald-Tribune*, what Ehrlich called "intelligent and decent newspapers," the *Daily News* eschewed "decent criticism or constructive criticism" in favor of "appealing to the lowest instincts of its readers, who are attracted to this sheet through its loud and misleading headlines, teasing pictures, cheap and sensational stories." Ehrlich pleaded with the FCC to deny the *Daily News* a radio license, claiming that it would be a "sacrilege and crime" if the paper was "given a chance also to pollute and poison the beautiful air of our great invention the—RADIO."[33]

New York liberals soon created two parallel movements to challenge the *Daily News* application. The Peoples Radio Foundation (PRF), a corporation organized for the purpose of obtaining an FM license to present programming supporting labor and working class interests, led one of the movements. Founding members included artist Rockwell Kent, poet Langston Hughes, and Joseph Brodsky, a renowned labor lawyer and defense attorney for the Scottsboro Boys, and the organization quickly attracted support from many prominent labor, ethnic, and fraternal organizations in New York City. PRF supporters began developing programming for the station and went so far as to rent out theaters in New York City to stage live performances of a number of its proposed radio programs. Working in front of what writer and PRF supporter Eugene Konecky claimed were "packed houses," PRF volunteers presented the kinds of programs that it hoped to put on the air, including one drama entitled "Heil, Columbia!" that "dramatized with music, sound effects and documentary dialogue" the recent race riots in Columbia, Tennessee.[34]

These publicity campaigns had an immediate effect. Hundreds of New Yorkers wrote letters to the FCC to support the PRF application, in which many expressed beliefs that the PRF could provide a genuine alternative to corporate broadcasting. One such New Yorker, Jack Anderson Spanagel, claimed that the city needed a "real *People's* radio station" that was "not subject to the desires of a trust" or "under the watchful censorship of a newspaper which is bound to be controlled by its big business advertisers." What Spanagel wanted, and claimed the PRF could offer, was a station that would "constantly campaign for the kind of America our Declaration of Independence and Preamble to the Constitution speak of," and that would "exemplify the term 'public interest' in the fullest degree." Many New Yorkers looked to a PRF station as an antidote to everything that they felt was wrong with contemporary commercial radio. Walter Kraus saw it as a chance to "escape from the endless outpourings of soap operas, unfunny comedians and bad music, biased news comments and other drivel all wrapped up in layers of tasteless and misleading commercials." With "advertising agencies and Wall Street owned networks" controlling radio, Kraus felt, the PRF represented a commitment to the public over advertisers. Folk singers Pete Seeger and Lee Hays wrote a similar letter of support.[35]

Supporters of the PRF also believed that the station would bring some much needed diversity to the New York airwaves and that it offered a solution to the problems of newspaper control and media consolidation. Listener Bernard Silverman saw the PRF as a way around the fact that the "Newspaper and Commercial interests . . . so largely dominate radio in New York." The PRF offered the "one chance in many years for the little guys to break into the highly monopolized radio field." Some also framed this opposition to media consolidation as a specific argument against the *New York Daily News*. Thomas Lockard wrote to the FCC that the *Daily News* was "one of the foulest papers in the country. . . . It has been one of the worst instruments of evil and the fomenting of dissention (sic) in New York City for a long time. It would be an outrage to permit an organ of expression such as a radio station to fall into the hands of the *Daily News*. A greater disservice to the people could scarcely be imagined." Another New Yorker wrote to the FCC that the PRF would provide quality broadcasting and that there was "*no* need for a radio station owned by the *Daily News* to translate printed scandal and bigotry into sound." Though their reasons for supporting the Peoples Radio Foundation were varied, what united all the group's supporters were the shared beliefs that New York radio was controlled by too few corporations and ripe for improvement with a new PRF station.[36]

Alongside the PRF campaign, the American Jewish Congress (AJC) initiated the second organized challenge to the *Daily News* application. Though many AJC supporters were in agreement with the PRF's desire to bring a noncommercial voice to the New York airwaves, its campaign was based more specifically on criticisms of what the group believed was the paper's record of anti-Semitic reporting. For AJC members in the wake of World War II and the Holocaust, the campaign against the *Daily News* was one element of a broader campaign against anti-Semitism and racial discrimination. The AJC, one of a handful of the most prominent Jewish organizations in the country, had existed since 1918 but was revitalized after World War II by a membership committed to more strident public opposition against intolerance. The AJC's main strategy involved legal campaigns for civil rights, which it undertook in a variety of venues, including suits against Columbia Medical School for discrimination against Jewish applicants, a California school board that segregated Mexican Americans, and a variety of states and municipalities that it accused of housing discrimination.[37]

In June 1946, the AJC began a major public relations campaign against the *Daily News* radio application by cosponsoring a petition with the NAACP, New York State Citizens Political Action Committee, City-wide Citizens Committee on Harlem, Committee of Catholics for Human Rights, and Methodist Federation for Social Services, asserting that "we are firmly convinced that the news, columns and editorials published in the *Daily News* have incited racial and religious animosities and have often revealed a striking similarity to propaganda emanating from Nazi and fascist sources." The petition was widely circulated and copies were forwarded to the FCC with hundreds of signatures.[38]

These sentiments were echoed by hundreds of New Yorkers inspired by the AJC to write letters to the FCC opposing the grant of a license to the *Daily News*. Many letters were similar in tone and sentiment to those written on behalf of the PRF, though AJC supporters were much more likely to draw attention to the ethnic and religious politics of the *Daily News* content. Sondra Vitrio argued that the paper had "incited racial and religious animosities" and claimed that its reporting bore a "striking resemblance to Nazi and Fascist propaganda." Tessa Weinstein called the paper's views "detrimental to the American way of life. It is a known fact that the *Daily News* is unreliable in its presentation of facts and that it actually lies. It is prejudiced racially and if given an FM outlet would be a menace to a decent society." Another listener wrote that "Goebbels would have been pleased by this application. We needn't open any more avenues of propaganda to fascists, anti-Semites, and vicious journalists." For many New Yorkers, the problem with the *Daily News* as a potential radio broadcaster was not just that it would create an even greater degree of corporate control of the local airwaves, but that it would encourage bigotry and prejudice over the airwaves. After winning a war against fascism and Nazism, many Americans looked at domestic racial injustice in increasingly critical terms, and attitudes like the ones many believed were promoted by the *Daily News* came to seem ever more offensive and dangerous.[39]

The AJC extended this public campaign against the *Daily News* by also attempting to involve itself directly in the FCC's licensing proceedings. The

AJC filed formal petitions to this effect in early 1946, charging that a *Daily News* radio station would not be in the public interest because the paper's past conduct meant that it would use a radio station as a "means of furthering its hostility to those of the Jewish faith and to other minority groups." *Daily News* representatives responded that the FCC was "without power or jurisdiction" to consider the AJC complaint because the Communications Act of 1934 forbade the Commission from exercising the "power of censorship," and in this case the company argued that any consideration of "past activity in the newspaper publishing field . . . would constitute an abridgement of freedom of the press." As the company claimed, the FCC would be creating a policy that veered perilously close to prior restraint. While not prohibiting newspapers from publishing certain kinds of material or opinions, what the *Daily News* argued that the Commission would be doing if it granted the AJC's request was telling newspapers that, if they wanted to become radio broadcasters, the articles and commentary printed in their pages with full Constitutional protection might be used against them in a licensing hearing. This, the *Daily News* claimed, was a form of coercion and a way of forcing papers to hesitate when printing controversial material lest it come back to haunt them later. The argument proved successful, and the AJC petition to intervene was denied, giving the *Daily News* a victory over the AJC as the hearings to parcel out the five New York City FM licenses began.[40]

The FCC convened its hearings on 8 July 1946 at the Federal Courthouse in New York City. On the second day of testimony, *Daily News* general manager F. M. Flynn presented the paper's case for why it should receive a broadcasting license. "We think that our experience in serving the public for some 27 years," Flynn asserted, "qualifies us to enlarge and expand on that service, and continue the coverage of the New York market in a public service way, such as we have developed on the newspaper." Marcus Cohn, the attorney for Unity Broadcasting, one of the other applicants, questioned Flynn about the paper's editorial policies and political views. Over vigorous objection from *Daily News* attorney Percy Russell that this violated the First Amendment and took the matter "far afield . . . from any legitimate interpretation of the issues in this case," J. Alfred Guest, the presiding examiner, allowed the testimony to proceed, stating that the Commission was "in no position to refuse to consider the method of operation of the newspaper . . . [or] the background of individuals who are applicants for licenses." Cohn's questions to Flynn were brief, but the line of argument he introduced soon became one of the central issues of the case. Indeed, taken together with the Peoples Radio

Foundation application, the AJC case against the *Daily News* made the other fifteen applicants in many ways participants in a legal sideshow. Even the other newspaper applicants were subject to only cursory cross-examination and limited criticism.[41]

With F. M. Flynn's testimony apparently completed, the FCC hearing suddenly took a theatrical turn. After J. Alfred Guest asked if there were any further questions, a member of the audience stood up. "My name is Will Maslow," the man announced. "I appear here on behalf of the American Jewish Congress. I ask leave of the Trial Examiner to cross examine Mr. Flynn." Percy Russell objected that the AJC had no standing to question witnesses, but Guest allowed him to speak briefly. Maslow stated that he was there to combat the "series of self-serving declarations made on behalf" of the *Daily News* and to present material showing that the paper was unfit to be a broadcaster. When Maslow tried to cross-examine Flynn, Guest told him he could not since he was not a party to the hearing or a representative of one that was. Bernard Fein, one of the other applicants present, stood up and announced that he "should like to cross examine this witness" and "would like to designate Mr. Maslow as my associate to handle that cross examination." Percy Russell protested this as "just an outright subterfuge" and argued that Fein was abusing his cross-examination privileges. Examiner Guest called a five-minute recess and, upon resumption, was greeted by PRF attorney Joseph Brodsky standing up to announce that the PRF was "entirely willing, if Mr. Maslow is satisfied, to retain him as co-counsel with me in our behalf in this proceeding." When Guest inquired as to when Brodsky decided to retain Maslow, he replied, "Seven and a half minutes ago." William Standard of NMU Broadcasting became the third party to retain Maslow on the spot, sending Russell into a fit. Brodsky defended what Russell apoplectically denounced as "collusion and subterfuge" by calling Russell's statements "loose remarks" made by "fine looking gentlemen who are attorneys for rich organizations." Brodsky maintained that he had a "right at any time, anywhere, to retain counsel. . . . And it is no conspiracy when I do something which I have a lawful right to do for the purpose of accomplishing a lawful objective."[42]

After some deliberation, the FCC decided to allow the AJC to present a formal case for why it felt that the *Daily News* should not get a broadcast license. Ten days later, Maslow began this presentation, charging that the *Daily News* would carry all of its alleged biases onto the radio. Louis Caldwell, the long-time attorney for the *Daily News*' parent Tribune Company, gave an impassioned argument against the decision to allow a newspaper's editorial policies to be considered in a licensing hearing, a move that he presented as a grave danger to press freedom. If the FCC went forward with the course it was taking, Caldwell cautioned, newspapers would have their reporting and editorial perspectives scrutinized during licensing hearings. This, he claimed, was a "usurpation of power" by the FCC and potentially "one of the most severe and deadly blows to freedom of the press that can ever be struck."[43]

Maslow's response was that, in order for the FCC to decide if the *Daily News* would be a good broadcaster, it had an "obligation" to examine the paper's "editorial policies and . . . news content" in order to determine if the paper would, "as it promises, operate a station without bias in this cosmopolitan city." In fact, Maslow claimed, the paper had "done its best to discredit minority groups" and created "strife in the community" through its news reporting. Though the paper portrayed itself as an aspiring public servant over the airwaves, Maslow argued that its record as a newspaper was clear evidence against this. The printed record, Maslow claimed, was a "better indication of how it will act when it receives a license than its promises of programming which we know are not binding upon it."[44]

To buttress its case against the *Daily News*, the AJC introduced a series of articles and columns printed in the *Daily News* between 1938 and 1946 that the organization believed supported the claim that the paper had been overtly and consistently anti-Semitic. The set of articles included items from September and October 1944 that Maslow claimed contained "wholly unnecessary references to the Jewishness of Sidney Hillman." Maslow acknowledged that Hillman was a prominent labor organizer and public figure and that the paper had a "perfect right to attack" him if it chose to. The FCC should, however, "consider the character of a newspaper which refers to the fact that he had a rabbinical education or the fact that he was an ex-rabbinical student, in making a particularly nasty remark about the Christians of the country having to clear their religion with Sidney Hillman, persisting in linking his name with other Jews, and solely other Jews, in Government." Maslow also cited another series of reports that allegedly "contained nine references to the allegedly excess number of Jews in the Federal Government."[45]

Joseph Brodsky, the attorney and Secretary-Treasurer of the PRF, joined the AJC's attack on the *Daily News* as he portrayed his station as a better alternative. Brodsky claimed that the PRF station had a "people's policy" that was "dedicated to the elimination of discrimination because of color, because of religion, and therefore a policy which fights Negro discrimination, a policy which fights anti-Semitism, a policy which fights discrimination because of alien birth." The *Daily News*, Brodsky claimed, "does not represent the policy that I here enunciated," and he cautioned that the paper would almost certainly have a "policy in its radio broadcasting which parallels its policy in its newspaper." The FCC could choose a station like the one proposed by the PRF, Brodsky claimed, a station that reflected the "hopes, the ambitions and the dreams of the people of America, and the people of my city," or it could choose a broadcaster like the *Daily News*, which would promote "prejudices which are prevalent and which . . . are anti-American, such as anti-Semitic prejudice or anti-Catholic prejudice."[46]

To portray the *Daily News* as unfit to broadcast, the AJC also submitted a content analysis of the paper conduced by AJC member and sociology professor Alexander Pekelis. Pekelis randomly selected three months each from 1945 and 1946 and consulted the *Daily News*, *New York Times*, *New York Herald Tribune*, *New York Daily Mirror*, and *PM*. Pekelis counted the number and length of stories and then analyzed the way that racial issues were framed, and what he testified that he found was consistent bias on the part of the *Daily News* in the way it wrote stories about not only Jews but also African Americans. For example, Pekelis stated, the *Daily News* would go out of its way to mention the race of a crime suspect if that person happened to be African American, a practice he claimed to have found was not followed by other papers.[47]

After presenting the Pekelis analysis, the AJC concluded its case with sweeping charges against the *Daily News* and a plea to the FCC to keep the paper off the air. The United States, the AJC claimed, had "adopted a unique system of radio regulations unparalleled in other countries." This system was a "most daring experiment, substantially based on the belief that a properly selected set of private licensees prompted by the profit motive is capable of performing a delicate public duty." This system demanded that the FCC be vigilant in "selecting licensees who can reasonably be expected to live up to such standards and thus serve the public interest." In order to do this, the Commission had to be allowed to "inquire into the specific communications background of the applicants and examine their past performances, particularly in the areas of public information, education of public taste and enlightenment of public opinion." The AJC dismissed the *Daily News* claim that this violated the First Amendment, pointing out that some applicants inevitably were denied in all comparative hearings. If the FCC upheld the *Daily News* contention that its past conduct as a publisher could not be considered, the

AJC claimed, this would "create the paradoxical situation" in which newspapers would be the only types of applicants to be "exempted from the obligation to show that they are intellectually and morally qualified to become the holders of an important public trust." The *Daily News* certainly had the right to continue expressing its editorial views in print but, in the matter at hand, there were five channels available and seventeen applicants for them, and "hence there must be twelve denials of freedom to broadcast." Because the paper had "consistently conveyed a distorted image of American Jews," it was thus simply "more proper to classify the *Daily News* with the rejected twelve than with the privileged five."[48]

AJC representatives continued to make these kinds of claims in public as well, as Alexander Pekelis argued in a letter to the *New York Times* that the *Daily News* had used its record as a newspaper as evidence of its qualifications to be a broadcaster, in the process claiming that it would approach radio with the same ethic that it approached publishing. As Pekelis saw it, the *Daily News* "invited the Commission to look into what it had done in print in order to find out what it intended to do on the air." When the Commission actually did this, Pekelis claimed, the paper "resented it," and he criticized it for trying to "have it both ways." The paper simply could not "invoke its newspaper policy to support its case and at the same time prevent its opponents from examining that policy." Legal scholar Zechariah Chafee agreed in *Government and Mass Communications*, his two-volume work for the Commission on the Freedom of the Press produced while the *Daily News* case was ongoing. The evidence of the "*Daily News* in print is surely relevant to the *Daily News* on the air," Chafee stated, and he dismissed the paper's First Amendment claims. What the FCC was doing was an "essential part of its job of parceling out the air in 'the public interest.'"[49]

In response, *Daily News* representatives and allies continued to defend the paper from the FCC scrutiny of its record in print. In its own newspaper, the *Daily News* coverage of the case consistently presented the paper as embroiled in a fight over free speech against false allegations.[50] Arguing before the FCC, the *Daily News* was even more assertive. F. M. Flynn of the *Daily News* vigorously challenged the allegations that his paper was racist or anti-Semitic. "I am convinced," Flynn stated emphatically, that the *Daily News* "has never had, nor does it now have any programs or plan" of anti-Semitism, nor "any policy or plan of discrimination against any minority group." Flynn claimed that the paper strove to represent "probably the greatest melting pot in the world" thus would never "want to have such an intent" as to be racist or anti-Semitic. Flynn not only defended his paper's content but also attacked the AJC's sampling methods. Out of the thousands of articles and columns that the *Daily News* had printed between 1938 and 1946, Flynn claimed, the AJC selected but a handful, certainly not enough to "substantiate a charge as sweeping as the one made." The entire AJC case, the *Daily News* claimed, was a "revolutionary formula of governmental regimentation of ideas" and an "abuse of the administrative process."[51]

As the AJC and *Daily News* offered competing perspectives on both the content of the paper's coverage and the legality of its admissibility as evidence, the FCC's hearings generated criticism from observers across the country. Senator Homer Capehart, a Republican from Indiana, argued that it was not within the FCC's powers to make any judgments of newspapers' content. There were "places for the proper judgment and determination," of whether newspaper reports were "false, unfair, misleading or prejudicial," Capehart claimed, but FCC chambers were not among them. If the "time should ever come" when newspapers could be "judged and dictated by a government agency in Washington," Capehart stated, "then God help America." Journalist Arthur Krock also felt that the hearing was a dangerous imposition of federal administrative authority onto newspapers. "The proper judges" of a newspaper, Krock claimed, "are its readers, not any part of the government."[52]

A number of publishers were similarly uneasy about the constitutional issues raised in the case. On 10 October 1946, John S. Knight, publisher of several metropolitan dailies including the *Chicago Daily News*, *Miami Herald*, and *Detroit Free Press*, described the hearings in an editorial as proceedings that "should cause every true lover of freedom to pause and consider whether he is aware of the methods being employed by the government and left-wing zealots to limit freedom of speech and political action." Knight claimed that the decision by the Commission to consider a paper's content when deciding whether to award a broadcast license was a dangerous encroachment on freedom of speech. "Reduced to simpler language," Knight claimed, this would mean that "the government can deny a radio license to a newspaper if it does not happen to like that newspaper's editorial policies or news content." For Knight, a longtime advocate for a critical and independent press, this represented some of the worst examples he had seen in the period of the state trying to exert undue influence over the press. The FCC's goal, Knight stated, was a "revolutionary doctrine" meaning that "an agency of government might undertake to punish newspapers considered unfriendly to the administration in power."[53]

Knight repeated this argument two weeks later in a speech at the annual

National Association of Broadcasters convention in Chicago. The American press enjoyed substantial freedoms, Knight stated, yet it was "forced to be constantly upon the alert against bureaucratic regulation and decree." In the *Daily News* case, Knight told the audience, the FCC "ruled that the editorial policies and news content of that newspaper were proper subjects of inquiry." This was, Knight claimed, a "very real threat to press freedom," especially if it caused "weak publishers" to "start bending the knee to government in order to win approval for their broadcasting ventures." This dangerously overreaching federal authority had to be fought on every front, Knight argued, in order to give other media the same protection, and to make sure that government regulation of broadcasting was not allowed to bleed into the newspaper world.[54]

As public debate swirled around the case, the *Daily News* filed a motion in November 1946 to dismiss the AJC testimony, and in April 1947, the Commission reached a decision in its favor. The amount of articles and editorials submitted by the AJC, the FCC ruled, was "too sparse a selection of material to have any probative value" to show that the *Daily News* was consistently biased against Jews and African Americans, and the Commission found the content analysis unpersuasive. Commissioner Clifford Durr issued a lengthy dissent, stating that he was puzzled that the other commissioners could dismiss the AJC material as insufficient. Durr was convinced that the articles submitted showed not just "bias and prejudice but also a lack of that sense of public responsibility which should be expected of a broadcast licensee." The *Daily News*, he claimed, had consistently printed articles that were full of "prejudice and hostility." Durr blasted what he saw as hypocrisy on the part of the *Daily News*, remarking that the paper had tried to use its record as a newspaper as "affirmative evidence of its qualifications to operate a radio station." This, Durr claimed, was asking the FCC to assess the quality of content published in a newspaper, which was exactly what the AJC was doing. Durr also dismissed the paper's First Amendment defense, stating that there was nothing in the amendment that mandated that the FCC "ignore the past behavior of an applicant merely because it has been evidenced in the operation of a newspaper rather than the operation of a manufacturing plant, department store, filling station, or some other line of business." The FCC had to decide who was best qualified to be a broadcaster, Durr stated, and this was always going to involve denying some license applications, freedom of speech considerations notwithstanding. However much anyone might like to and feel qualified to be a broadcaster, Durr asserted, the Bill of Rights "cannot expand the radio spectrum."[55]

On the same day that the FCC issued this proposed decision striking the AJC testimony from the record, it issued another proposed decision granting the five FM licenses to applicants WMCA, American Broadcasting Company (ABC), Unity Broadcasting, North Jersey Broadcasting, and the *Daily News*. Several of the applicants who were denied filed exceptions, and the AJC also filed a motion to protest its testimony being stricken. In response, further hearings were held in June 1947. Will Maslow and the AJC vigorously protested the proposed decision, claiming that the Commission had a "clear duty to deny" the *Daily News* application because of its conduct as a newspaper, conduct that certainly would "carry over to the air" if it received a license. The *Daily News* continued to assert that the FCC had the right only to inquire into the "financial qualifications of an applicant, his honesty, and things of that kind." Anything else was a violation of the First Amendment.[56] After deliberating further, the FCC delivered a surprising reversal and denied the *Daily News* application. Instead, the Commission proposed to award the license to a radio corporation set up by the Board of Missions and Extensions of the Methodist Church, along with the other four parties in the original proposed decision. North Jersey Radio and the *Daily News* then filed exceptions, and more hearings were held in late 1947 and early 1948, with the main parties restating their main arguments.[57]

On 7 April 1948, the FCC issued its two final decisions, the first relating to the admissibility of the AJC evidence, the other giving the final decision on who was to actually get the licenses. On the AJC matter, the majority ultimately agreed with Clifford Durr's previous dissent, ruling that it was "within the proper scope of inquiry in a radio licensing proceeding" to consider "an applicant's previous activities," even if this meant critically assessing newspaper content. The "fairness with which a licensee deals with particular racial or religious groups in the community," the FCC decided, was "clearly a substantial aspect of his operation in the public interest." If the FCC could not consider newspaper content, it claimed, this would "give newspapers a preferred position over all others who may seek to become licensees of radio stations by requiring a more limited inquiry into their qualifications." Considering the past conduct of any applicant was justified, the FCC claimed, regardless of "whether it be publishing newspapers, selling edible oil, or any other type of business."[58]

After ruling that the AJC claims and findings were admissible evidence, the Commission decided to not award the *Daily News* a license while granting the applications of WMCA, ABC, North Jersey Radio, North Jersey Broadcasting, and Unity Broadcasting. Although the AJC case against the *Daily News* was ultimately successful, the related application of the PRF was denied. The FCC's decision did contain some additional progressive elements, however, as Unity Broadcasting was owned by the International Ladies Garment Workers Union, giving labor interests some representation on the New York airwaves. This, combined with the rejection of the *Daily News*, represented a clear desire by the FCC to encourage some diversity of ownership and content on New York's FM dial. More importantly, in considering the public sentiment of New Yorkers about the *Daily News* application, the FCC displayed a real sensitivity to public opinion when it considered whether or not a broadcaster would serve the public interest of a particular community. At least some degree of diversity on the radio, the American Jewish Congress demonstrated, could be achieved through collective civic action.[59]

Journalists, Public Service, and Citizen Opposition to William Randolph Hearst

As it administered the contentious New York City FM hearings, the FCC was also faced with a high-profile license renewal case in Baltimore, Maryland, involving WBAL, a station owned by *Baltimore American* and *Baltimore News-Post* publisher William Randolph Hearst. Hearst had owned the station since 1934, and when the license came up for renewal in 1946 a group calling itself Public Service Radio Corporation (PSRC) mounted a challenge by filing an application of its own for the same frequency. The case pitted a group of local citizens organized to encourage diverse media ownership against a large media corporation and, like the *Daily News* proceeding, the group asked the FCC to assess a newspaper publisher's fitness to operate a radio station in the public interest. Unlike the *Daily News* hearing, however, the Baltimore case was not a comparative hearing for a newly available license but instead a direct challenge to an existing broadcaster. The odds were not in the PSRC's favor, as the FCC rarely denied license renewals. In fact, out of the thousands of renewal applications the Commission had processed since 1934, it had denied fewer than twenty to date. In the Baltimore case, the PSRC was asking the FCC to decide two things: whether WBAL's program service had been so poor that it ought to lose its license, and whether that license should then go to an organization promising different and allegedly higher-quality programming.[60]

The PSRC was a group of Baltimore-area citizens organized for the specific purpose of challenging the WBAL license. The owners of the largest stakes in the company were journalists Drew Pearson and Robert Allen. The pair had collaborated for more than a decade and had produced such works as the gossipy political books *Washington Merry-Go-Round* and *More Merry-Go-Round*, and *The Nine Old Men*, a critique of the Supreme Court written at the height of Franklin Roosevelt's animosity toward the Court in 1937. Pearson and Allen also produced a popular syndicated newspaper column and had partnered as radio commentators as well. In many respects, the Pearson-Allen leadership of the PSRC was a modification of the long-standing publisher discourse promoting newspapers as the best class of station owners. Pearson and Allen believed that a newspaper background was an ideal one for a radio station owner, but they also believed that it was the journalist rather than the publisher who was best suited for radio. Newspaper work, Pearson and Allen believed, cultivated public responsibility and demanded a commitment to the public interest, but they believed that the owners of newspaper corporations had become detached from these concerns as they sought increasing profits. Radio, the pair believed, offered the possibility of bringing fresh and diverse perspectives to the public, but only if the medium could be freed from the control of large corporations. As they challenged Hearst, Pearson and Allen argued that professional journalists could do a better job operating a radio station than could corporate media owners.

The Public Service Radio Corporation's name reflected the commitment of Pearson and Allen to provide quality broadcasting to Baltimore. It was also an obvious reference to the FCC's recently published and controversial *Public Service Responsibility of Broadcast Licensees*. The report, also known as the Blue Book, was the product of a yearlong investigation of ways for the FCC to establish more rigorous standards for assessing programming quality during license renewal hearings, and it was one of the FCC's major post-World War II initiatives. The Blue Book research was directed by the British-born Charles Siepmann, who had come to the United States in 1937 with the support of a Rockefeller Foundation grant to study educational broadcasting after a decade-long career at the British Broadcasting Corporation. Siepmann later taught at Harvard from 1939 to 1942 and in 1946 became a professor of education and communication at New York University. The Blue Book's most significant claims were that American broadcasting was dominated by advertisers and sorely lacking in noncommercial and educational programming, and its most significant recommendation was that the FCC should not renew the licenses of stations that it found had not fulfilled their public service responsibilities.[61]

The broadcast industry in general was furious at the report, with *Broadcasting* calling it "as masterfully evasive as it is vicious" and announcing that "Radio censorship is here." The magazine claimed that the report had probably "been in the minds of many men who have served on the FCC, and on the old FRC" and speculated that its "first lines probably took form in the mind of James Lawrence Fly, former chairman of the Commission." Siepmann did little to quell the controversy that his report stirred up and in fact went out of his way to incite further ire from the industry. Soon after the Blue Book's publication, Siepmann authored a book entitled *Radio's Second Chance* in which he elaborated on some of his Blue Book findings and provided advice to readers on how they could improve their local airwaves, including involving themselves in license renewal proceedings. Siepmann asserted that the FCC had the "clearly established" power to "pass judgment on past program service" when it considered license renewals. Since the airwaves were public property, Siepmann advised his readers, it was the FCC's job to *"safeguard the public against the control of stations by persons in any sense unfitted for the task of operating in the public interest."* What Siepmann did, in essence, was to encourage ordinary Americans to act upon the criticisms of corporate broadcasting that he had developed while conducting research for the FCC.[62]

For WBAL, the challenge to its license by the PSRC in the wake of the FCC's *Public Service Responsibility of Broadcast Licensees* was made more threatening because of the fact that WBAL had come under particularly heavy criticism as one of the case studies featured in the Blue Book. Siepmann had chosen five stations to represent the ways that the public interest was poorly served by commercial radio stations and to suggest that the FCC take a more detailed look at programming when deciding on license renewals. Though the Blue Book stated that the case studies were not chosen for any particular reason, Hearst Radio strongly took offense at WBAL's inclusion among Siepmann's five. WBAL saw the newly competitive licensing hearing as a government plot to use the report against it, charging that the PSRC application was filed as a "direct result of the false, distorted and misleading discussion of the operation of Station WBAL" in the Blue Book. Industry observers thought the same way, and *Broadcasting* saw the hearing as a "top-level test of FCC's Blue Book policies."[63]

The crux of the case that the PSRC offered for why it should be given WBAL's frequency was the claim that it could provide the service to Baltimore that the Blue Book claimed the station was not. PSRC principals Drew Pearson and Robert Allen made this case repeatedly to the FCC during the licensing proceedings. Of the two men, Pearson was the more well known to the general public, having started his journalistic career at the *Baltimore Sun* in the late 1920s and achieving national notoriety for the Washington books that he and Allen had written, a fame that was amplified as he became a nationally syndicated newspaper columnist and a radio broadcaster.[64] Pearson found radio intriguing because it offered a chance to become the manager of a media corporation, something that he believed was financially impossible through newspaper publishing. Pearson claimed that he had for "a good many years" wanted to extend his journalistic activities more into radio, but he "wanted to be active in a radio station" as an owner, Pearson stated, "rather than as a radio commentator." His original plan was to "get a small station in Rockville or Gaithersburg and build it up and see what impact a radio station could have on a community." Radio had a tremendous amount of unfulfilled potential, he believed. Though there were some good stations, "radio on the average in the United States has been for profit and for entertainment to the exclusion or perhaps neglect of education . . . [and] moral uplift." Radio might fill some of the gaps that had opened up as formerly influential social institutions waned, Pearson thought. There seemed to be a "whale of an opportunity" to use radio to improve local communities, and "help to make up for the fact that the churches have slid backward, unfortunately in recent years." Schools were also "having a hard time keeping up with the tremendous advance of technical life," Pearson stated, and he wanted radio to "supply" what "those other mediums of influence on American life" were not.[65]

Pearson's desire to own a radio station was in many ways a product of the same background and motivation that had led him into the profession of journalism. His father Paul had been a professor of public speaking at Swarthmore College and the director of a Chautauqua company that did tours of the east coast. Drawing upon the tradition of the lyceum movement, Chautauqua began in 1874 as a Methodist summer camp on the New York lake from which it drew its name, and within ten years was attracting as many as 100,000 visitors annually to hear sermons and lectures from some of the country's leading intellectuals and preachers. Pearson's father was instrumental not only in taking the Chautauqua model and making it a portable event but also in expanding its program to include theatrical entertainment and political speeches. By the 1920s, progressive politicians such as Hiram Johnson and Robert La Follette were making regular and popular appearances on the traveling Chautauqua circuit, and some contemporaries saw Chautauqua as an antidote to an overzealously commercialized press in the way that Drew Pearson would in the 1940s. Sociologist Edward A. Ross, for example, wrote to Paul Pearson in 1923 that "newspapers generally are becoming less loyal to the people and more subservient to the interests from whom they hope for advertising," and he praised Pearson for providing a way for Americans to stay better informed.[66]

Pearson's background shaped many of his ideas about radio, as he saw public culture as something that could be enlightening if its producers had commitments to education and uplift. In this regard, Pearson claimed that WBAL approached radio entirely as a commercial venture, a philosophy that meant profits were stressed at the expense of the public interest. WBAL had the "thesis of radio" that it was mainly "entertainment, and education and moral leadership takes a second or third place," and Pearson's plan was to "reverse that." The station that he would run would "still have entertainment, which is necessary, but let us call that the sugar coating around the pill." The core mission of the station would be inspired by his ideas about the social function that Chautauqua meetings used to hold. Chautauqua, Pearson felt, had "disappeared because radio came in. You no longer have your community sessions of that kind. You have very few radio stations that make a great hobby and business of working for the community." Properly utilized, radio might extend the idea of "the old Chautauqua" onto a mass scale. Part of the attraction for Pearson of obtaining the frequency held by WBAL was not only that he believed his station could do better broadcasting, but also the fact that the station had a powerful license that could reach millions of listeners. Pearson's radio plans were ambitious and he believed that "you either had to do it right, or not at all, and you had to have a large wavelength. In other words, 50,000 watts were required." This was what WBAL had, and Pearson claimed that he was "just audacious enough to think" that he might "do a better job" with it.[67]

Pearson's main partner in the campaign against WBAL was his longtime collaborator Robert Allen, who shared many criticisms of Hearst as a broadcaster and hopes for what a new station might do instead. Like Pearson, Allen had been drawn to journalism by a deep commitment to public service. Allen believed that publishers who shared this as their main motivation had steadily disappeared over the course of his career, and like Pearson he saw radio broadcasting as a way to recapture some of this older spirit of journalism. WBAL thus offered a perfect opportunity for Allen, who saw Baltimore as a "uniquely available field for a newspaper man" and the kind of "great metropolis" where he felt he could "move in and really do things, things along the type of journalism I was brought up on." Recalling the "old" *New York World*, the *St. Louis Post-Dispatch*, and the "old" *Milwaukee Journal*, Allen testified to the FCC that these papers were "dynamic. They meant something . . . Baltimore offers that kind of a field now." It was ultimately a "great opportunity town for my kind of newspaper guy." As he talked to people in Baltimore, Allen remarked, he found that "everywhere I touched, I got a sharp, caustic, and hostile reaction. Here is a great facility, the largest station in that community," and he found very few satisfied listeners. Allen discovered that many in Baltimore were "constantly talking about the over-commercialization, and all we get is this and that, somebody selling something," and he remarked that "you become conscious very quickly of an overemphasis on that aspect of the programming." With the right strategy, Allen felt, Baltimore "would support" the "kind of paper or . . . radio station" that he and Pearson were planning. "It is a big metropolitan city, and there is a big void there in that kind of militant journalism."[68]

Pearson and Allen's campaign against WBAL soon attracted substantial support from influential Baltimore residents, some of whom became active in the management of the PSRC. For example, Elizabeth Holt Downs, president of Maryland League of Women Voters, had become a regular follower of FCC policy during James Fly's tenure as chairman. In February 1946, Downs told the FCC, she saw an item in *Broadcasting* discussing the WBAL license renewal proceedings and began talking to people about the possibility of mounting a challenge to it. Dissatisfied with the station's service record, she thought that she might get a group together to possibly "have some people appear and say we did not think WBAL's license should be renewed, because they certainly had given us—up to that time—no discussion of public issues." Like Pearson and Allen, Downs did not just want to criticize the station, but rather wanted to get it off the air entirely. Downs began exploring fundraising opportunities in Baltimore to back a campaign against WBAL "because we knew it would take considerable money." When she discovered that Pearson and Allen were already organizing just such a group, Downs became active in the PSRC management and a minority stockholder in the corporation.[69]

Blue Book author Charles Siepmann was similarly and publicly supportive of the PSRC application. Under the auspices of the Anti-Defamation League of B'Nai B'Rith, he published a short book entitled *The Radio Listener's Bill of*

Rights in which he encouraged listeners to challenge the licenses of stations that they believed delivered poor service. "Radio is yours," Siepmann argued, "to make, or to mar by default of ignorance, indifferences or inertia." Of his work on the Blue Book, Siepmann wrote that it "aroused the industry to fury but largely escaped the attention of the listening public. You should read it."[70] Siepmann turned specifically to the WBAL proceeding in a December 1946 article in *The Nation*. What was "exciting and important about this case," Siepmann argued, was that it presented an "opportunity for a community to make its wishes the decisive factor in determining the commission's verdict," as the Blue Book had made quality program service a key consideration for the FCC in license renewals. It also opened the door for citizens' groups to claim that stations had been presenting poor programming. The case was a "rare opportunity to test whether democracy works," Siepmann argued. "The people of Baltimore and Maryland, and listeners far afield within the service area of this powerful station, now have the chance to register their will. The decision should be theirs."[71]

In response to Siepmann and the PSRC, Hearst Radio representatives attacked the portrayal that WBAL had received in the Blue Book, calling it a "deliberately unfair and misleading picture," and trying to get the entire matter dismissed on these grounds. The Blue Book treatment of WBAL was slanderous, Hearst Radio claimed, and "Common justice requires that, insofar as it is able to do so, the Commission rectify this bitterly unfair and wholly unwarranted injury." Hearst representatives blamed the Blue Book for inciting the controversy that led to the PSRC challenge, claiming that, without it "there would have been no Pearson and Allen application. Without the Pearson and Allen application, Hearst would have been granted the renewal of license for Station WBAL without a hearing." Criticizing the PSRC application and attacking the Blue Book was a two-pronged Hearst strategy, as the corporation not only asked for a renewal but also a "complete investigation of the false, distorted and misleading" portrait of WBAL and an "appropriate retraction" as well. The FCC denied the requests and ordered the comparative hearing to proceed.[72]

As the FCC began assessing WBAL's service to Baltimore, it found a mixed record among different segments of the population. Many local elites supported WBAL, perhaps out of lingering fealty and fear toward Hearst. For example, Michael Curley, archbishop of Baltimore and Washington, said that he had always known the station to be "most cooperative in giving free time" and "very willing to lend its facilities for the use of Catholic

Programs." John Rutherford, the clerk of the Baltimore City Court, claimed that it would be a "tragedy for the people of this community to lose the services of this outstanding and most useful station." Robert Fich, a U.S. Representative from Pennsylvania, told the FCC that he often listened to the station while driving back and forth to Washington from his home in Pennsylvania. "For a good, all-around station that will keep me advised all the way from Pennsylvania to Washington without changing my dial, I know of no better station than WBAL in Baltimore," Fich stated. Mayor Thomas D'Alessandro, Jr., of Baltimore went so far as to issue a proclamation declaring that September 1947 was to be "WBAL Month in Baltimore" to celebrate the "continuous service to the people in the City of Baltimore" that the station had offered.[73]

Ordinary citizens were less inclined to express support for WBAL. Norman Williams wrote that the Hearst corporation could "feed the nation all sorts of bunk through Hearst Radio," and pointed out that Hearst papers devoted "a lot of space . . . to blasting Communism" but at the same time reported "hardly anything . . . about those firms which did business with Nazi Germany in the cartel agreements." Williams expressed admiration for the work the FCC had done in writing and publishing the Blue Book, remarking that he "would like to see every monopoly tie up between press and radio chains broken to insure freedom of speech and press." In the comparative hearing at hand, he felt, the PSRC offered the better alternative, and it was "only fair to support Drew Pearson, as he has told the truth more times than not." Another listener remarked of WBAL that "taking this station out of the hands of the Hearst interests will be a forward step" for the Baltimore media.[74]

The FCC held twenty-eight days of hearings between November 1947 and February 1948 on the WBAL license and PSRC challenge, during which Hearst defended WBAL's programming and commitment to public service. Hearst representatives repeatedly criticized the Blue Book and petitioned for the entire licensing hearing to be postponed until the Commission issued a formal withdrawal of the criticisms it published in the report. At one juncture, the company went so far as to file a lawsuit against the FCC over the issue. It was "impossible to obtain a fair hearing" in the face of the Blue Book allegations, Hearst Radio attorney William Dempsey claimed. In an appeal in federal court, WBAL claimed that the Blue Book exposed it to "public shame, obloquy, contumely, odium, contempt, ridicule, aversion, degradation and disgrace," but the court denied the plea and refused to stop the FCC proceeding.[75]

Public Service Radio Corporation representatives presented a detailed case arguing that they could offer better service to Baltimore than WBAL. Charging that WBAL sacrificed public service for commercial gain, PSRC promised to devote substantially more broadcasting time to local politics, public affairs, and high-quality musical and dramatic programming. All of this, Pearson, Allen, and Downs claimed, was a move away from a business model stressing profitability to one that combined public service with financial sustainability. PSRC also made an aggressive but ultimately unsuccessful effort to have the aging William Randolph Hearst himself brought to Washington to give testimony, hoping that bringing the controversial media mogul to the stand would galvanize opposition to WBAL.

When the FCC reviewed the voluminous case record, it offered an ultimately ambivalent assessment of WBAL's programming. The Commission found that, "when compared to what might be termed as ideal programming," what WBAL offered was "unbalanced with respect to an overabundance of commercial programs," and "lacked a desirable amount of time devoted to local activities and to sustaining programs." PSRC, the Commission felt, offered both a slate of high-quality proposed programming and a plan for a better integration of ownership and management, with Pearson and Allen much more likely to take an active role in station affairs than William Randolph Hearst did. Ultimately, though, the Commission was hesitant to not renew the applications of existing stations, noting in this case that there were "risks attendant on the execution of the proposed programming of Public Service Radio Corporation, excellent though the proposal may be," and the FCC chose what it stated was a barely satisfactory station instead of licensing a new station that promised better service. The FCC also remarked that newspaper ownership was not a deciding issue in the decision. Though it was a "factor which is considered," the Commission found no evidence that "common control of WBAL and the Baltimore newspaper has been employed adversely to the interests of the listening public, and an inference can reasonably be drawn that these conditions which have previously obtained can continue."[76]

Commissioner Wayne Coy dissented from the majority opinion, arguing that WBAL's record was "certainly not one of superior service to the community," nor was the station's programming "of outstanding quality such as that proposed by Public Service Radio Corporation." Moreover, Coy argued, the decision to renew the WBAL license flew in the face of the Commission's attempts to ensure diverse ownership. With Hearst also owning a newspaper in Baltimore as part of extensive nationwide media holdings, Coy felt that it would be more in the service of the public interest to give the license to the PSRC. Coy also wanted the FCC to be more rigorous in assessing the programming of existing licensees, something that it had both the right and responsibility to do. "The Communications Act," Coy stated, "makes it explicitly clear that a license creates no property right in the licensee and confers no vested right in the use of the licensed facilities." The Commission need not give any credence to the fact that Hearst was the existing licensee, Coy stated, as "licensees should not be permitted to utilize their investment in broadcast facilities as a reason for retaining their facilities when they have not utilized those facilities in rendering a real public service to their community."[77]

Coy's dissent connected to a reformist strain of FCC policy that traced back to the mid-1930s. Like Irvin Stewart, James Lawrence Fly, and Clifford Durr before him, Coy wanted the FCC to aggressively apply the "public interest, convenience, and necessity" standard when it considered new and renewal license applications, and he wanted the FCC to take seriously the desires of local citizens to have more diversity of ownership in their local media. Sometimes successful, but often not, these commissioners consistently pushed for the denial of newspaper applications for radio licenses in a struggle to create the kind of diversity on the dial they thought might best serve the public. As television crept onto the American media landscape, however, the results of this struggle tended to favor corporations more than the public.

The American Communications Conspiracy?

In economist Ronald Coase's seminal 1959 article "The Federal Communications Commission," Coase cited the *New York Daily News* case as alarming evidence of federal regulation gone astray. The *Daily News*, Coase speculated, might have had its radio application denied by the FCC as punishment for its past conduct as a newspaper. "What seems clear" from the outcome of the case, Coase argued, "is that a newspaper which has an editorial policy approved of by the Commission is more likely to obtain a radio or television license than one that does not. The threat to freedom of the press in its strictest sense is evident." For Coase, the *Daily News* case ultimately demonstrated the perils of too much government regulation of the media, and it was also evidence of the greater desirability of a private property approach to spectrum allocation than the existing system in which the FCC had the power to grant and revoke licenses.[78]

Supporters of the Peoples Radio Foundation drew the opposite conclusion from the outcome of the *Daily News* case. This was not evidence of unhinged regulation, PRF supporters believed, but evidence of an FCC that was too amenable to corporate broadcasting and too hesitant to encourage real diversity on the airwaves. In July 1947, just months after the FCC had denied the PRF application for a broadcasting license in New York, one of the organization's key members, attorney Joseph Brodsky, suffered a fatal heart attack at work while preparing a legal defense for suspects under investigation by the House Un-American Activities Committee. In October, the PRF directors met and decided that, after the unsuccessful application and in the wake of Brodsky's death, they should "dissolve the corporation." They also voted to set aside some of their remaining funds to publish a book entitled *The American Communications Conspiracy*, hoping to "perpetuate the ideals of democracy and public service" that Brodsky had championed in his life and work. The book, written by PRF member Eugene Konecky, a former advertising manager at an NBC-affiliated radio station, was a critical and often venomous attack on the American media. "Joe," Konecky wrote of his deceased colleague, "dreamed of a radio station dedicated to broadcasting the truth. He listened to the radio news reports and read the newspapers. To him they were a two-headed monopoly monster of deadly lies."[79]

The American Communications Conspiracy leveled sweeping charges against corporate radio owners for delivering poor public service. Ultimately, Konecky claimed, radio was a tool of big business interests that had hijacked the medium from the people and obscured the fact that they were actually using public property to perpetuate their social and political domination. Konecky claimed that "control of the stations, their policies and programs, is concentrated in the hands of relatively small and powerful groups," which he listed as "Sponsors, advertising agencies, network owners and executives, the Radio Manufacturers of America, radio engineers, NAB, FCC, station owners." All of these groups, Konecky claimed, "participate in shaping the dominant policies" that governed American broadcasting, policies that he claimed "constitute expressions of the ideology and objectives of the capitalist class and its dominant groups."[80]

Though *The American Communications Conspiracy* was a deeply polemical work, it was also a deeply researched assessment of American broadcasting. Konecky demonstrated a thorough knowledge of the technological and political development of American broadcasting, and his unabashedly ideological account of corporate-dominated radio history was amply documented. One of the major problems that Konecky highlighted in radio history was ownership of stations by newspapers, and he devoted a substantial section of his book to the issue. "Newspaper direct and indirect control of broadcasting," Konecky asserted, was "part of the communications monopoly" and was, "in the widest sense . . . integrated into Big Business domination of American life." Newspapers, he argued, had been profoundly influential in helping to develop the model of privately operated, advertiser-supported, and profit-oriented American broadcasting, and Konecky was deeply troubled by the political implications of this system. The "problem of the rapidly increasing spread of newspaper control in broadcasting," he argued, was "one of the basic issues of our times." If this claim seemed "exaggerated" to readers, Konecky asserted, he urged them to consider whether the "existence of a supermonopoly of the two main mass media of public information and communications—the press and broadcasting" was "important in deciding the alternatives of war and peace, security or chaos, democracy or Fascism." For Konecky, it was profoundly important.[81]

The relationship between newspapers and radio in the late 1940s was almost totally harmonious, Konecky claimed, and he described it as a "deep-sea unity between the monopoly owners." AM had long been taken over by big business, Konecky stated, and now FM and television were becoming so as well. "The most significant aspect of the history of radio is the story of the persistent efforts of monopoly to gain control of broadcasting," Konecky argued, and he implored his readers to not allow the "stupid, blind, greedy and insane tactics of the press-radio mob to bewilder us." The kind of campaign that the PRF took part in to reform the American media was part of a broader struggle for democracy in the United States, as Konecky saw it. The campaign to improve the media was inseparable from the "struggle of the trade unions against the Taft-Hartley law, from the fight for civil rights and abolition of the un-American Committee, from the battle to restore the FDR policies, and from the necessity to build a powerful democratic and anti-monopoly coalition of labor, the exploited farmers, the oppressed national groups, the Negro people and the progressive sections of professional and small business." This broader campaign against injustice in all its forms was what drove the PRF to try to set up their station, Konecky concluded. That the government refused to support it and others like it, despite the outpourings of support from thousands of ordinary Americans who organized and fought to improve their local media, was to him both conspiracy and tragedy.[82]

Others involved in pursuing broadcast reform during the time Konecky was writing his book found a similar dissatisfaction with the direction of FCC policy. Cases like the *New York Daily News* matter proved to be the exceptions as the FCC granted almost five hundred AM and FM licenses to newspapers in the five years after World War II. And in the case of the PSRC, the FCC declined to act on the recommendations of its own Blue Book that it do much more to consider the commitment of station licensees to provide quality local programming. In general, the post-World War II FCC took on an increasingly conservative and pro-corporate character that drifted far from and even rejected its New Deal activist stance under James Lawrence Fly. This decreasing activism by the FCC boded ill for those concerned about media consolidation, and for those who desired to keep local media markets as diverse as possible by preventing newspapers from owning radio stations. It also would bode ill for those concerned about the development of the new media of the post-World War II period: television.[83]

The Persistence of Print: Newspapers and Broadcasting in the Age of Television

In the late 1940s, the *Chicago Tribune*, a pioneer in radio broadcasting since the 1920s, went on television. During a televised dedication ceremony for WGN-TV's new transmitter in 1949, *Tribune* publisher Robert McCormick announced that a new era was dawning in America because of television. The "age-old human limitations of voice and vision have been utterly outmoded and overcome," McCormick claimed, and now a "man's personal appearance," with all its "clues to his personality" would be made visible to his audience. Speakers could be "pictured intimately . . . upon an electronic screen" and "widely scrutinized," giving audiences more and better information about significant people and events. To make this information not just audible but now visible was to create, McCormick claimed, "something new in the world." McCormick was certain that television, like radio before it, could improve the quality of American life, as "each new extension of the range of human communication permits a wider and a freer exchange of knowledge and ideas."[1]

Robert McCormick was not alone in believing that television was initiating a major cultural shift in America. In the 1940s, many commentators began issuing hyperbolic proclamations about the new medium of television and the changes it would bring about. In 1945, radio playwright Arch Oboler wrote what he called a "requiem for radio" in *Variety* magazine. Television, Oboler proclaimed, "will supplant 'blind' broadcasting even as sound pictures did way with the silent movies. To deny this is to whistle in the dark of wish-thinking." NBC president Merlin Aylesworth predicted a similar death for radio in *Look* magazine in 1949, stating that "within three years the broadcast of sound, or ear radio, over giant networks will be wiped out. Powerful network television will take its place, completely overshadowing the few weather reports and recorded programs left to the remaining single, independent ear radio stations." For observers like Mc-Cormick, Oboler, and Aylesworth, television promised to connect audiences to people and events more directly and intimately than ever before, and the zeal with which Americans took to television seemed to confirm the optimism behind many of these assessments. Between 1946 and 1950, annual sales of television sets in the United States went from just 6,000 to 7.4 million, an average of over 20,000 per day. Over 52 million sets were sold in the decade after 1946, and by the end of the 1950s 90 percent of American homes contained a television. In 1951, *New York Times* television critic Jack Gould remarked that television had "become the colossus of the world of entertainment, information, and education." Just as many predicted that radio would supplant print in the 1920s, television seemed poised to supplant radio in the 1940s and 1950s.[2]

Despite the evidence of television's quick and widespread success, however, not all observers were willing to immediately and confidently report the death of radio. In 1951, William S. Hedges, the pioneering figure behind the *Chicago Daily News* station WMAQ, remarked that radio still "can do a job that nothing else can do, not even television." Radio, Hedges felt, "will always have a place in many bathrooms, kitchens, dining-rooms where television may never penetrate." American homes also had multiple sets, as children had receivers in their rooms, "mama has one in the kitchen," and there was "probably one in the bedroom or the bathroom." This, while the lone television set was "down in the living-room." When the TV was turned off, Hedges stated, the radio sets kept "right on working." For Hedges, it was not just that Americans still had radio sets that they were going to use, but also that the medium still had unique and appealing characteristics that would keep it vibrant. Radio was "beyond all question the best scenic designer that has ever been created. The listener creates the scene as he believes it to be. There are no flaws in it at all; there are no imperfections. He creates in his mind the way in which he thinks it really is." Former FCC chairman James Lawrence Fly was similarly confident that radio would remain vital and wrote to *Look* in response to Merlin Aylesworth's article that, even though

"TV is here to stay," he urged Americans to "not throw away" their radios. In fact, he wrote, "If you do not have a good one, buy it now. You will use it for a long time to come."[3]

The rise of rock 'n' roll and the Top-40 format in the 1950s demonstrated the continuing adaptability and popularity of radio in the televisual age. Technological advances enabled radios to be made cheaper, smaller, and more portable. American homes and cars nearly all had radios, and millions of Americans began taking portable radios to beaches, ballparks, and all manner of public spaces. In fact, during the 1950s over 137 million radio sets were sold, more than double the 66 million television sets sold. Television, rather than creating an entirely new visual culture that broke with all that came before it, became one element—though certainly an important element—of a larger ecological system of media already in place.[4]

The partnership between newspapers and radio that characterized much of media history before television continued into the 1940s and 1950s. As was the case in 1920, the *Detroit News* and radio station WWJ exemplified the cooperation between newspapers and broadcasting. In 1946, the paper launched a "million dollar expansion program" to begin television broadcasting. *News* publisher William J. Scripps remarked that the program "follows a long-established policy" that the paper had of trying "constantly to render a public service through WWJ." The new *Detroit News* television station, Scripps claimed, would be operated according to the "same public service" standards that the paper and radio station had always aspired to. Similar partnerships sprang up across the country, as other radio pioneers such as the *Fort Worth Star-Telegram* and *St. Louis Post-Dispatch* set up television stations soon after World War II. As had been the case with radio, publishers took care to maintain what they saw as higher standards in accepting advertisements and acting in the public interest. Joseph Pulitzer, Jr., remarked that the "television screen will be consciously or unconsciously associated with the *Post-Dispatch*, calling for the same excellence and distinction we strive for in the paper. If television is to render a public service, commercialism must be subordinated to principles of good journalism."[5]

Moves by newspapers into television took place across the country and, by 1950, newspapers owned 40 of the 97 (40 percent) television stations on the air. In 1953, they owned 88 of the 138 (64 percent) stations in operation (see Appendix). Newspapers' prominent roles in directing the new medium were widely noted, as *Business Week* remarked that the "newspaper business, for all its reputation, isn't so stodgy as you may think." Reminding readers that when publishers were "confronted with the menace of radio back in the twenties" they "decided that if they couldn't lick 'em, at least they could join 'em. And they did—by buying or founding station after station." Publishers then "did the same thing when FM came along," and were now "doing it for the third time with television." And, in each instance the results were often commercially successful. As media executive Frank Arnold noted in 1951, broadcasting had "supplemented" many newspapers "to the degree that today our best newspapers are enjoying a larger and more widespread circulation and greater demand for news than the period prior to the advent of broadcasting."[6]

For American audiences, newspapers' appeal also endured after World War II even as they purchased millions of television and radio sets. In mid-1945, after the delivery staffs of eight of New York City's newspapers went on strike, sociologist Bernard Berelson conducted numerous interviews with local residents about what it meant to them to miss the paper on a daily basis. For many, it was not just the loss of information about daily events that bothered them, but also the fact that their daily ritual of reading had been taken away. One remarked that "I feel awfully lost. I like the feeling of being in touch with the world at large." Others were troubled and even despondent, confessing that "I sat around in the subway, staring, feeling out of place," and that, "I am suffering! Seriously! I could not sleep, I missed it so." In 1952, sociologists C. Wright Mills and Harvey Zorbaugh found that newspapers retained a wide readership and tremendous appeal alongside radio listening and television viewing. As Mills noted, "there is no Sunday morning without the funnies" for most people, and he reported that many people read the Sunday paper at their own pace, often keeping it around the house and perusing it into Monday. After more than thirty years of living with electronic media, and while incorporating a new visual medium into their daily lives, Americans remained regular and even voracious newspaper readers.[7]

In the early years of American television, newspapers not only remained an important part of daily life but also significant institutional actors in the process of broadcast policymaking. Concerns about newspaper ownership of broadcasting stations were pervasive in the post-World War II period for both radio and television. Almost immediately after the war ended, the CIO began lobbying Congress to enact legislation limiting to 25 percent the number of FM licenses that could be granted to either newspapers or current AM licensees. In 1947, CIO vice president Richard Leonard testified before Congress that there were "100 cities or towns in the country where the only newspaper owns the only radio station," and he claimed that it was "intolerable in a democratic system that one person or corporation shall have the sole and unchallenged control over the two principal media of communication in any given community." Reform groups continued to pressure the federal government to protect media diversity at both the national and local levels.[8]

The record of postwar reform movements was mixed in terms of its effect on the radio industry, but the record in television was largely one of failure for critics of commercial broadcasting. Much to the chagrin of the American Jewish Congress and Peoples Radio Foundation, newspaper-television cross-ownership came to New York City when the *New York Daily News* was granted a television license in 1947. The hearing, which overlapped with the controversial FM proceeding, involved five applicants for four available television licenses, including several of the same parties. Though the AJC and PRF won the fight against the *Daily News* in FM, they lost the battle in television. This was indicative of trends at the national level and, on the whole, FCC policy for television was much more favorable than not to large media corporations.[9]

This line of policymaking became the cause for much lament in the 1960s. Fred Friendly, Edward R. Murrow's producer on *See It Now* in the 1950s and a key figure in the development of American public broadcasting in the 1960s, blasted the pro-corporate direction of the FCC, which he in 1967 called a "tower of jello on the Potomac." Friendly believed that James Fly had come "closer to winning than anybody" in making the FCC into an agency that could make "radio and eventually television the instrument of national purpose that it is, and not just a tool to move goods with." But, Friendly claimed, "the broadcast industry has been captured by mercantile society, lock, stock and electronic barrel." Others bemoaned the lack of a law prohibiting newspaper ownership of radio in broadcasting's early years. Clarence Dill, one of the chief architects of American radio law, remarked in 1964 that he wished that he had had the foresight to get a prohibition on newspaper ownership written into the Communications Act of 1934, but stated that it was just something that few could tell at the time would develop into the kind of problem that it had become. "I can see a number of things that we could have done that would have been a good thing for the country, but we couldn't foresee them, because we had no way of knowing about the developments. One of them was this matter of a newspaper and a radio station being owned by the same owner." If he had been able to recognize then how much trouble newspaper-radio ownership would cause later, Dill remarked, he would have pushed to ban it during the period when the structures of American broadcast regulation were being established. It was "a matter of competition," Dill remarked, and "that's the American way of doing things." Had he been able to prevent newspaper ownership of radio starting in the 1930s, Dill believed, "it would have been a good thing."[10]

Soon after Dill and Friendly's laments, the Federal Communications Commission, in a burst of reformist activity in the late 1960s and early 1970s, issued a series of decisions aimed at promoting diversity in local media ownership. After a lengthy proceeding in Jackson, Mississippi, the FCC revoked the license of WLBT-TV, the local NBC affiliate, on the grounds that the station had provided generally poor service to and shown consistent bias against African Americans. In Chicago, the FCC supported local campaigns to prevent two classical music radio stations from being sold to owners that many citizens claimed would provide poor service to the city's listeners. In January 1969, the FCC declined the renewal application of WHDH, a Boston television station owned by the *Boston Herald-Traveler*, despite finding that the station had provided acceptable programming. The decision was the exact opposite of the one that the FCC had reached in the Baltimore proceeding between Public Service Radio Corporation and William Randolph Hearst's corporation in 1951, as this time the commission declined the renewal of the newspaper applicant in an attempt to diversify local media ownership. The *Herald-Traveler* appealed the decision all the way to the Supreme Court, stating that losing the television station would be a catastrophic loss of revenue for the newspaper, which would probably go bankrupt without it. The paper's court challenges were unsuccessful, and in early 1972 the paper stopped broadcasting on WHDH. Several months later, as it had argued that it would have to without revenue from television, the *Herald-Traveler* stopped publishing altogether.[11]

Other FCC actions around the time of the *Herald-Traveler* case prompted further anxiety among newspaper publishers. In August 1968, the Department of Justice sent the FCC a memo urging the Commission to consider bans on corporations owning more than one AM, FM, or television station in the same market and on newspaper-broadcast cross-ownership. The Justice Department stated that the "clear effect of combined ownership of similar broadcast media in the same local market is to reduce the diversity of news and information sources available," and it urged the FCC to rectify the situation either through general rulemaking or through the denial of future license applications and renewals from publishers or broadcasters already operating stations in particular markets. The memorandum's "implication was clear," one journalist noted. Either the FCC "would do something about this concentration," or the Justice Department would intervene and try to take care of matters itself through court proceedings.[12]

The FCC soon took action, also motivated strongly by commissioner Nicholas Johnson, who had joined the Commission in 1966. In 1968, Johnson wrote in *The Atlantic* that he was "philosophically wedded to the fundamental importance of 'the marketplace of ideas' in a free society," and that he was determined to revitalize the FCC's commitment to this ideal. The FCC, Johnson claimed, was "directly empowered to keep media ownership patterns compatible with a democracy's need for diversified sources of opinion and information." Johnson wrote the mass-market paperback *How to Talk Back to Your Television Set* in 1970, in which he encouraged ordinary Americans to become involved in FCC proceedings in order to improve their local media. In 1971, Johnson's celebrity as an FCC Commissioner and crusader for media reform made him the subject of a lengthy *Rolling Stone* cover story complete with Annie Leibovitz photographs.[13]

Following Nicholas Johnson, the FCC in 1970 considered banning newspaper-broadcast cross-ownership as part of a broader set of new rules designed to limit broadcast ownership concentration. The plan saw little activity until 1974, when the Commission took up the issue with renewed vigor. Some of the motivation against cross-ownership came from citizens groups and reformist commissioners, but there was also some prodding from the Nixon White House. In particular, the *Washington Post* charged that Richard Nixon had targeted the paper for reprisal after the Watergate story broke by encouraging the FCC to deny license renewals for two television stations in Florida that the company owned. In May 1974, the House Judiciary Committee's impeachment investigation uncovered White House transcripts from September 1972 in which Nixon claimed that the *Post* was "going to have damnable, damnable problems" with its Florida license renewals. The process was "going to be goddamn active," Nixon fumed. The "game has to be played awfully rough." Nicholas Johnson remarked that, while Nixon never explicitly told him to target the *Post*, "I know of no one at the FCC or in the broadcasting industry at the time who did not assume that the President and his men had either ordered, known about—or at least greeted with glee—the Florida challenges at the FCC." The motivations behind campaigns for broadcast ownership reforms in the 1970s were in many ways quite similar to those in the 1940s, except that in the early 1970s it was a Republican (Nixon) pushing for the policy change, while in the early 1940s it was a Democrat (Roosevelt). Media ownership remained a significant issue in the political process across eras, and a particular concern to members of both parties in all branches of government.[14]

With these various motivations, the FCC forged ahead with its general consideration of its media ownership rules throughout 1974. Criticism of the proceeding from broadcasters and publishers was heated, and the FCC heard testimony and considered comments and studies from almost two hundred parties. In 1975, the Commission issued its new set of rules barring future newspaper-broadcast cross-ownership and ordering divestiture of broadcast holdings "in instances where the degree of media concentration ... could be labeled as egregious," a standard that applied to seven television stations and nine radio stations around the country. The controversial rules were upheld by the District of Columbia Court of Appeals, which found them to be a "rational attempt to promote the highly valued goal of diversity." Over further protests from the National Association of Broadcasters and the American Newspaper Publishers Association, the Supreme Court upheld the rules in 1978.[15]

This regulatory activism in the 1960s and 1970s ultimately proved temporary, and since this high water mark of federal limitations on media ownership there has been a steady erosion of this kind of reformist broadcast regulation in the United States, a trend culminating with the Telecommunications Act of 1996, in which the FCC removed many of its remaining numerical limits on broadcast ownership. This led almost immediately to a frenzy of merger activity that has created historically high levels of concentrated ownership in radio and television. The newspaper-broadcast cross-ownership ban has remained, however, much to the chagrin of many publishers and broadcasters. In 2001, a Republican-dominated FCC under chairman Michael Powell (son of then Secretary of State Colin Powell) began attempts to loosen many of the few remaining ownership caps, including the cross-ownership rule. Powell had hoped to push the rules through quietly, but was quickly surprised by strong bipartisan opposition in Congress and massive public outcry from both liberal and conservative citizens and groups united against large media corporations and seeking diverse media ownership in their communities. On 2 June 2003, the FCC passed the new regulations in a 3–2 party-line vote, with Republicans in the majority. Public opposition to the plan continued afterward while other activists pursued a court challenge, and in June 2004, a federal appeals court ordered the FCC to halt its deregulatory plan.[16]

In the years since Michael Powell's unsuccessful deregulatory effort, a number of commentators have suggested that the FCC needs to go forward with removing the ban on newspaper-broadcast cross ownership. If newspaper publishers claimed in the 1920s to be among the few parties who could afford the operating expenses required to operate quality radio stations, a claim might be made today that radio and television station owners might be among the few parties who can afford the expenses required to operate quality newspapers. Given the precarious situation of the newspaper business in contemporary America, there may be valid reasons for removing the ban on newspaper-broadcast ownership, despite some of the monopoly issues involved. This is a debate worth having in our time, but only if serious consideration is also given to local interests and proponents of diverse media ownership. As legal scholar C. Edwin Baker argues, media policy should be both "inclusionary" and "participatory." All Americans, Baker argues, "should be able to experience some significant media as in some sense 'theirs' and not experience their media interests as marginalized," and there should be "more and more fairly distributed opportunities to participate in the public sphere." Ordinary Americans, in the metaphorical marketplace of ideas, should have access to that marketplace not simply as consumers.[17]

As the public opposition to Michael Powell's policy goals demonstrated, many Americans want ownership diversity in their media and remain uncomfortable with policy decided on the bases of benefits to corporations and alleged economic efficiency. These debates remain open, and one might hope that the FCC will continue to consider noneconomic perspectives about media policy in its decision-making process. As was the case with early radio, media ownership remains a tremendously important political issue, one that demands more qualitative debate about the relationship between media and democracy. One might also ask that the FCC commit to giving ordinary citizens more say in media ownership debates, the privilege of which it has demonstrated only an irregular commitment. However the current debates proceed, they should not cause us to overlook how important the issue of newspaper ownership of radio was in an era before television, a time when Americans were confronting what many felt to be an amazing and occasionally frightening new technology in radio broadcasting.[18]

Media consolidation had, by the time television arrived on the scene, already become a major problem for the federal government and many ordinary Americans. The number of radio and television stations has always been limited by the breadth of the electromagnetic spectrum, and there were no new newspapers on the way, attorney Morris Ernst claimed in 1944. "We are finished, finished forever in the United States with the inauguration of a newspaper in a metropolitan center," Ernst stated. "Inheritance taxes being what they are, we have seen the last of the Marshall Fields." Ernst was largely correct, as the number of existing American newspapers dropped steadily from the early days of radio to the early days of television. Though circulation doubled from 1920 to 1953, the number of daily newspapers in the United States declined from 2,042 to 1,785. More importantly, the number of cities with competing daily newspapers shrank from 552 to only 87. The decades since have seen further declines in these areas, and by 1996 only 19 cities in the United States (1.3 percent of the total) had more than one daily newspaper. In more recent years, proclamations of the "death of newspapers" have become increasingly common and some major metropolitan areas may soon lack even a single local printed daily.[19]

Some observers see little reason to bemoan these trends and are instead optimistic about what they see as the liberating potential of the Internet. For its proponents, the Internet removes many of the most serious problems in "old media" like newspapers, radio, and television, and the problem of scarcity on the radio and television dials becomes a thing of the past as digital technology enables the number of channels to increase to seemingly limitless ends. The Internet also removes the barriers to entry to broadcasting, the argument goes, as aspiring broadcasters no longer need a governmentally granted license to reach the public but can disseminate audio and video digitally over wired and wireless networks. If A. J. Liebling's conception of press freedom was limited to the owners of printing presses, aspiring publishers now need only a personal computer and an Internet connection to realize this.[20] The Internet has created a situation where, as the title of one recent work on the subject puts it, *We're All Journalists Now*, should we care to be. To legal scholar Yochai Benkler, one of the most thoughtful advocates of the Internet's liberating potential, the Internet is a "radical reversal" of the structural development of the mass media. "For more than 150 years," Benkler argues, "new communications technologies have tended to concentrate and commercialize the production and exchange of information, while extending the geographic and social reach of information distribution networks." The Internet, on the other hand, is "the first modern communications medium that expands its reach by decentralizing the capital structure of production and distribution of information, culture, and knowledge."[21]

Though there are reasons to share Benkler's optimistic attitude about the Internet, there remain many reasons to be skeptical as well. The increased amount of information immediately available in the Internet age has not necessarily increased the amount of reliable information available. The Internet also has not ended the problem of concentrated media ownership, and in many areas the market for Internet service is controlled by a small number of firms. Large corporations such as Google, Apple, and Microsoft have become extremely powerful and profitable as a result of the Internet.[22] Barriers to accessing the Internet remain, as minorities and poor Americans often find it difficult to afford a computer and regular Internet service. This "digital divide," as scholars call it, remains a significant problem if the alleged promise of the Internet is to be realized.[23] And finally, though the Internet has allowed any aspiring "journalist" to have a public voice, it remains unclear whether there will emerge a sustainable model to fund in-depth reporting of public affairs, or whether this "journalism" contributes to a more informed and open-minded or simply a more polarized electorate.[24]

In the first half of the twentieth century, the invention and adoption of electronic broadcasting expanded and changed the quantity and variety of information that was a part of daily life in the United States. First as sound and later with pictures, broadcasting made the business of information and ideas more profitable for the corporations fortunate enough to get licenses. Throughout this history, newspapers have been central to the process of shaping the development of radio and television as industries and objects of state regulation. That they were as influential as they were is perhaps not surprising, given that newspapers were the country's dominant mass medium in the decades when broadcasting first developed. The spectacular growth of some of these multimedia corporations that combined newspapers and broadcasting (and later other media as well) is also perhaps not unexpected, given the broader trends toward corporate consolidation in a variety of American industries over the last century. That these trends will continue to define the structure of the American media and the corporations that provide us with our daily knowledge of the world around us, in all its seriousness and frivolity, remains to be seen. It is not unexpected that they will, but it is also not automatic. Given a more reformist FCC and an engaged citizenry—two developments that have existed at times in the past and shown clear signs of blossoming in the twenty-first century—Americans may well see that their media comes to better reflect the diversity of their country.

Newspaper Ownership of American
Broadcasting Stations, 1923–1953

The table shows stations that were actually broadcasting, not all those authorized but not yet on the air.

	AM Radio			FM Radio			Television		
	Total	Newspaper	Percent	Total	Newspaper	Percent	Total	Newspaper	Percent
1923	573	60	10.5						
1924	535	38	7.1						
1925	571	33	5.8						
1926	528	38	7.2						
1927	694	38	5.5						
1928	691	41	5.9						
1929	614	34	5.5						
1930	612	36	5.9						
1931	612	68	11.1						
1932	608	78	12.8						
1933	610	80	13.1						
1934	591	90	15.2						
1935	583	106	18.2						
1936	627	144	23.0						
1937	652	184	28.2						
1938	692	201	29.0						
1939	729	226	31.0						
1940	770	252	32.7						
1941	835	283	33.9	29	5	17.2			
1942	788	284	36.0	65	6	9.2			
1943	909	280	30.8	51	10	19.6			
1944	906	277	30.6	55	10	18.2			
1945	913	268	29.4	58	14	24.1	6	0	0.0
1946	956	271	28.3	55	13	23.6	6	0	0.0
1947	1119	316	28.2	172	38	22.1	7	1	14.3
1948	1640	451	27.5	930	262	28.2	20	9	45.0
1949	1925	466	24.2	714	271	38.0	51	13	25.5
1950	2088	491	23.5	768	272	35.4	97	40	41.2
1951	2235	488	21.8	746	233	31.2	107	45	42.1
1952	2319	482	20.8	644	194	30.1	108	49	45.4
1953	2387	469	19.6	713	195	27.3	138	88	63.8

Sources: For 1923–1930, Malcolm Willey and Stuart Rice, *Communication Agencies and Social Life* (New York: McGraw-Hill, 1933), 196. For 1931–1934, Federal Communications Commission, "Summary of Record in re: Orders 79 and 79-A," 21 January 1944, 5, Box 1939, Docket 6051, FCCDCF, NACP; and *Broadcasting Yearbook, 1940* (1 February 1940): 11. For 1935–1953, *Broadcasting Yearbook, 1935–1953*. Data for 1923–1934 for June; data for 1935–1953 for January.

Archival Abbreviations and Acronyms

Columbia University Oral History Research Office Collection, New York
(CUOHROC)
    Radio Pioneers Project (RPP)
    James Lawrence Fly Project (JLFP)

Rare Book and Manuscript Library, Columbia University, New York
(Columbia)
    Edwin H. Armstrong Papers (Armstrong Papers)
    James Lawrence Fly Papers (Fly Papers)
    Elliott Sanger Papers (Sanger Papers)

William Randolph Hearst Papers, BANC MSS 77/121c, The Bancroft
Library, University of California, Berkeley (Hearst Papers)

Herbert Hoover Papers, Herbert Hoover Presidential Library, West Branch,
Iowa (Hoover Papers)

National Archives, College Park, Md. (NACP)
    Records of the Federal Communications Commission, Docketed
    Case Files, Record Group 173 (FCCDCF)
    Records of the Federal Communications Commission, Office of
    the Executive Director, General Correspondence 1927–46, Record
    Group 173 (FCCOED-GC)

Records of the Federal Communications Commission, Radio Intelligence Division, Commissioners, Correspondence and Reports, 1940–46, Record Group 173 (FCC-RID)

National Archives, Washington, D.C. (NADC)
Records of the United States Court of Appeals, District of Columbia Circuit, General Docket, Official Trial Transcripts and Related Records, 1893–1956, Record Group 276 (USCA)
Records of the United States Supreme Court, Appellate Case Files, Record Group 267 (USSC)

Library of Congress, Washington, D.C. (LOC)
Joseph Pulitzer Papers, Manuscript Division (Pulitzer Papers)
Raymond Clapper Papers, Manuscript Division (Clapper Papers)
National Broadcasting Company Papers, Motion Picture, Broadcasting, and Recorded Sound Division (NBC-MPBRSD)

American Civil Liberties Union Records, The Roger Baldwin Years, Public Policy Papers, Seeley G. Mudd Manuscript Library, Department of Rare Books and Special Collections, Princeton University Library, Princeton, N.J. (ACLU Records)

Tribune Archives, Colonel Robert R. McCormick Research Center, First Division Museum at Cantigny, Wheaton, Ill. (Tribune Archives)

State Historical Society of Wisconsin, Madison (SHSW)
Donald Wells Anderson Papers (Anderson Papers)
William S. Hedges Papers (Hedges Papers)
Charles A., Elizabeth, and Charles E. Kading Papers (Kading Papers)
Mass Communications Ephemera Collection (MCEC)
Mass Communications Small Collections (MCSC)
National Association of Broadcasters Records (NAB)
National Broadcasting Company Records (NBC)

Library of American Broadcasting, Hornbake Library, University of Maryland, College Park (LAB)
Dick Dorrance Papers (Dorrance Papers)

Notes

Introduction. Underwriting the Ether:
Newspapers and the Origins of American Broadcasting

1. Reminiscences of William E. Scripps, May 1951, 6–7, RPP, CUOHROC.

2. Reminiscences of Thomas E. Clark, 24 May 1951, 4–5, 27–28, RPP, CUOHROC; Reminiscences of William E. Scripps, May 1951, 18, 20, RPP, CUOHROC; Arthur Pound, *The Only Thing Worth Finding: The Life and Legacies of George Gough Booth* (Detroit: Wayne State University Press, 1964), 227–29.

3. Reminiscences of William E. Scripps, May 1951, 22–24, RPP, CUOHROC.

4. Reminiscences of Thomas E. Clark, 24 May 1951, 29–32, RPP, CUOHROC; Reminiscences of William E. Scripps, May 1951, 23–25, RPP, CUOHROC; R. J. McLauchlin, "What the Detroit 'News' Has Done in Broadcasting," *Radio Broadcast* 1 (June 1922): 136–37; *Detroit News*, 1 September 1920, quoted in Erik Barnouw, *A Tower in Babel: A History of Broadcasting in the United States*, vol. 1, *To 1933* (New York: Oxford University Press, 1966), 63; Mitchell Charnley, *News by Radio* (New York: Macmillan, 1948), 1–4.

5. Alan Trachtenberg, *The Incorporation of America: Culture and Society in the Gilded Age* (New York: Hill and Wang, 1982), 3–4; Douglas Craig, *Fireside Politics: Radio and Political Culture in the United States, 1920–1940* (Baltimore: Johns Hopkins University Press, 2000); Robert Horwitz, *The Irony of Regulatory Reform: The Deregulation of American Telecommunications* (New York: Oxford University Press, 1989).

6. Between 1920 and 1955, the American population rose from 106.5 million to 165.3 million, a 55 percent increase, while daily newspaper circulation rose from 27.8 million to 56.1 million, a 102 percent increase. See U.S. Bureau of the Census, *Historical Statistics of the United States, Colonial Times to 1970, Bicentennial Edition*, 2 vols. (Washington, D.C.: Government Printing Office, 1975), 9, 809; and Carl Kaestle and Janice Radway, "A Framework for the History of Publishing and Reading in the United States,

1880–1940," in Carl Kaestle and Janice Radway, eds., *A History of the Book in America*, vol. 4, *Print in Motion: The Expansion of Publishing and Reading in the United States, 1880–1940* (Chapel Hill: University of North Carolina Press, 2009), 7–21.

7. Paul Lazarsfeld, "Some Notes on the Relationship Between Radio and the Press," *Journalism Quarterly* 18 (March 1941): 10, emphasis in original; Paul Lazarsfeld, *Radio and the Printed Page: An Introduction to the Study of Radio and Its Role in the Communication of Ideas* (New York: Duell, Sloan and Pearce, 1940), 4. On the complementarities of reading and listening, see also Walter Ong, *Orality and Literacy* (New York: Routledge, 2002 [1982]), 133–35.

8. For eloquent analyses of radio from this perspective, see Douglas Kahn and Gregory Whitehead, eds., *Wireless Imagination: Sound, Radio, and the Avant-Garde* (Cambridge, Mass.: MIT Press, 1992); Edward Miller, *Emergency Broadcasting and 1930s American Radio* (Philadelphia: Temple University Press, 2003); and John Durham Peters, *Speaking into the Air: A History of the Idea of Communication* (Chicago: University of Chicago Press, 1999), chaps. 4–5. For perspectives on the development of radio broadcasting in the context of the evolution of recorded sound and the act of listening in American life, see Jonathan Sterne, *The Audible Past: Cultural Origins of Sound Reproduction* (Durham, N.C.: Duke University Press, 2003); David Suisman, *Selling Sounds: The Commercial Revolution in American Music* (Cambridge, Mass.: Harvard University Press, 2009); David Suisman and Susan Strasser, eds., *Sound in the Age of Mechanical Reproduction* (Philadelphia: University of Pennsylvania Press, 2010); Emily Thompson, *The Soundscape of Modernity: Architectural Acoustics and the Culture of Listening in America, 1900–1933* (Cambridge, Mass.: MIT Press, 2002); and Steve J. Wurtzler, *Electric Sounds: Technological Change and the Rise of the Corporate Mass Media* (New York: Columbia University Press, 2007).

9. Clifford Doerksen, *American Babel: Rogue Radio Broadcasters of the Jazz Age* (Philadelphia: University of Pennsylvania Press, 2005); Susan Smulyan, *Selling Radio: The Commercialization of American Broadcasting, 1920–1934* (Washington, D.C.: Smithsonian Institution Press, 1994).

10. Robert McChesney, *Telecommunications, Mass Media, and Democracy: The Battle for Control of U.S. Broadcasting, 1928–1935* (New York: Oxford University Press, 1993), 14–16, 72–80; Hugh Slotten, "Radio's Hidden Voice: Noncommercial Broadcasting, Extension Education, and State Universities During the 1920s," *Technology and Culture* 49 (January 2008): 1–20.

11. Noah Arceneaux, "The Wireless in the Window: Department Stores and Radio Retailing in the 1920s," *Journalism and Mass Communication Quarterly* 83 (Autumn 2006): 581–95; Noah Arceneaux, "A Sales Floor in the Sky: Philadelphia Department Stores and the Radio Boom of the 1920s," *Journal of Broadcasting and Electronic Media* 53 (March 2009): 76–89.

12. James Young, "Is the Radio Newspaper Next?" *Radio Broadcast* 7 (September 1925): 575; Paul Starr, *The Creation of the Media: Political Origins of Modern Communications* (New York: Basic Books, 2004).

13. The small group of significant analyses of newspaper ownership of radio includes Mickie Edwardson, "Convergence, Issues, and Attitudes in the Fight over Newspaper-Broadcast Cross-Ownership," *Journalism History* 33 (Summer 2007): 79–92; Gwenyth Jackaway, *Media at War: Radio's Challenge to the Newspapers, 1924-1939* (Westport, Conn.: Praeger, 1995); Harvey Levin, *Broadcast Regulation and Joint Ownership of Media* (New York: New York University Press, 1960); Robert McChesney, "Press-Radio Relations and the Emergence of Network, Commercial Broadcasting in the United States, 1930–1935," *Historical Journal of Film, Radio and Television* 11 (March 1991): 41–57; and Christopher Sterling, "Newspaper Ownership of Broadcast Stations, 1920–68," *Journalism Quarterly* 46 (Summer 1969): 227–36, 254. Less comprehensive analyses of the subject include Warren Agee, "A Study of Cross-Channel Ownership of Communications Media" (M.A. thesis, University of Minnesota, 1949); Warren Agee, "Cross-Channel Ownership of Communication Media," *Journalism Quarterly* 26 (December 1949): 410–16; John Harold Dunn, "Government Efforts to Separate Press and Radio Ownership, 1937–1944" (M.A. thesis, University of Wisconsin, 1948); George Gerling, "Trends in the Early Relationships Between Newspapers and Radio Broadcasting" (M.A. thesis, University of Wisconsin, 1946); Howard Gilbert, "Newspaper-Radio Joint Ownership: Unblest Be the Tie That Binds," *Yale Law Journal* 59 (June 1950): 1342–50; John August Grams, "An Analysis of Federal Communications Commission Actions in the Licensing of Newspaper-Affiliated Broadcasting Stations to 1970" (Ph.D. dissertation, University of Wisconsin, 1973); Clifford Jene Leabo, "The 1941 Newspaper-Radio Hearings-FCC Gambit" (M.A. thesis, University of Minnesota, 1972); Harvey Levin, "Cross-Channel Ownership of Mass Media: A Study in Social Valuation" (Ph.D. dissertation, Columbia University, 1953); Harvey Levin, "Competition Among Mass Media and the Public Interest," *Public Opinion Quarterly* 18 (Spring 1954): 62–79; Harvey Levin, "Economies of Cross Channel Affiliation of Media," *Journalism Quarterly* 31 (Spring 1954): 167–74; Rudolph Michael, "History and Criticism of Press-Radio Relationships," *Journalism Quarterly* 15 (March 1938): 178–84, 220; Robert Montgomery, "An Objective Study of Newspaper Interests in Radio Broadcasting" (M.S. thesis, University of Wisconsin, 1949); Daniel Toohey, "Newspaper Ownership of Broadcast Facilities," *Federal Communications Bar Journal* 20 (1966): 44–57; Paul Wagner, "The Evolution of Newspaper Interest in Radio," *Journalism Quarterly* 23 (June 1946): 182–88; and Maryland Wilson, "Broadcasting by the Newspaper-Owned Stations in Detroit, 1920–1927" (Ph.D. dissertation, University of Michigan, 1952). On the more recent history of newspaper-broadcast cross-ownership, see Eric Klinenberg, *Fighting for Air: The Battle to Control America's Media* (New York: Metropolitan Books, 2007), chap. 9; and Robert McChesney, *The Problem of the Media: U.S. Communication Politics in the Twenty-First Century* (New York: Monthly Review Press, 2004), chap. 7.

14. In this sense, it is important to understand the term "new media" as a historical concept rather than as a synonym for the Internet or digital media, as it is used in much contemporary discourse. Media historians Lisa Gitelman and Geoffrey Pingree argue that, for many scholars, "to study 'new media' is to study *today's* new media," when in

reality "All media were once 'new media.'" Lisa Gitelman and Geoffrey Pingree, "Introduction: What's New About New Media?" in Lisa Gitelman and Geoffrey Pingree, eds., *New Media, 1740–1915* (Cambridge, Mass.: MIT Press, 2003), xi, emphasis in original. See also Lisa Gitelman, *Always Already New: Media, History, and the Data of Culture* (Cambridge, Mass.: MIT Press, 2006).

15. Jürgen Habermas, *The Structural Transformation of the Public Sphere: An Inquiry into a Category of Bourgeois Society*, trans. Thomas Burger (Cambridge, Mass.: MIT Press, 2000 [1962]), 51, 170–71.

16. Michael Schudson, "Toward a Troubleshooting Manual for Journalism History," *Journalism and Mass Communication Quarterly* 74 (Autumn 1997): 463–76; David Paul Nord, "A Plea for Journalism History," *Journalism History* 15 (Spring 1988): 8–15.

17. Michael Schudson, "News, Public, Nation," *American Historical Review* 107 (April 2002): 481–95; Jeffrey Pasley, *The Tyranny of Printers: Newspaper Politics in the Early Republic* (Charlottesville: University of Virginia Press, 2001), 2.

18. Notable exceptions include James Baughman, *The Republic of Mass Culture: Journalism, Filmmaking, and Broadcasting in America Since 1941* (Baltimore: Johns Hopkins University Press, 2006 [1992]); and Michele Hilmes, *Hollywood and Broadcasting: From Radio to Cable* (Urbana: University of Illinois Press, 1990).

19. George Stone, "Radio Has Gripped Chicago," *Radio Broadcast* 1 (October 1922): 503; M. H. Aylesworth, "The Modern Stentor," 1928, 20, 3, Commerce Period Papers, Box 490, Folder Radio Correspondence, Press Releases, Misc. 1928–1964 & Undated, Hoover Papers; Hadley Cantril and Gordon Allport, *The Psychology of Radio* (New York: Harper & Brothers, 1935), vii, 4.

20. Some excellent recent works examining aspects of early radio history that fit this description include William Barlow, *Voice Over: The Making of Black Radio* (Philadelphia: Temple University Press, 1999); Susan Douglas, *Listening In: Radio and the American Imagination* (Minneapolis: University of Minnesota Press, 2004 [1999]); Michele Hilmes, *Radio Voices: American Broadcasting, 1922–1952* (Minneapolis: University of Minnesota Press, 1997); Jason Loviglio, *Radio's Intimate Public: Network Broadcasting and Mass-Mediated Democracy* (Minneapolis: University of Minnesota Press, 2005); Kathy Newman, *Radio Active: Advertising and Consumer Activism, 1935–1947* (Berkeley: University of California Press, 2004); Alexander Russo, *Points on the Dial: Golden Age Radio Beyond the Networks* (Durham, N.C.: Duke University Press, 2010); and Barbara Savage, *Broadcasting Freedom: Radio, War, and the Politics of Race, 1938–1948* (Chapel Hill: University of North Carolina Press, 1999).

21. David Thorburn and Henry Jenkins, "Introduction: Toward an Aesthetics of Transition," in David Thorburn and Henry Jenkins, eds., *Rethinking Media Change: The Aesthetics of Transition* (Cambridge, Mass.: MIT Press, 2003), 2–3. Other scholarly works emphasizing longer term continuity in media history include Alfred D. Chandler, Jr., and James W. Cortada, eds., *A Nation Transformed by Information: How Information Has Shaped the United States from Colonial Times to the Present* (New York: Oxford University Press, 2000); Daniel Czitrom, *Media and the American Mind: From Morse to*

McLuhan (Chapel Hill: University of North Carolina Press, 1982); Susan Douglas, *Inventing American Broadcasting, 1899-1922* (Baltimore: Johns Hopkins University Press, 1987); Richard R. John, *Spreading the News: The American Postal System from Franklin to Morse* (Cambridge, Mass.: Harvard University Press, 1995); Richard R. John, *Network Nation: Inventing American Telecommunications* (Cambridge, Mass.: Belknap Press of Harvard University Press, 2010); Carolyn Marvin, *When Old Technologies Were New: Thinking About Electric Communication in the Late Nineteenth Century* (New York: Oxford University Press, 1988); and Joshua Meyerowitz, *No Sense of Place: The Impact of Electronic Media on Social Behavior* (New York: Oxford University Press, 1985).

22. Warren Susman, *Culture as History: The Transformation of American Society in the Twentieth Century* (New York: Pantheon, 1984), 253-54, emphasis in original.

23. Benedict Anderson, *Imagined Communities: Reflections on the Origin and Spread of Nationalism* (London: Verso, 2006 [1983]), 35, 40. On the idea of "print culture," see Elizabeth Eisenstein, *The Printing Press as an Agent of Change: Communications and Cultural Transformations in Early-Modern Europe* (New York: Cambridge University Press, 1979); Adrian Johns, *The Nature of the Book: Print and Knowledge in the Making* (Chicago: University of Chicago Press, 1998); and Elizabeth Eisenstein and Adrian Johns, "AHR Forum: How Revolutionary Was the Print Revolution?" *American Historical Review* 107 (February 2002): 84-128. On the variety of ways to conceptualize the relationship between producers of media content and their audiences, see Richard Butsch, *The Citizen Audience: Crowds, Publics, and Individuals* (New York: Routledge, 2008).

24. Starr, *The Creation of the Media*, 130-39, 169-70; Michael Schudson, *Discovering the News: A Social History of American Newspapers* (New York: Basic Books, 1978), 31-35; Daniel Walker Howe, *What Hath God Wrought: The Transformation of America, 1815-1848* (New York: Oxford University Press, 2007), 694-98. For a comparative perspective on how book and magazine publishers navigated this process, see Scott Casper, Jeffrey Groves, Stephen Nissenbaum, and Michael Winship, eds., *A History of the Book in America*, vol. 3, *The Industrial Book, 1840-1880* (Chapel Hill: University of North Carolina Press, 2007).

25. Douglas, *Inventing American Broadcasting*, 8-10, 19-23; John, *Network Nation*, 178; R. Ernest Dupuy, "WHB," *Radio News* 5 (October 1924): 498-505.

26. W. E. Ingersol, Testimony Before the FCC, 25 September 1941, 1313-16, 1331-32, 1327, Box 1933, Docket 6051, FCCDCF, NACP.

27. David Nasaw, *The Chief: The Life of William Randolph Hearst* (Boston: Houghton Mifflin, 2000), xiii-xiv, 256-57; Hearst Radio Service Bulletin, 8 October 1930, 1, Carton 36, Folder 4, Hearst Papers.

28. Stephen Petacci, Testimony Before the FCC, 21 September 1936, 37-38, Box 850, Docket 3763, FCCDCF, NACP.

29. Don Elias, Testimony in United States Senate, 80th Cong., 1st sess., *To Amend the Communications Act of 1934, Hearings Before a Subcommittee of the Committee on Interstate and Foreign Commerce on S.1333* (Washington, D.C.: Government Printing Office, 1947), 432.

30. "Freedom of the Hot Air," *Editor & Publisher* 66 (21 April 1934): 18.

31. This line of legal proceedings began before radio. During World War I, the International News Service (INS) began selling news to clients that it had taken from previously published Associated Press (AP) reports. AP sued INS, and in 1918 the Supreme Court ruled that AP retained property rights in news even after it was published and ordered INS to stop the practice. See Margaret Blanchard, *Revolutionary Sparks: Freedom of Expression in Modern America* (New York: Oxford University Press, 1992), 145. In the early 1930s, AP and newspaper publishers also brought successful suits in South Dakota, Washington, and Louisiana charging broadcasters with "news piracy" for doing radio newscasts with items taken directly from newspapers. See Louise Benjamin, *Freedom of the Air and the Public Interest: First Amendment Rights in Broadcasting to 1935* (Carbondale: Southern Illinois University Press, 2001), 174–78.

32. Jackaway, *Media at War*, chap. 2.

33. Frank Arnold, "Cooperation and the Secret of Success," *Editor & Publisher* 70 (5 June 1937): 32.

34. Roy Roberts, Testimony Before the Federal Communications Commission, 18 September 1941, 1001, 1011, 1009, 1031, Box 1933, Docket 6051, FCCDCF, NACP.

35. Sidney Kaye, Testimony in United States Senate, 78th Cong., 1st sess., *To Amend the Communications Act, Hearings Before a Subcommittee of the Committee on Interstate and Foreign Commerce on S.814* (Washington, D.C.: Government Printing Office, 1944), 412.

36. *St. Louis Post-Dispatch* Advertisement, *Broadcasting Yearbook, 1936* (10 February 1936): 4.

37. Joseph Pulitzer to Ralph Coghlan, 29 March 1945, 2, Box 108, Folder Radio and Television Advertising, 1930–1946, Pulitzer Papers, LOC; Joseph Pulitzer to Ralph Coghlan, 24 January 1943, ibid.; Daniel Pfaff, *Joseph Pulitzer II and the Post-Dispatch: A Newspaperman's Life* (University Park: Pennsylvania State University Press, 1991), 333–34; Justin Miller, "A Judge Views Radio," Letter to the Editor, *St. Louis Post-Dispatch*, undated [1945], Box 108, Folder Radio and Television Advertising, 1930–1946, Pulitzer Papers, LOC.

38. Isabelle Keating, "Pirates of the Air," *Harper's* 169 (August 1934): 472; "The Press and the People—A Survey," *Fortune* 20 (August 1939): 65, 70.

39. Ben Bagdikian, *The New Media Monopoly* (Boston: Beacon Press, 2004), 9. The book was a revised edition of a book that Bagdikian originally published in 1983 and has gone through several revisions. The substance of Bagdikian's critique has stayed consistent between the first and most recent printed version. For a critical perspective on Bagdikian's data and conclusions, see Eli Noam, *Media Ownership and Concentration in America* (New York: Oxford University Press, 2009), 18–22.

40. G. S. Boggel to James Fly, 29 July 1941, Box 245, File 45-4, FCCOED-GC, NACP; G. H. Banks to James Fly, 25 July 1941, ibid.; A. J. Liebling, *The Press* (New York: Pantheon, 1983 [1961]), 32–33.

41. Joy Elmer Morgan to James Fly, 22 July 1941, Box 245, File 45-4, FCCOED-GC,

NACP; Bernard Geelan to James Fly, 15 February 1944, Box 246, File 45-4, ibid.; Josh Lee to Franklin Roosevelt, 18 March 1938, Box 245, File 45-4, ibid.; James Wolfe to El-bert Thomas, 27 November 1944, 1, Box 246, File 45-4, ibid.

42. John Durham Peters, "The 'Marketplace of Ideas:' A History of the Concept," in Andrew Calabrese and Colin Sparks, eds., *Toward a Political Economy of Culture: Capitalism and Communication in the Twenty-First Century* (Lanham, Md.: Rowman & Littlefield, 2004), 72, 80. The analysis below of Morris Ernst's use of the "marketplace of ideas" concept is at odds with Peters, who claims that it was not employed by "any lead-ing theorists of free expression before 1950" (72). On the recent history of the concept, see Philip Napoli, *Foundations of Communications Policy: Principles and Process in the Regulation of Electronic Media* (Cresskill, N.J.: Hampton Press, 2001), chap. 5.

43. *Abrams v. U.S.*, 250 U.S. 616 (1919), 630; Louis Menand, *The Metaphysical Club: A Story of Ideas in America* (New York: Farrar, Straus and Giroux, 2001), 65-67, 428-31.

44. *Abrams v. U.S.*, 630.

45. Starr, *The Creation of the Media*, 77-82, 267-94; Margaret Blanchard, "Filling in the Void: Speech and Press in State Courts Prior to *Gitlow*," in Bill Chamberlain and Charlene Brown, eds., *The First Amendment Reconsidered: New Perspectives on the Mean-ing of Freedom of Speech and Press* (New York: Longman, 1982): 14-59; David Rabban, *Free Speech in Its Forgotten Years* (New York: Cambridge University Press, 1997); Fred Friendly, *Minnesota Rag: The Dramatic Story of the Landmark Supreme Court Case That Gave New Meaning to Freedom of the Press* (New York: Random House, 1981).

46. *Mutual Film Corporation v. Industrial Commission of Ohio*, 236 U.S. 230 (1915), 241, 244; Starr, *The Creation of the Media*, 311-15; Garth Jowett, "'A Capacity for Evil': The 1915 Supreme Court *Mutual* Decision," in Matthew Bernstein, ed., *Controlling Hollywood: Censorship and Regulation in the Studio Era* (New Brunswick, N.J.: Rutgers University Press, 1999): 16-40; Louise Benjamin, "Defining the Public Interest and Pro-tecting the Public Welfare in the 1920s: Parallels Between Radio and Movie Regulation," *Historical Journal of Film, Radio and Television* 12 (August 1992): 87-101. Film did not receive full constitutional protection until 1952.

47. David Sarnoff, "Uncensored and Uncontrolled," *The Nation* 119 (23 July 1924): 90; David Sarnoff, Testimony in U.S. House of Representatives, 68th Cong., 1st sess., *To Regulate Radio Communication: Hearings Before the Committee on the Merchant Marine and Fisheries on H.R. 7357* (Washington, D.C.: Government Printing Office, 1924), 160; Editorial, "Free & Uneasy," *Broadcasting* 15 (15 December 1938): 44.

48. Melvin Urofsky, *Louis D. Brandeis: A Life* (New York: Pantheon, 2009), 300; Ger-ald Berk, *Louis D. Brandeis and the Making of Regulated Competition, 1900-1932* (New York: Cambridge University Press, 2009), 1, 41, 66.

49. John Dewey, *Liberalism and Social Action* (Amherst, Mass.: Prometheus Books, 2000 [1935]), 17, 53-54, 35.

50. Fred Roddell, "Morris Ernst," *Life* 16 (21 February 1944): 102; Morris Ernst, "Radio Censorship and the 'Listening Millions,'" *The Nation* 122 (28 April 1926): 473; Morris Ernst, Testimony Before the FCC, 2 October 1941, 1421, Box 1933, Docket 6051,

FCCDCF, NACP; "Memorandum by Morris Ernst Prepared at the Request of the Board of Directors at the Special Meeting Held Thursday, Oct. 9, 1941," 6, Vol. 2351, Reel 203, Correspondence—Censorship—Press-Radio—1942, Entry 7—Mimeographed Material, ACLU Records.

51. Arthur Garfield Hays, Testimony Before the FCC, 30 January 1942, 3129–30, Box 1936, Docket 6051, FCCDCF, NACP.

52. Dewey, *Liberalism and Social Action*, 34–35.

53. James Lawrence Fly, "Freedom of Speech and the Press," Talk at Cornell University, 20 September 1944, 3, 5–7, emphasis in original, Box 39, Folder Cornell University—Public Lecture—9/20/44, Fly Papers, Columbia; Mickie Edwardson, "James Lawrence Fly's Fight for a Free Marketplace of Ideas," *American Journalism* 14 (Winter 1997): 19–39.

54. Adam Candeub, "Media Ownership Regulation, the First Amendment, and Democracy's Future," *University of California Davis Law Review* 41 (April 2008): 1547–1612; Philip Napoli, "Deconstructing the Diversity Principle," *Journal of Communication* 49 (Autumn 1999): 7–34; Robert Entman and Steven Wildman, "Reconciling Economic and Non-Economic Perspectives on Media Policy: Transcending the 'Marketplace of Ideas,'" *Journal of Communication* 42 (Winter 1992): 5–19.

55. *Abrams v. U.S.*, 630; *Detroit News*, 1 September 1920, quoted in Barnouw, *A Tower in Babel*, 63.

56. The specific parameters of this regulation have changed dramatically from the early days of radio to the present. For an excellent summary of media ownership laws, see Candeub, "Media Ownership Regulation," 1555–61.

57. C. Edwin Baker, *Media Concentration and Democracy: Why Ownership Matters* (New York: Cambridge University Press, 2007), 48.

58. Frederick Allen, "Newspapers and the Truth," *Atlantic Monthly* 129 (January 1922): 44; Walter Lippmann, *Public Opinion* (New York: Free Press, 1997 [1922]), 228, 158, 19. Lippmann's views were not met uncritically, and his exchange of ideas with John Dewey in the 1920s about the relationship between journalism and democracy remains one of the most incisive discourses about the subject. See Brett Gary, *The Nervous Liberals: Propaganda Anxieties from World War I to the Cold War* (New York: Columbia University Press, 1999), 23–46; Christopher Lasch, *The True and Only Heaven: Progress and Its Critics* (New York: Norton, 1991), 360–68; Ronald Steel, *Walter Lippmann and the American Century* (New York: Vintage, 1981), 171–85; and Robert Westbrook, *John Dewey and American Democracy* (Ithaca, N.Y.: Cornell University Press, 1991), 293–318. The best articulated positions by the original authors are Walter Lippmann, *The Phantom Public* (New York: Harcourt, Brace, 1925); and John Dewey, *The Public and Its Problems* (New York: Henry Holt, 1927).

59. Edward Purcell, *The Crisis of Democratic Theory: Scientific Naturalism and the Problem of Value* (Lexington: University Press of Kentucky, 1973); David Ciepley, *Liberalism in the Shadow of Totalitarianism* (Cambridge, Mass.: Harvard University Press, 2006).

60. Blanchard, *Revolutionary Sparks*, 145–48; Schudson, *Discovering the News*, 157–58; Frank Parker Stockbridge, "Newspapers Called On to Help Suppress Broadcasting Frauds," *American Press* 48 (August 1930): 1, 36.

61. "Radio Makes Better Citizens," *Wireless Age* 10 (October 1922): 26.

62. Harry Kursh, Letter to the Editor, *New York Times*, 17 November 1947, 20.

63. William J. Scripps, Testimony Before the FCC, 19 April 1948, 956, Box 4, Docket 8516, FCCDCF, NACP.

Chapter 1. Power, Politics, and the Promise of New Media: Newspaper Ownership of Radio in the 1920s

1. R. J. McLauchlin, "What the Detroit 'News' Has Done in Broadcasting," *Radio Broadcast* 1 (June 1922): 136–38; "Radio Experts' Rules Completed," *Editor & Publisher* 54 (11 March 1922): 30; Thomas Ormsbee, "Newspapers Capitalize Radio Craze in Manifold Ways," *Editor & Publisher* 54 (22 April 1922): 16; "A Newspaper Radio 'Beat,'" *Literary Digest* 75 (21 October 1922): 28; Winfield Barton, "What Broadcasting Does for a Newspaper," *Radio News* 4 (February 1922): 345–56; "Brian Collins, "The New Orleans Press-Radio War and Huey P. Long, 1922–1936" (M.A. thesis, Louisiana State University, 2002), 2.

2. Clayton Koppes, "The Social Destiny of Radio: Hope and Disillusionment in the 1920s," *South Atlantic Quarterly* 68 (Summer 1969): 363–76; Eunice Fuller Barnard, "Radio Politics," *New Republic* 38 (19 March 1924): 91–92; George Stone, "Radio Has Gripped Chicago," *Radio Broadcast* 1 (October 1922): 503; Erik Barnouw, *A Tower in Babel: A History of Broadcasting in the United States*, vol. 1, *To 1933* (New York: Oxford University Press, 1966), 78–79; "The Broadcasting of News by the Daily Papers," *Radio Broadcast* 4 (November 1923): 100.

3. J. H. Morecroft, "Radio Currents: An Editorial Interpretation," *Radio Broadcast* 1 (May 1922): 3.

4. Susan Douglas, *Listening In: Radio and the American Imagination* (Minneapolis: University of Minnesota Press, 2004 [1999]), 58, 74.

5. Stone, "Radio Has Gripped Chicago," 505–6; Barnouw, *A Tower in Babel*, 88–90; Michele Hilmes, *Radio Voices: American Broadcasting, 1922–1952* (Minneapolis: University of Minnesota Press, 1997), 54.

6. W. S. Gilmore, "Radio Serves This Newspaper," *The Quill* 19 (June 1931): 15.

7. Dudley Siddall, "Who Owns Our Broadcasting Stations?" *Radio Broadcast* 6 (February 1925): 709; "A Newspaper Radio 'Beat,'" 27–28.

8. Reminiscences of Edwin Lloyd Tyson, May 1951, 18–19, RPP, CUOHROC; Reminiscences of Rex G. White, 1951, 3–4, RPP, CUOHROC.

9. Susan Smulyan, *Selling Radio: The Commercialization of American Broadcasting, 1920-1934* (Washington, D.C.: Smithsonian Institution Press, 1994), 1, 39–41; Robert McChesney, *Telecommunications, Mass Media, and Democracy: The Battle for Control of U.S. Broadcasting, 1928-1935* (New York: Oxford University Press, 1993), 14–15; Reminiscences of Herbert Ponting, May 1951, 1–2, 9–10, RPP, CUOHROC; Noah Arceneaux,

"Department Stores and the Origins of American Broadcasting, 1910–1931" (Ph.D. dissertation, University of Georgia, 2007).

10. Reminiscences of Herbert Ponting, May 1951, 2, RPP, CUOHROC; William S. Hedges, "Enemies or Allies?" *The Quill* 19 (February 1931): 5–6.

11. This was a widespread practice among American newspapers. For a detailed study of the specialty sections on radio broadcasting in American newspapers, see Randall Patnode, "Heralding Radio: The Social Construction of Broadcasting by Newspaper Specialty Sections, 1922–1926" (Ph.D. dissertation, University of North Carolina, 1999). On the cultural significance of newspaper coverage of radio broadcasting, see Catherine Covert, "'We May Hear Too Much': American Sensibility and the Response to Radio, 1919–1924," in Catherine Covert and John Stevens, eds., *Mass Media Between the Wars: Perceptions of Cultural Tension, 1918–1941* (Syracuse, N.Y.: Syracuse University Press, 1984), 199–220.

12. Reminiscences of Elton Plant, 25 May 1951, 27–28, RPP, CUOHROC.

13. Ormsbee, "Newspapers Capitalize Radio Craze in Manifold Ways," 16.

14. Alfred D. Chandler, Jr., *The Visible Hand: The Managerial Revolution in American Business* (Cambridge, Mass.: Belknap Press of Harvard University Press, 2002 [1977]); Olivier Zunz, *Making America Corporate, 1870–1920* (Chicago: University of Chicago Press, 1990).

15. Reminiscences of William S. Hedges, 1951, 8–9, RPP, CUOHROC; William S. Hedges to Martin Codel, 7 April 1932, 1, Box 1, Folder Correspondence, 29 April 1926–31 December 1935, Hedges Papers, SHSW.

16. Reminiscences of William S. Hedges, 1951, 9–11, RPP, CUOHROC; William S. Hedges to Raymond Guy, 7 January 1958, Box 1, Folder Correspondence, April 1935–April 1958, Hedges Papers, SHSW; Interview with Judith Waller, 1 June 1951, 6, 8, MCSC, SHSW; William S. Hedges, quoted in Barton, "What Broadcasting Does for a Newspaper," 344.

17. Reminiscences of William S. Hedges, 1951, 15–17, RPP, CUOHROC; Melvin Patrick Ely, *The Adventures of Amos 'n' Andy: A Social History of an American Phenomenon* (Charlottesville: University of Virginia Press, 2001 [1991]), 56–58.

18. Robert R. McCormick to Hulbert Taft, 1 November 1927, Box 95, Folder Radio, General, 1924–1953, Series I-60—Robert R. McCormick, Business Correspondence, 1927–1955, Tribune Archives; Marc Rose, "Radio or Newspaper—Can Both Survive," *The Nation* 119 (24 December 1924): 699–700; Richard Norton Smith, *The Colonel: The Life and Legend of Robert R. McCormick, 1880–1955* (Boston: Houghton Mifflin, 1997), 267–69.

19. "Confidential Survey for Newspaper-Radio Committee, July 1941," 6, Box 50, Folder 7, Series XI-175—*Chicago Tribune*—Kirkland and Ellis Files, Tribune Archives; Daniel Calibraro and John Fink, *WGN: A Pictorial History* (Chicago: WGN Inc., 1961), 18–19; Advertisement, "W-G-N's Achievements During 1925," *Chicago Tribune*, 28 December 1925, 22.

20. Edward J. Larson, *Summer for the Gods: The Scopes Trial and America's*

Continuing Debate Over Science and Religion (New York: Basic Books, 1997); James Walter Wesolowski, "Before Canon 35: WGN Broadcasts the Monkey Trial," *Tennessee Historical Quarterly* 34 (Winter 1975): 395, 398; "W-G-N to Bring Evolution Case to Your Home," *Chicago Tribune*, 28 June 1925, D7; "Broadcast of Scopes Trial Unprecedented," *Chicago Tribune*, 5 July 1925, C6; "W-G-N Will Take Scopes Trial to Record Audience," *Chicago Tribune*, 12 July 1925, 3; Michael Lienesch, *In the Beginning: Fundamentalism, the Scopes Trial, and the Making of the Antievolution Movement* (Chapel Hill: University of North Carolina Press, 2007), 146–47; Edward Caudill, *The Scopes Trial: A Photographic History* (Knoxville: University of Tennessee Press, 2000).

21. Charles McGovern, *Sold American: Consumption and Citizenship, 1890–1945* (Chapel Hill: University of North Carolina Press, 2006), 9–10; Roland Marchand, *Advertising and the American Dream: Making Way for Modernity, 1920–1940* (Berkeley: University of California Press, 1985), 88–94. See also Simon Bronner, ed., *Consuming Visions: Accumulation and Display of Goods in America, 1880–1920* (New York: Norton, 1989); Lizabeth Cohen, *Making a New Deal: Industrial Workers in Chicago, 1919–1939* (New York: Cambridge University Press, 1990); Pamela Laird, *Advertising Progress: American Business and the Rise of Consumer Marketing* (Baltimore: Johns Hopkins University Press, 1998); William Leach, *Land of Desire: Merchants, Power, and the Rise of a New American Culture* (New York: Vintage, 1993); T. J. Jackson Lears, *No Place of Grace: Antimodernism and the Transformation of American Culture, 1880–1920* (Chicago: University of Chicago Press, 1994 [1981]); and Susan Strasser, *Satisfaction Guaranteed: The Making of the American Mass Market* (Washington, D.C.: Smithsonian Institution Press, 1989).

22. Clifford Doerksen, *American Babel: Rogue Radio Broadcasters of the Jazz Age* (Philadelphia: University of Pennsylvania Press, 2005), 13–16; Daniel Horowitz, *The Morality of Spending: Attitudes Toward the Consumer Society in America, 1875–1940* (Baltimore: Johns Hopkins University Press, 1985), 134–35; Lee De Forest, quoted in Editorial, "Indirect Radio Advertising," *Editor & Publisher* 57 (14 March 1925): 20; Editorial, "Radio Advertising," *Editor & Publisher* 58 (14 November 1925): 32; Barnouw; *A Tower in Babel*, 177.

23. Interview with Judith Waller, 1 June 1951, 22–A, MCSC, SHSW; Daniel Pfaff, "Joseph Pulitzer II and Advertising Censorship, 1929–1939," *Journalism Monographs* 77 (July 1982): 1, 7, 11; Reminiscences of Edwin Lloyd Tyson, May 1951, 24–25, RPP, CUOHROC. For similar statements about WWJ's advertising standards, see Harry Bannister, *The Education of a Broadcaster* (New York: Simon and Schuster, 1965), 21–22.

24. Editorial, "Radio Advertising," *Editor & Publisher* 57 (4 October 1924): 20; Arthur Robb, "Should Newspapers Sell Advertisers Time on Their Radio Stations," *Editor & Publisher* 58 (6 June 1925): 3–4; Editorial, "Press Radio Advertising," *Editor & Publisher* 58 (6 June 1925): 24.

25. Upton Sinclair, *The Brass Check: A Study of American Journalism*, Introduction by Robert McChesney and Ben Scott (Urbana: University of Illinois Press, 2003 [1920]), 318; Kevin Mattson, *Upton Sinclair and the Other American Century* (Hoboken, N.J.:

John Wiley, 2006); Anthony Arthur, *Radical Innocent: Upton Sinclair* (New York: Random House, 2006), 181–82; Michael Schudson, *Discovering the News: A Social History of American Newspapers* (New York: Basic Books, 1978), chap. 4.

26. Reminiscences of Joseph Haeffner, May 1951, 1–4, RPP, CUOHROC; Reminiscences of Alfred Kirchhofer, 21 May 1951, 1–6, RPP, CUOHROC; "Daily Presses Plea for Radio Rights," *Editor & Publisher* 62 (2 November 1929): 28; "Asks Right to Broadcast," *New York Times*, 7 August 1929, 46; "Buffalo Stirs Up a Radio Problem," *New York Times*, 24 November 1929, XX16; Alfred Kirchhofer, quoted in Arthur Robb, "New Radio Station of Buffalo News Trophy of Victory over Monopoly," *Editor & Publisher* 63 (18 October 1930): 5; Editorial, "Radio," *Editor & Publisher* 63 (2 May 1931): 30.

27. Hugh Slotten, *Radio and Television Regulation: Broadcast Technology in the United States, 1920–1960* (Baltimore: Johns Hopkins University Press, 2000), chap. 1.

28. Ellis Hawley, "Herbert Hoover, the Commerce Secretariat, and the Vision of an 'Associative State,'" *Journal of American History* 61 (June 1974): 119, 127; Ellis Hawley, *The Great War and the Search for a Modern Order: A History of the American People and Their Institutions, 1917–1933* (New York: St. Martin's, 1979), 100–104; Louise Benjamin, "Working It Out Together: Radio Policy from Hoover to the Radio Act of 1927," *Journal of Broadcasting and Electronic Media* 42 (Spring 1998): 221–36.

29. Statement by the Secretary of Commerce at the Opening of the Radio Conference on 27 February 1922, 1, Commerce Period Papers, Box 489, Folder Radio Correspondence, Press Releases, Misc. 1922 January–March, Hoover Papers; Minutes of Open Meetings of Department of Commerce Conference on Radio Telephony, Washington, D.C., 27, 28 February 1922, 91, Commerce Period Papers, Box 496, Folder Radio: Conferences, National-First (27 February 1922), Minutes, Hoover Papers; "Radio Conference to Zone the Air," *Editor & Publisher* 54 (4 March 1922): 12.

30. U.S. Department of Commerce, Recommendations of the National Radio Committee, 24 March 1923, Commerce Period Papers, Box 496, Folder Radio: Conferences, National-Second (20–24 March 1923), Hoover Papers; "Urge Wide Reforms in Broadcasting," *New York Times*, 25 March 1923, S5; Sam Bell, "Radio Meeting Allots 390–430 Wave to Newspaper Broadcasters," *Editor & Publisher* 55 (24 March 1923): 6.

31. U.S. Department of Commerce, *Recommendations for Regulation of Radio Adopted by the Third National Radio Conference* (Washington, D.C.: Government Printing Office, 1924), 6–7, 9–11.

32. Proceedings of the Third Radio Conference, 6–10 October 1924, 20, Commerce Period Papers, Box 496, Folder Radio: Conferences—Third (6 October 1924), Proceedings, Hoover Papers.

33. "Hoover Calls Conference to Solve Radio Problems," *New York Times*, 11 October 1925, XX18; *Proceedings of the Fourth National Radio Conference and Recommendations for Regulation of Radio* (Washington, D.C.: Government Printing Office, 1926), ii–iii; "Radio Problems and Conference Recommendations," An Address by Secretary of Commerce Hoover Broadcast from Washington, D.C., 12 November 1925, Commerce

Period Papers, Box 496, Folder Radio: Conferences—National—Fourth (9–11 November 1925), Hoover Papers.

34. Hugh Aitken, "Allocating the Spectrum: The Origins of Radio Regulation," *Technology and Culture* 35 (October 1994): 700–702; *Hoover v. Intercity Radio Co.*, 286 F. 1003 (1923), 1007.

35. Aitken, "Allocating the Spectrum," 702–6; *United States v. Zenith Radio Corporation et al.*, 12 F.2d 614 (1926); "Hoover Asks Help to Avoid Air Chaos," *New York Times*, 10 July 1926, 1; Editorial, "New Towers of Babel," *Editor & Publisher* 59 (20 November 1926): 26.

36. *Tribune Company v. Oak Leaves Broadcasting Station*, reprinted in *Congressional Record*, 69th Cong., 2nd sess., 1926, 68, pt. 1: 216–17; "New Stations Jeopardized by Chicago Court Decision," *New York Times*, 28 November 1926, XX16.

37. *Tribune Company v. Oak Leaves Broadcasting Station*, 219; Philip Kinsley, "Court Fixes Radio Rights on the Air; W-G-N Wins," *Chicago Tribune*, 18 November 1926, 1, 16; Aitken, "Allocating the Spectrum," 710–12; Louise Benjamin, "The Precedent That Almost Was: A 1926 Court Effort to Regulate Radio," *Journalism Quarterly* 67 (Autumn 1990): 584. *Tribune* publisher Robert McCormick never entirely gave up hope that he might someday obtain full property rights for his radio station. In 1946, McCormick wrote to radio pioneer Edwin Armstrong that "the history of land titles is that a possession finally became recognized as a right. And those of us who live two or three hundred years may hope to have the same happen in radio." Robert R. McCormick to Edwin H. Armstrong, 2 April 1946, Box 1—Cataloged Correspondence, Folder McCormick, Robert R., Armstrong Papers, Columbia. The case has also remained a touchstone for academic economists advocating a property-rights approach to radio regulation, for example Ronald Coase, "The Federal Communications Commission," *Journal of Law and Economics* 2 (October 1959): 1–40; and Thomas Hazlett, "The Rationality of U.S. Regulation of the Broadcast Spectrum," *Journal of Law and Economics* 33 (April 1990): 133–75.

38. Marvin Bensman, *The Beginning of Broadcast Regulation in the Twentieth Century* (Jefferson, N.C.: McFarland, 2000), 207–8; David Moss and Michael Fein, "Radio Regulation Revisited: Coase, the FCC, and the Public Interest," *Journal of Policy History* 15 (Fall 2003): 389–416; United States Senate, 69th Cong., 1st sess., *Radio Control: Hearings Before the Senate Committee on Interstate Commerce on S.1 and S.1754* (Washington, D.C.: Government Printing Office, 1926), 130, 132–33.

39. Mary Mander, "The Public Debate About Broadcasting in the Twenties: An Interpretive History," *Journal of Broadcasting* 28 (Spring 1984): 169–70, 178–84.

40. *Congressional Record*, 69th Cong., 1st sess., 1926, 67, pt. 5: 5558.

41. Moss and Fein, "Radio Regulation Revisited," 402–3, 407–9.

42. Walter Strong to Calvin Coolidge, 8 February 1927, Commerce Period Papers, Box 497, Folder Radio: Federal Radio Commission, Applications & Endorsements, Bail-Bake, Hoover Papers; Edwin Emery, *History of the American Newspaper Publishers Association* (Minneapolis: University of Minnesota Press, 1950), 199; William S. Hedges

to Martin Codel, 7 April 1932, 2, Box 1, Folder Correspondence, 29 April 1926–31 December 1935, Hedges Papers, SHSW; "Urges Federal Radio Law," *New York Times*, 20 November 1926, 23; "Broadcasters Urged to Ask State Courts for Protection," *New York Times*, 28 November 1926, XX21; Radio Industry Asks Emergency Control," *New York Times*, 4 December 1926, 1; "Increasing Number of Broadcasters Creates More Disturbance and Big Problem for the Ether's Traffic Cops," *New York Times*, 12 December 1926, XX16; "Who Shall Control Radio is Problem Facing Congress," *New York Times*, 12 December 1926, XX21.

43. Morton Keller, *Regulating a New Economy: Public Policy and Economic Change in America, 1900–1933* (Cambridge, Mass.: Harvard University Press, 1990), 84–85; Douglas Craig, *Fireside Politics: Radio and Political Culture in the United States, 1920–1940* (Baltimore: Johns Hopkins University Press, 2000), chap. 3; Susan Douglas, *Inventing American Broadcasting, 1899–1922* (Baltimore: Johns Hopkins University Press, 1987), 276–85; Hugh Aitken, *The Continuous Wave: Technology and American Radio, 1900–1932* (Princeton, N.J.: Princeton University Press, 1985), chap. 5; Daniel Rodgers, *Atlantic Crossings: Social Politics in a Progressive Age* (Cambridge, Mass.: Harvard University Press, 1998).

44. Gabriel Kolko, *The Triumph of Conservatism: A Reinterpretation of American History, 1900–1916* (New York: Free Press, 1963); Gabriel Kolko, *Railroads and Regulation, 1877–1916* (New York: Norton, 1970 [1965]); Martin Sklar, *The Corporate Reconstruction of American Capitalism, 1890–1916: The Market, the Law, and Politics* (Cambridge: Cambridge University Press, 1988).

45. Louise Benjamin, *Freedom of the Air and the Public Interest: First Amendment Rights in Broadcasting to 1935* (Carbondale: Southern Illinois University Press, 2001), chap. 5; Richard R. John, *Network Nation: Inventing American Telecommunications* (Cambridge, Mass.: Belknap Press of Harvard University Press, 2010), 411–12; Radio Act of 1927, PL 632, 69th Cong., 2nd sess., 23 February 1927, reprinted in Barnouw, *A Tower in Babel*, 305, 307–9, 312; Moss and Fein, "Radio Regulation Revisited," 400–401; "Amended Radio Bill Submitted to House," *New York Times*, 28 January 1927, 7; Craig, *Fireside Politics*, 57–58.

46. Silas Bent, "Radio Steals the Press' Thunder," *The Independent* 119 (9 July 1927): 34; "Radio Bill Called Air 'Magna Charta,'" *New York Times*, 20 February 1927, 17.

47. Walter Strong to Herbert Hoover, 27 February 1928, Commerce Period Files, Box 497, Folder Radio: Federal Radio Commission, Correspondence, 1928–1929, Hoover Papers; Herbert Hoover to Walter Strong, 28 February 1928, ibid.; Hugh Slotten, "Radio's Hidden Voice: Noncommercial Broadcasting, Extension Education, and State Universities During the 1920s," *Technology and Culture* 49 (January 2008): 1–20; McChesney, *Telecommunications, Mass Media, and Democracy*, 21; Jennifer Profitt and Michael Brown, "Regulating the Radio Monopoly: Ewin Davis and His Legislative Debates, 1923–1928," *Journal of Radio Studies* 11 (June 2004): 100–115.

48. McChesney, *Telecommunications, Mass Media, and Democracy*, 24–25. On Caldwell's legal career in the 1920s and 1930s, see Robert McChesney, "Free Speech and Democracy! Louis G. Caldwell, the American Bar Association and the Debate over

the Free Speech Implications of Broadcast Regulation, 1928–1938," *American Journal of Legal History* 35 (October 1991): 351–92. Caldwell also wrote two influential law review articles expounding on the theories he had tried to put into action at the FRC and in private practice. See Louis Caldwell, "The Standard of Public Interest, Convenience or Necessity as Used in the Radio Act of 1927," *Air Law Review* 1 (July 1930): 295–330; and "Principles Governing the Licensing of Broadcasting Stations," *University of Pennsylvania Law Review* 79 (December 1930): 113–57.

49. M. C. Martin, Memorandum Re: Tribune Legal Services, 16 November 1928, 1, Box 15, Folder 5, Series XI-173—*Chicago Tribune*, Business Manager Files, 1926–1955, Tribune Archives. Caldwell's ability to influence broadcast regulation in favor of the *Tribune* was widely noted. William S. Hedges remarked to *Chicago Daily News* publisher Walter Strong that Caldwell's presence in Washington was "nothing more or less than to maintain an insidious lobby for WGN." William S. Hedges to Walter Strong, 26 February 1931, 3, Presidential Period, Subject Files, Box 148, Folder Federal Radio Commission, Correspondence, 1931 May, Hoover Papers.

50. McChesney, *Telecommunications, Mass Media, and Democracy*, 72; Elizabeth Fones-Wolf, *Waves of Opposition: Labor and the Struggle for Democratic Radio* (Urbana: University of Illinois Press, 2006), 19–21; Nathan Godfried, *WCFL: Chicago's Voice of Labor, 1926–78* (Urbana: University of Illinois Press, 1997), chaps. 2–3; Jesse Walker, *Rebels on the Air: An Alternative History of Radio in America* (New York: New York University Press, 2001), 38.

51. *Congressional Record*, 70th Cong., 2nd sess., 1929, 70, pt. 2: 1240–41.

52. United States Senate, 71st Cong., 2nd sess., *Hearings Before the Committee on Interstate Commerce on S.6, a Bill to Provide for the Regulation of the Transmission of Intelligence by Wire or Wireless* (Washington, D.C.: Government Printing Office, 1930), 1643, 1647; *Congressional Record*, 71st Cong., 2nd sess., 1930, 72, pt. 9: 9184.

53. Paul Starr, *The Creation of the Media: Political Origins of Modern Communications* (New York: Basic Books, 2004), 1–2, 4, emphasis in original; Yochai Benkler, *The Wealth of Networks: How Social Production Transforms Markets and Freedom* (New Haven, Conn.: Yale University Press, 2006), 188–89.

54. Ben Fisher, "Radio and the Newspaper: An Analysis of Their Relationship," *Oregon Exchanges* 14 (October 1930): 10; Frank Parker Stockbridge, "Radio vs. the Press: Will the Newspapers Control Broadcasting?" *Outlook and Independent* 156 (31 December 1930): 692, 694.

55. M. H. Aylesworth, Untitled Memorandum to the Board of Directors of the National Broadcasting Company, 19 April 1935, 2, Topical Files, Folder 29—Broadcast Ads-Newspapers, NBC-MPBRSD, LOC; M. H. Aylesworth, "The Press and Radio, the Radio Viewpoint," Speech at American Society of Newspaper Editors Annual Meeting in Washington, D.C, 19 April 1930, printed in American Society of Newspaper Editors, *Problems of Journalism: Proceedings of the Eighth Annual Meeting of the American Society of Newspaper Editors* (Atlantic City, N.J.: American Society of Newspaper Editors, 1930), 145, 149.

Chapter 2. New Empires: Media Concentration in the 1930s

1. W. E. Macfarlane, Address to the Fall Convention of the American Newspaper Publishers Association, 12 November 1930, reprinted in "Broadcast Advertising Out of Hand," *Editor & Publisher* 63 (15 November 1930): 9.

2. Karl Bickel, *New Empires: The Newspaper and the Radio* (Philadelphia: Lippincott, 1930), 37, 43, 53, 79.

3. H. O. Davis, *The Empire of the Air: The Story of the Exploitation of Radio for Private Profit, With a Plan for the Reorganization of Broadcasting* (Ventura, Calif.: Ventura Free Press, 1932), 98; *Citizen Kane*, dir. Orson Welles, 119 min., Mercury Productions, 1941; David Nasaw, *The Chief: The Life of William Randolph Hearst* (Boston: Houghton Mifflin, 2000), 322–23, 405.

4. Harold Innis, *Empire and Communications* (Oxford: Clarendon Press, 1950), 3.

5. Lee de Forest, *Father of Radio: The Autobiography of Lee de Forest* (Chicago: Wilcox & Follet, 1950), 4. De Forest's statement is the source of the title of the monographic history of radio that later became the basis for filmmaker Ken Burns's documentary of the same title. See Tom Lewis, *Empire of the Air: The Men Who Made Radio* (New York: HarperCollins, 1991).

6. David Welky, *Everything Was Better in America: Print Culture in the Great Depression* (Urbana: University of Illinois Press, 2008); Bruce Lenthall, *Radio's America: The Great Depression and the Rise of Modern Mass Culture* (Chicago: University of Chicago Press, 2007); Douglas Craig, *Fireside Politics: Radio and Political Culture in the United States, 1920–1940* (Baltimore: Johns Hopkins University Press, 2000), 17.

7. Gwenyth Jackaway, *Media at War: Radio's Challenge to the Newspapers, 1924–1939* (Westport, Conn.: Praeger, 1995), 86–87.

8. "Publishers Warned of Radio Dangers," *Editor & Publisher* 63 (25 April 1931): 19, 26; Editorial, "Radio," *Editor & Publisher* 63 (2 May 1931): 30.

9. Brian Collins, "The New Orleans Press-Radio War and Huey P. Long, 1922–1936" (M.A. thesis, Louisiana State University, 2002), 48; "Radio Program Listings Dropped by Three Waterbury Newspapers," *Editor & Publisher* 63 (14 February 1931): 18; "Radio Programs Back in Condensed Form," *Editor & Publisher* 63 (21 February 1931): 8; Jerome Walker, "Editors Sharply Divided on How to Handle Radio Programs," *Editor & Publisher* 63 (21 March 1931): 44; Editorial, "The Radio Case," *Editor & Publisher* 63 (18 April 1931): 54; Robert Mann, "Trade Names Barred in Radio Programs by New York City Newspapers," *Editor & Publisher* 64 (25 July 1931): 5, 42; Robert Mann, "Trade Names Fading From Radio Programs Survey of 65 Dailies Reveals," *Editor & Publisher* 64 (22 August 1931): 5–6; Howard London, "Radio Programs Getting Scant Space," *Editor & Publisher* 66 (30 September 1933): 9; "2 Charlotte Papers Ban Radio News," *Editor & Publisher* 66 (11 November 1933): 8; Editorial, "Radio Programs," *Editor & Publisher* 66 (11 November 1933): 24.

10. "Radio 'Lifting' of News Attacked," *Editor & Publisher* 63 (17 January 1931): 9, 43; Arthur Robb, "Keep News from Radio, S.N.P.A. Urges," *Editor & Publisher* 65 (23 July 1932): 7–8, 20; "A.P. Sues Radio Station In Move to End 'News Pirating' by Broadcasters," *Editor & Publisher* 65 (4 March 1933): 3.

11. Jackaway, *Media at War*; Gwenyth Jackaway, "America's Press-Radio War of the 1930s: A Case Study in Battles Between Old and New Media," *Historical Journal of Film, Radio and Television* 14 (August 1994): 299–314. See also George Lott, Jr., "The Press-Radio War of the 1930s," *Journal of Broadcasting* 14 (Summer 1970): 275–86; Giraud Chester, "The Press-Radio War: 1933–1935," *Public Opinion Quarterly* 13 (Summer 1949): 252–64; and Russell Hammargren, "The Origin of Press-Radio Conflict," *Journalism Quarterly* 13 (March 1936): 91–93.

12. Jackaway, *Media at War*, 8; Editorial, "Fake Radio News," *Editor & Publisher* 66 (7 October 1933): 24; Editorial, "The Radio Menace," *Editor & Publisher* 66 (4 November 1933): 6; Editorial, "Radio's Slender Base," *Editor & Publisher* 66 (20 January 1934): 20; Editorial, "Irresponsible Radio News," *Editor & Publisher* 67 (26 May 1934): 22; "False Radio Reports Alarmed Public," *Editor & Publisher* 67 (21 July 1934): 7; Editorial, "Spot News and Radio," *Editor & Publisher* 64 (26 March 1932): 24.

13. T. R. Carskadon, "The Press-Radio War," *New Republic* 86 (11 March 1936): 133; "Plan to End Radio News Competition Formed at New York Conference," *Editor & Publisher* 66 (16 December 1933): 3, 53; Excerpt from Proceedings of 1934 Annual Convention of American Newspaper Publishers Association, Report of Radio Committee, 1–2, Box 1936, Docket 6051, FCCDCF, NACP; "Press-Radio Agreement in Operation," *Editor & Publisher* 66 (3 March 1934): 7.

14. Arthur Robb, "Radio as Newspaper Competitor Theme of Coming Publishers' Meetings," *Editor & Publisher* 63 (11 April 1931): 6.

15. Joseph Pulitzer to L. K. Nicholson, 15 November 1932, Box 46, Folder Associated Press—Radio, 1926–40, Pulitzer Papers, LOC; A. G. Lincoln to Joseph Pulitzer, 31 January 1933, ibid.

16. F. A. Miller to E. H. Harris, January 1934, quoted in "Radio-Press Proposal is Referred to Committee for Revision," *Editor & Publisher* 66 (20 January 1934): 8; W. E. Macfarlane to Robert McCormick, 13 January 1934, Box 20, Folder 2, Series XI-173 —*Chicago Tribune*, Business Manager Files, 1926–1955, Tribune Archives.

17. Volney Hurd, "Can Press Stop Progress by 'Air Brakes'?," *Broadcasting* 6 (15 May 1934): 20; Clarence Dill, "Dill Calls Press-Radio Program Failure," *Broadcasting* 7 (1 October 1934): 15, 49.

18. Isabelle Keating, "Radio Invades Journalism," *The Nation* 140 (12 June 1935): 677; Carskadon, "The Press-Radio War," 132.

19. William S. Hedges, "What Television Will Mean to Newspapers, Explained by Chicago News Broadcast Chief," *American Press* 48 (July 1930): 5; Robert McChesney, "Press-Radio Relations and the Emergence of Network, Commercial Broadcasting in the United States, 1930–1935," *Historical Journal of Film, Radio and Television* 11 (March 1991): 43–46; "Press Control of Radio Favored," *Editor & Publisher* 63 (25 April 1931): 37, 108; Alf Pratte, "Going Along for the Ride on the Prosperity Bandwagon: Peaceful Annexation Not War Between the Editors and Radio: 1923–1941," *Journal of Radio Studies* 2 (1993/1994): 123–39.

20. John Ryan, *The Production of Culture in the Music Industry: The ASCAP-BMI*

Controversy (Lanham, Md.: University Press of America, 1985), 17, 27–38; Erik Barnouw, *A Tower in Babel: A History of Broadcasting in the United States*, vol. 1, *To 1933* (New York: Oxford University Press, 1966), 119–21; Michele Hilmes, *Radio Voices: American Broadcasting, 1922–1952* (Minneapolis: University of Minnesota Press, 1997), 72; David Suisman, *Selling Sounds: The Commercial Revolution in American Music* (Cambridge, Mass.: Harvard University Press, 2009), 170–75, 251.

21. H. Dean Fitzer to Quin Ryan, 10 September 1932, 1–2, Box 18, Folder 7, Series XI-173—*Chicago Tribune*, Business Manager Files, 1926–1955, Tribune Archives; William S. Hedges to Frank Knox, 20 October 1932, 1–2, Box 1, Folder Correspondence, 29 April 1926–31 December 1935, Hedges Papers, SHSW; Typescript, "Report of Meeting, Newspaper-Owned Radio Stations, Sherman Hotel, Chicago, Oct. 19, 1932," ibid.; George Manning, "Dill Warns Dailies Owning Stations," *Editor & Publisher* 65 (19 November 1932): 8; "Press-Owned Stations Organized," *Editor & Publisher* 68 (13 July 1935): 7, 40.

22. Speech Transcript of Charles Webb, ANPA Annual Meeting, New York, N.Y., 26 April 1933, 2, Box 15, Folder 57, NBC, SHSW; George Brandenburg, "Radio Rendering Valuable Aid in Circulation Promotion Work," *Editor & Publisher* 70 (9 October 1937): 9; E. P. Schwartz, "Uses Radio to Reach Non-Readers," *Editor & Publisher* 68 (27 July 1935): 9; "Says Ownership of Radio Station an Asset to Small City Daily," *Editor & Publisher* 70 (13 February 1937): 29.

23. Paul R. Kelly, "Radio Prized Ally, Not Competitor, Says Daily Owning Two Stations," *Editor & Publisher* 68 (27 July 1935): 10; Fred Gaertner, Jr., "Station WWJ Strong Promotion Arm for Detroit News Since 1920," ibid., 6; Walter Damm, "Goodwill Leading Product of WTMJ," ibid., 7; John Paschall, "Newspapers Are Best Broadcasters Says Atlanta Journal Editor," ibid., 10; Roy Roberts, "K.C. *Star*'s Station Part of Paper," ibid., 11; Ted Dealey, "No Rivalry Between Radio and Press, But Mutual Freedom Fight—Dealey," ibid., 7, emphasis in original.

24. William Randolph Hearst to Emile Gough, 22 April 1930, 2–3, emphasis in original, Carton 36, Folder 1, Hearst Papers; William Randolph Hearst to Emile Gough, 22 October 1930, 1–2, ibid.

25. Emile Gough, "Report to Mr. William Randolph Hearst on Radio and Its Relation to His Newspapers," 24 September 1930, 2, 6, Carton 36, Folder 2, Hearst Papers; Typescript, "Report on Hearst Radio Enterprises," undated, c.a. 1935, Box 37, Folder 30, NBC, SHSW; "Hearst Interests Buy WBAL and Seek More Radio Outlets," *Broadcasting* 7 (1 December 1934): 8; Memorandum, Niles Trammell to R. C. Patterson, 23 November 1934, 1, Box 28, Folder 6, NBC, SHSW; Emile Gough to J. V. Connolly, 24 January 1933, Box 1938, Docket 6051,FCCDCF, NACP; Nasaw, *The Chief*, 391.

26. "Radio Not Newspaper's Competitor—Williamson," *The United States Publisher & Printer* 8 (June 1930): 12; M. H. Aylesworth, Typescript, "Hearst Radio in Relationship to the National Broadcasting Company," 18 March 1935, 3, 8–9, Box 37, Folder 39, NBC, SHSW.

27. M. H. Aylesworth to Roy Howard, 14 January 1935, 1, Box 41, Folder 33, NBC,

SHSW; Lenox Lohr to Albert Lasker, 10 March 1937, 1, Box 55, Folder 21, ibid.; Niles Trammell to J. S. McCarrens, 18 April 1941, Box 82, Folder 26, ibid.

28. E. M. Nockels, "The Tribune, Caldwell and Property Rights," *Federation News*, 5 September 1931, 6, Box 95, Folder WCFL, 1931, Series I-60, Robert R. McCormick, Business Correspondence, 1927–1955, Tribune Archives; W. E. MacFarlane to Leo Fitzpatrick, 6 September 1933, Box 22, Folder 1, Series XI-173—*Chicago Tribune*, Business Manager Files, 1926–1955, Tribune Archives; Federal Communications Commission, *Report on Chain Broadcasting* (Washington, D.C.: Government Printing Office, 1941), 26–28.

29. M. H. Aylesworth, Untitled Memorandum, 19 April 1935, 3, Topical Files, Folder 29—Broadcast Ads-Newspapers, NBC-MPBRSD, LOC; Advertisement, "NBC Salutes the Newspaper," *Editor & Publisher* 68 (27 July 1935): 34–35.

30. "Newspaper Ownership and Control of Radio Stations," *Broadcasting* 9 (15 August 1935): 12; "Newspapers Seeking Radio Stations," *Editor & Publisher* 68 (14 December 1935): 24.

31. "Scripps-Howard Buying WCPO As 'Proving Ground' for Radio," *Editor & Publisher* 68 (21 September 1935): 12; Sol Taishoff, "Scripps-Howard Enters Broadcasting Field," *Broadcasting* 9 (15 September 1935): 5; Editorial, "Seeing the Light," *Broadcasting* 9 (15 September 1935): 30; "Newspaper Groups Expanding Activities in Broadcast Field," *Broadcasting* 11 (15 October 1936): 32.

32. McChesney, "Press-Radio Relations and the Emergence of Network, Commercial Broadcasting," 45–46; "Radio vs. Newspapers," *Business Week*, 21 December 1932, 12.

33. William Randolph Hearst to E. J. Gough, 22 October 1930, 3, Carton 36, Folder 1, Hearst Papers; Frank Gannett to Charles M. Saltzman, 22 November 1930, Presidential Period, Subject Files, Box 148, Folder Federal Radio Commission, Correspondence, 1930, November–December, Hoover Papers; Frank Gannett to George Akerson, 2 November 1930, ibid.; Frank Gannett to Walter Newton, 8 November 1932, Presidential Period, Subject Files, Box 149, Folder Federal Radio Commission, Correspondence, 1932 September–1933, Hoover Papers.

34. Nancy Unger, *Fighting Bob La Follette: The Righteous Reformer* (Chapel Hill: University of North Carolina Press, 2000), 184–85, 258; Philip La Follette, *Adventure in Politics: The Memoirs of Philip La Follette*, ed. Donald Young (New York: Holt, Rinehart and Winston, 1970), 51–55; Richard Hofstadter, *The Age of Reform: From Bryan to F.D.R.* (New York: Vintage, 1955), 269–70.

35. Philip La Follette to Charles A. Kading, 26 June 1928, Box 2, Folder Correspondence—1928 June, Kading Papers, SHSW.

36. Glenn Roberts, Testimony Before the Federal Radio Commission, 17 November 1930, 5, Box 14, Folder 4, Anderson Papers, SHSW; Glenn Roberts, Testimony Before the Federal Radio Commission, 19 November 1930, 218–20, ibid.

37. Elisha Hanson, Testimony Before the Federal Radio Commission, 17 November 1930, 6, ibid.

38. A. M. Brayton to Walter Newton, 3 June 1930, 2–3, Presidential Period, Subject Files, Box 149, Folder Federal Radio Commission, Correspondence, 1932, April-June, Hoover Papers.

39. Walter Goodland to George Vits, 2 February 1931, Presidential Period, Subject Files, Box 148, Folder Federal Radio Commission, Correspondence, 1931, February, Hoover Papers; George Vits to Walter Newton, 4 February 1931, ibid.; Herbert Hoover, Untitled Memorandum, 8 February 1931, ibid.; Herbert Hoover, Untitled Memorandum, 17 February 1931, ibid.

40. Julius Liebman to Walter Newton, 17 June 1931, Presidential Period, Subject Files, Box 148, Folder Federal Radio Commission, Correspondence, 1931, June-July, Hoover Papers; Stephen Bolles to Walter Newton, 29 August 1931, Presidential Period, Subject Files, Box 148, Folder Federal Radio Commission, Correspondence, 1931, August-September, Hoover Papers.

41. Jonathan Kasparek, *Fighting Son: A Biography of Philip F. La Follette* (Madison: Wisconsin Historical Society Press, 2006), 133; A. M. Brayton to Walter Newton, 8 April 1932, Presidential Period, Subject Files, Box 149, Folder Federal Radio Commission, Correspondence, 1932, April-June, Hoover Papers.

Chapter 3. Reshaping the Public Sphere: The New Deal and Media Concentration

1. Elisha Hanson, "Official Propaganda and the New Deal," *Annals of the American Academy of Political and Social Science* 179 (May 1935): 176.

2. Ibid., 178.

3. Lawrence Levine and Cornelia Levine, *The People and the President: America's Conversation with FDR* (Boston: Beacon Press, 2002), 12, 10. On Roosevelt's success on the radio, see Robert J. Brown, *Manipulating the Ether: The Power of Broadcast Radio in Thirties America* (Jefferson, N.C.: McFarland & Company, 1998), 7–127; Douglas Craig, *Fireside Politics: Radio and Political Culture in the United States, 1920–1940* (Baltimore: Johns Hopkins University Press, 2000), 154–57; William Leuchtenburg, *Franklin D. Roosevelt and the New Deal* (New York: Harper & Row, 1963), 330–32; and Vincent Roscigno and William Danaher, *The Voice of Southern Labor: Radio, Music, and Textile Strikes, 1929–1934* (Minneapolis: University of Minnesota Press, 2004), chap. 3.

4. Hanson, "Official Propaganda and the New Deal," 176.

5. Jason Scott Smith, *Building New Deal Liberalism: The Political Economy of Public Works, 1933–1956* (New York: Cambridge University Press, 2006); Ronald Tobey, *Technology as Freedom: The New Deal and the Electrical Modernization of the American Home* (Berkeley: University of California Press, 1996); William Stott, *Documentary Expression and Thirties America* (Chicago: University of Chicago Press, 1986 [1973]), 102–18.

6. Harold Ickes, *America's House of Lords: An Inquiry into the Freedom of the Press* (New York: Harcourt, Brace, 1939), 129; Editorial, "Freedom of the Air," *New York Herald Tribune*, 15 January 1936, 18.

7. Robert McChesney, *Telecommunications, Mass Media, and Democracy: The Battle for Control of U.S. Broadcasting, 1928–1935* (New York: Oxford University Press, 1993);

Glen O. Robinson, "The Federal Communications Act: An Essay on Origins and Regulatory Purpose," in Max Paglin, ed., *A Legislative History of the Communications Act of 1934* (New York: Oxford University Press, 1989), 3; Susan Brinson, *The Red Scare, Politics, and the Federal Communications Commission, 1941–1960* (Westport, Conn.: Praeger, 2004), 26–27.

8. Martin Codel, "Dill and Davis Seen Powers in Radio Rule Under Roosevelt," *Broadcasting* 3 (15 November 1932): 8; George Manning, "Dill Warns Dailies Owning Stations," *Editor & Publisher* 65 (19 November 1932): 8.

9. Burton Wheeler, Interviewed by Ed Craney, Butte, Montana, 30 September 1964, 6, Oral History Transcript AT-17, LAB; McChesney, *Telecommunications, Mass Media, and Democracy*, 227; S. Howard Evans, *Report on Radio Broadcasting*, 24 April 1935, 17, 37, Box 992, Docket 4063, FCCDCF, NACP; George Henry Payne, "Safeguarding the Public Interest," address at Cornell University, 21 August 1935, printed in George Henry Payne, *The Fourth Estate and Radio and Other Addresses* (Boston: Microphone Press, 1936), 29.

10. Editorial, "Fast and Loose Radio," *Editor & Publisher* 67 (15 December 1934): 38; "Newspaper, Chain Ownership Data Requested by Congress," *Broadcasting* 12 (15 January 1937): 12; U.S. Senate, 74th Cong., 1st sess., *Confirmation of Members of the Federal Communications Commission, Hearings Before a Subcommittee of the Committee on Interstate Commerce* (Washington, D.C.: Government Printing Office, 1935), 195; *Congressional Record*, 74th Cong., 1st sess., 1935, 79, pt. 13: 14310–11, 14315.

11. On the concept of localism in American broadcasting history, see Robert Hilliard and Michael Keith, *The Quieted Voice: The Rise and Demise of Localism in American Radio* (Carbondale: Southern Illinois University Press, 2005).

12. Daniel Toohey, "Newspaper Ownership of Broadcast Facilities," *Federal Communications Bar Journal* 20 (1966): 44–57; *United States Broadcasting Corp. et al.*, 2 F.C.C. 208 (17 December 1935), 235–36, 241.

13. *Mason City Broadcast Company, et al.*, 3 F.C.C. 116 (24 July 1936), 118; Untitled Clipping, *Mason City Globe Gazette*, 18 January 1933, Box 758, Folder 1, Docket 3259, FCCDCF, NACP; Lee Loomis, Testimony Before the FCC, 23 January 1936, 145, Box 758, Folder 2, ibid.

14. Exception to Examiner's Report No. I-216, 18 April 1936, 1, 4, Box 758, Folder 1, ibid.; *Mason City Broadcast Company, et al.*, 123.

15. Tri-State Broadcasting Company, "Petition to Intervene in re: Application of Dorrance D. Roderick," 7 April 1936, 2, Box 894, Docket 3858, FCCDCF, NACP; *Roderick*, 3 F.C.C. 616 (12 January 1937), 619.

16. *Roderick*, 626–27, 629; "Newspaper, Economic Issues Are Joined in KTSM Appeal," *Broadcasting* 12 (15 March 1937): 22, 58; James Butler, "FCC Member Opposes Tieup Between Newspapers and Radio," *Editor & Publisher* 70 (6 March 1937): 8.

17. Irvin Stewart, "The Public Control of Radio," *Air Law Review* 8 (April 1937):145.

18. *Telegraph Herald, et al.*, 4 F.C.C. 392 (2 July 1937); William Klauer, Testimony Before the FCC, 16 September 1936, 220, Box 957, Docket 3967, FCCDCF, NACP.

19. Telegraph Herald, Petition for Reconsideration Under Rule 104.4, 18 January 1936, 2–3, *Sanders Brothers Radio Station v. Federal Communications Commission*, U.S. Court of Appeals for the District of Columbia, No. 7087, Box 735, USCA, NADC; *Sanders Brothers Radio Station v. Federal Communications Commission*, 106 F.2d 321 (1939).

20. Federal Communications Commission, "Petition for a Writ of Certiorari to the United States Court of Appeals for the District of Columbia," October Term, 1939, 10–13, Box 1864, *Federal Communications Commission v. Sanders Brothers Radio Station*, U.S. Supreme Court No. 499, UCSC, NADC.

21. *Federal Communications Commission v. Sanders Brothers Radio Station*, 309 U.S. 470 (1940), 473–74.

22. Editorial, "The Newspaper Issue," *Broadcasting* 13 (15 December 1937): 48; Editorial, "For the Slaughter?" *Broadcasting* 13 (1 August 1937): 56; "New FCC Considers Policies in Two Newspaper-Radio Cases," *Broadcasting* 13 (1 December 1937): 32, 34; "FCC to Formulate Policy on Dailies' Stations," *Editor & Publisher* 70 (28 August 1937): 7.

23. Louis Liebovich, *Bylines in Despair: Herbert Hoover, the Great Depression, and the U.S. News Media* (Westport, Conn.: Praeger, 1994), 120–21, 125; John Tebbel and Sarah Miles Watts, *The Press and the Presidency: From George Washington to Ronald Reagan* (New York: Oxford University Press, 1985), 439–41.

24. Richard Steele, *Propaganda in an Open Society: The Roosevelt Administration and the Media, 1933–1941* (Westport, Conn.: Greenwood Press, 1985), chap. 2; "The Press and the Campaign," *New Republic* 87 (22 July 1936): 311–12. On publisher opposition to the NIRA, see Edwin Emery, *History of the American Newspaper Publishers Association* (Minneapolis: University of Minnesota Press, 1950), chap. 15; and Elisha Hanson, "The American Newspaper Publishers Association," *Public Opinion Quarterly* 2 (January 1938): 122–23.

25. David Nasaw, *The Chief: The Life of William Randolph Hearst* (Boston: Houghton Mifflin, 2000), 516–24; Richard Norton Smith, *The Colonel: The Life and Legend of Robert R. McCormick, 1880–1955* (Boston: Houghton Mifflin, 1997), 345–46; "Ickes Denounces Press in Chicago," *New York Times*, 22 October 1936, 16; Steele, *Propaganda in an Open Society*, 47; Louise Overacker, "Campaign Funds in the Presidential Election of 1936," *American Political Science Review* 31 (June 1937): 473–98.

26. Graham White, *FDR and the Press* (Chicago: University of Chicago Press, 1979), 49, 79, 138–40.

27. Franklin Roosevelt, quoted in White, *FDR and the Press*, 49; "The Press Loses the Election," *New Republic* 89 (18 November 1936): 62; "Public Opinion and the Press," *Commonweal* 25 (20 November 1936): 85–86; "Faith in Power of Editors Shaken," *Literary Digest* 122 (19 December 1936): 42; Stott, *Documentary Expression and Thirties America*, 78–80; George Seldes, *Lords of the Press* (New York: Julian Messner, 1938), 3.

28. Steele, *Propaganda in an Open Society*, 19; Gary Dean Best, *The Critical Press and the New Deal: The Press Versus Presidential Power, 1933–1938* (Westport, Conn.: Praeger, 1993), 24; Editorial, "Roosevelt, Radio Star," *Los Angeles Times*, 3 January 1936, A4; Betty Winfield, *FDR and the News Media* (Urbana: University of Illinois Press, 1990), 110.

29. Excerpt from Proceedings of 1936 Annual Convention of American Newspaper Publishers Association, Report of Radio Committee, 4, 1, 5, Box 1936, Docket 6051, FCCDCF, NACP. For further analysis of the federal government's alleged ability to control radio via the licensing system, see E. H. Harris, "Radio and the Press," *Annals of the American Academy of Political and Social Science* 177 (January 1935): 163–69; and Merrill Denison, "Freedom, Radio, and the FCC," *Harper's* 178 (May 1939): 629–40. On increasing anxiety about the possibility of a dictatorship emerging in the United States during this period, see Benjamin Alpers, *Dictators, Democracy, and American Public Culture: Envisioning the Totalitarian Enemy, 1920s–1950s* (Chapel Hill: University of North Carolina Press, 2003); and David Ciepley, *Liberalism in the Shadow of Totalitarianism* (Cambridge, Mass.: Harvard University Press, 2006). On 1930s American radio in comparative perspective, see Wolfgang Schivelbusch, *Three New Deals: Reflections on Roosevelt's America, Mussolini's Italy, and Hitler's Germany, 1933–1939* (New York: Picador, 2006), chaps. 2–3.

30. S. Res.149, 75th Cong., 1st sess., 6 July 1937, 4, 8; "Senate May Hold Post-Session Probe in Fall," *Broadcasting* 13 (15 July 1937): 15, 66; "Thorough Senate Radio Probe Seen Certain," *Broadcasting* 13 (15 August 1937): 9, 62; *Congressional Record*, 75th Cong., 3rd sess., 1938, 83, pt. 7: 7631.

31. H. Res. 365, 75th Cong., 2nd sess., 1 December 1937; *Congressional Record*, 75th Cong., 1st sess., 1937, 81, pt. 7: 7280–81; *Congressional Record*, 75th Cong., 1st sess., 1937, 81, pt. 8: 8656. McFarlane was unrelenting on this point, making similar remarks several times in 1938. See *Congressional Record*, 75th Cong., 3rd sess., 1938, 83, pt. 1: 205–10; 75th Cong., 3rd sess., 1938, 83, pt. 1: 561; 75th Cong., 3rd sess., 1938, 83, pt. 4: 3616–17.

32. "Radio Inquiry in Congress Unlikely," *Broadcasting* 11 (1 December 1936): 13; Editorial, "Senator Wheeler Speaks," *Broadcasting* 11 (1 December 1936): 44; "Legislation May Divorce Press From Radio Interests," *Editor & Publisher* 69 (5 December 1936): 8; "Wheeler Seeking Data on Press-Radio Situation," *Editor & Publisher* 70 (16 January 1937): 22; Hampson Gary, Memorandum to the Federal Communications Commission, re: Opinion of the General Counsel, 25 January 1937, 1, Box 20, Folder 9, Series XI-173 —*Chicago Tribune*, Business Manager Files, 1926–1955, Tribune Archives.

33. Gary, Memorandum to the Federal Communications Commission, 2, 9, Tribune Archives; "Shotgun Divorce of Radio-Press Threatened by Senator Wheeler," *Variety* 125 (17 February 1937): 36; "Broadcasters Dig Trenches for Fight," ibid., 36; Sol Taishoff, "Newspaper-Radio Problem Out in the Open," *Broadcasting* 12 (15 February 1937): 11; James Butler, "Press-Radio Divorce Up to Congress," *Editor & Publisher* 70 (20 February 1937): 9; Editorial, "Politics or Public Service—The Newspaper-Radio Issue," *Broadcasting* 12 (1 March 1937): 14; "Wheeler Radio-Press Bill Gets Reaction," *Broadcasting* 12 (1 March 1937): 15.

34. Alan Brinkley, *The End of Reform: New Deal Liberalism in Recession and War* (New York: Vintage, 1995), 19–21; David Kennedy, *Freedom from Fear: The American People in Depression and War, 1929–1945* (New York: Oxford University Press, 1999), 331; Leuchtenburg, *Franklin D. Roosevelt and the New Deal*, 231–38.

35. Kennedy, *Freedom from Fear*, 333–34; "Newspaper-Radio Legislation Delayed," *Broadcasting* 12 (15 March 1937): 22; "Newspapers End Antagonism to Radio," *Broadcasting* 12 (1 May 1937): 15.

36. "Is the Press Next," Extension of Remarks of Fred L. Crawford of Michigan in the House, *Congressional Record*, 75th Cong., 2nd sess., 1937, 82, Appendix pt. 1: 307, 309; Thomas L. Stokes, Typescript, 20 December 1937, Box 204, Folder Reference File—Radio, Clapper Papers, LOC.

37. H.R. 3892, 75th Cong., 1st sess., 28 January 1937, 1–2; *Congressional Record*, 75th Cong., 3rd sess., 1938, 83, pt. 6: 5914; "Cry Against Joint Ownership Revived as Minton Raps Press," *Broadcasting* 14 (1 May 1938): 68.

38. Otha Wearin and Alfred Kirchhofer, "Joint Ownership of Newspapers and Radio Stations," *Public Opinion Quarterly* 2 (April 1938): 300–301, 304.

39. Ibid., 304–5, 308.

40. George C. Willings to William Randolph Hearst, 16 February 1937, Carton 36, Folder 3, Hearst Papers; Louis Caldwell to W. E. Macfarlane, 4 February 1937, 1, Box 20, Folder 9, Series XI-173—*Chicago Tribune*, Business Manager Files, 1926–1955, Tribune Archives; W. E. MacFarlane to Robert McCormick, 8 February 1937, ibid.; E. M. Antrim to W. E. MacFarlane, 27 February 1937, ibid.; Charles Halleck to E. M. Antrim, 1 March 1937, ibid.

41. H. Res. 72, 76th Cong., 1st sess., 25 January 1939; S. Res. 94, 76th Cong., 1st sess., 6 March 1939.

42. Deposition of George Harvey, 28 October 1935, 2, Box 813, Docket 3489, FCCDCF, NACP; William Ottoway, Testimony Before the FCC, 31 March 1937, 3, Box 1106, Docket 4357, FCCDCF, NACP.

43. *Stevens and Stevens*, 5 F.C.C. 177 (2 March 1938), 180, 182; Jerome Heckman, "Diversification of Control of the Media of Mass Communication—Policy or Fallacy?" *Georgetown Law Journal* 42 (January 1954): 385.

44. Erik Barnouw, *The Golden Web: A History of Broadcasting in the United States*, vol. 2, *1933 to 1953* (New York: Oxford University Press, 1968), 78–81; Susan Douglas, *Listening In: Radio and the American Imagination* (Minneapolis: University of Minnesota Press, 2004 [1999]), chap. 7; Kennedy, *Freedom from Fear*, 418–20.

45. James Rorty, "Radio Comes Through," *The Nation* 147 (15 October 1938): 372–74. On Rorty's critique of commercial broadcasting, see James Rorty, *Order on the Air!* (New York: John Day, 1934); and Kathy Newman, *Radio Active: Advertising and Consumer Activism, 1935–1947* (Berkeley: University of California Press, 2004), 58–63.

46. Excerpt from Proceedings of 1939 Annual Convention of American Newspaper Publishers Association, Report of Radio Committee, 1, Box 1936, Docket 6051, FCCDCF, NACP; Leland Stowe, "War News on Radio Aided Newspaper Sales—Stowe," *Editor & Publisher* 71 (8 October 1938): 28. The broadcasting industry was likewise self-congratulatory. See Editorial, "War and Words," *Broadcasting* 17 (15 September 1939): 48.

47. Joseph Pulitzer to Lansing Ray, 17 May 1939, emphasis in original, Box 46, Folder Associated Press—Radio, 1926–40, Pulitzer Papers, LOC. See also Bruce Robert-

son, "ANPA Moves Toward Harmony with Radio," *Broadcasting* 16 (1 May 1939): 11, 68. For analysis of the key radio newscasters during the Munich Crisis, see David Culbert, *News for Everyman: Radio and Foreign Affairs in Thirties America* (Westport, Conn.: Greenwood Press, 1976).

48. Excerpt from Proceedings of 1938 Annual Convention of American Newspaper Publishers Association, Report of Radio Committee, 1–2, Box 1936, Docket 6051, FCCDCF, NACP.

49. "Ickes and Gannett Debate Free Press," *New York Times*, 13 January 1939, 14; "Town Hall Adds 25% to Its Following; 2,500,000 Now Taking Part in Programs," *New York Times*, 17 December 1939, 48; "'Demagogic' Attack on Press Answered by U.S. Editors," *Editor & Publisher* 72 (21 January 1939): 3, 30; "Ickes Charges News Distortion by Press in Air Debate," *Editor and Publisher* 72 (21 January 1939): 4, 17; "Gannett Defends U.S. Press, Calls It 'Free and Fair,'" *Editor & Publisher* 72 (21 January 1939): 5, 29; "3 Ickes Charges Denied; Called Untruths," *Editor & Publisher* 72 (21 January 1939): 6.

50. "Gannett Retorts to Ickes on Papers," *New York Times*, 7 February 1939, 13; S.S. McClure to Frank Gannett, 7 November 1939, 1, Box 68, Folder 49, NBC, SHSW; Pamphlet, "Open Letter from Frank Gannett to All Voters of Both Parties," undated, 1, 6, ibid.

51. "Address by Secretary Ickes Before National Lawyers Guild," *New York Times*, 11 February 1939, 2; "Ickes Broadens Attack on Press in New Speech," *Editor & Publisher* 72 (18 February 1939): 14.

52. Stephen Monchak, "Ickes Takes Field Again Tilting Hard at Columnists," *Editor & Publisher* 72 (15 April 1939): 7. Ickes was not the only critic close to the administration to slam newspapers, as Eleanor Roosevelt and Hugo Black both delivered highly publicized rebukes in 1939. See "Mrs. Roosevelt Warns Against U.S. Press Control," *Editor & Publisher* 72 (21 January 1939): 16; and Editorial, "'Free as the Press,'" *Broadcasting* 16 (15 May 1939): 44.

53. Ickes, *America's House of Lords*, 14, 123, 129. The fight between Ickes and the Gannett organization continued unabated throughout 1940. In November, Frank Tripp, the vice president and general manager of Gannett Newspapers, sent an open letter to Harold Ickes that was widely printed in American newspapers, in which Tripp claimed that Ickes's animosity toward the press had proven largely misplaced since Roosevelt had been reelected yet again. Ickes responded with an open letter of his own, telling Tripp that there was "this difference between us—you insist that the press is free and that everything is fine and dandy in the journalistic heaven, while I know, from harsh daily experience, that much of the press is neither free (it is free only from governmental discretion or control) nor fair." "Election Proved Freedom of Press, Tripp Says in Letter to Ickes," *Editor & Publisher* 73 (16 November 1940): 3, 29; "Ickes Replies to Tripp's 'Dear Harold' Letter," *Editor & Publisher* 73 (14 December 1940): 22.

54. "A Radio Interview on the Government Reporting Factually to the People," 9 May 1939, Franklin Delano Roosevelt, *The Public Papers and Addresses of Franklin D. Roosevelt*, vol. 8 (New York: Macmillan, 1941), 309; "Roosevelt Praises Radio, Raps

Press," *Broadcasting* 16 (15 May 1939): 9, 62; "Administration Still Opposed to Ownership by Newspapers," *Broadcasting* 16 (1 April 1939): 24; Editorial, "The Press Issue," *Broadcasting* 16 (15 April 1939): 44.

55. "Radio," *Time* 31 (16 May 1938): 25; Federal Communications Commission, Proposed Findings of Fact and Conclusions Submitted by Respondents, WM. C. Barnes and Jonas Weiland, 14 July 1939, 2, Box 1652, Docket 5497, FCCDCF, NACP; *Barnes and Weiland*, 8 F.C.C. 46 (10 January 1940), 54.

56. Winfield, *FDR and the News Media*, 127–28.

57. Editorial, "More About FM," *Editor & Publisher* 73 (6 July 1940): 20; Walter Johnson, "FCC Receiving Requests for FM Licenses," *Editor & Publisher* 73 (27 July 1940): 6; Walter Damm, "Radio Expert Sees FM As Big Opportunity for Newspapers," *Editor & Publisher* 73 (3 August 1940): 7; Editorial, "Closer Affinity," *Broadcasting* 18 (1 May 1940): 50.

Chapter 4. Reform Liberalism and the Media: The Federal Communications Commission's Newspaper-Radio Investigation

1. Ellis Hawley, *The New Deal and the Problem of Monopoly: A Study in Economic Ambivalence* (New York: Fordham University Press, 1995 [1966]), Part I–II; David Kennedy, *Freedom from Fear: The American People in Depression and War, 1929–1945* (New York: Oxford University Press, 1999), 181–89, 325–31; William Leuchtenburg, *Franklin D. Roosevelt and the New Deal* (New York: Harper & Row, 1963), 64–94, 144–46.

2. Hawley, *The New Deal and the Problem of Monopoly*, 389; Alan Brinkley, *The End of Reform: New Deal Liberalism in Recession and War* (New York: Vintage, 1995), 56–57.

3. Hawley, *The New Deal and the Problem of Monopoly*, 286–87, 421, 428; Brinkley, *The End of Reform*, 58–59. On the differences between Thurman Arnold and the Brandeisians, see Brinkley, *The End of Reform*, chap. 6.

4. Michael Conant, *Antitrust in the Motion Picture Industry: Economic and Legal Analysis* (Berkeley: University of California Press, 1960), chap. 5; Giuliana Muscio, *Hollywood's New Deal* (Philadelphia: Temple University Press, 1997), chap. 5.

5. *Associated Press et al. v. United States*, 326 U.S. 1 (1945), 7, 20. For extended analysis of the case, see Margaret Blanchard, "The Associated Press Antitrust Suit: A Philosophical Clash over Ownership of First Amendment Rights," *Business History Review* 61 (Spring 1987): 43–85.

6. Federal Communications Commission, *Report on Chain Broadcasting* (Washington, D.C.: Government Printing Office, 1941), 72. For a detailed analysis of the history of the *Report on Chain Broadcasting* and its aftermath, see Michael Socolow, "To Network a Nation: N.B.C., C.B.S., and the Development of National Network Radio in the United States, 1925–1950" (Ph.D. dissertation, Georgetown University, 2001), chap. 3; and Christopher Sterling, "Breaking Chains: NBC and the FCC Network Inquiry, 1938–1943," in Michele Hilmes, ed., *NBC: America's Network* (Berkeley: University of California Press, 2007), 85–97.

7. James Fly, Speech to 1940 National Independent Broadcasters Convention, quoted in *FM: A Bulletin of News and Notes on the Advancement of Frequency Modulation* 26 (1 November 1940): 3, Box 1, Folder 6, Dorrance Papers, LAB; Hugh Slotten, "'Rainbow in the Sky': FM Radio, Technical Superiority, and Regulatory Decision-Making," *Technology and Culture* 37 (October 1996): 686–94; "FCC Spotlight on the Press," *Newsweek* 17 (31 March 1941): 65–66; Raymond Nixon, "Trends in Daily Newspaper Ownership Since 1945," *Journalism Quarterly* 31 (Winter 1954): 7.

8. Reminiscences of Paul Porter, 13 July 1967, 18, JLFP, CUOHROC; Franklin D. Roosevelt to James Lawrence Fly, 3 December 1940, quoted in Erik Barnouw, *The Golden Web: A History of Broadcasting in the United States*, vol. 2, *1933 to 1953* (New York: Oxford University Press, 1968), 170. Though Roosevelt motivated the investigation, his public support of it was muted. According to James Rowe, one of Roosevelt's administrative assistants, the president told Fly that he would not be able to back him up publicly because of political pressures. As Rowe recalled, "Fly told me he'd had a meeting with the President and the President had said that he wanted Fly to conduct an investigation leading to the rule or proposal that newspapers could not own radio stations. And he said that the President told him this was what he wanted but that he could not admit it and that if Fly got in trouble, he was out on his limb—he couldn't do anything about it. He wanted him to do it." Reminiscences of James Rowe, 1 August 1967, 2, JLFP, CUOHROC.

9. Susan Brinson, *The Red Scare, Politics, and the Federal Communications Commission, 1941–1960* (Westport, Conn.: Praeger, 2004), 36. On the relative activism of the FCC during Fly's tenure, see also James Baughman, *Television's Guardians: The FCC and the Politics of Programming, 1958–1967* (Knoxville: University of Tennessee Press, 1985).

10. On Fly's career, see Mickie Edwardson, "James Lawrence Fly's Fight for a Free Marketplace of Ideas," *American Journalism* 14 (Winter 1997): 19–39; Mickie Edwardson, "James Lawrence Fly, the FBI, and Wiretapping," *The Historian* 61 (Winter 1999): 361–81; Mickie Edwardson, "James Lawrence Fly v. David Sarnoff: Blitzkrieg over Television," *Journalism History* 25 (Summer 1999): 42–52; Mickie Edwardson, "James Lawrence Fly's Report on Chain Broadcasting (1941) and the Regulation of Monopoly in America," *Historical Journal of Film, Radio, and Television* 22 (October 2002): 397–423; and Henry Pringle, "The Controversial Mr. Fly," *Saturday Evening Post* 216 (22 July 1944): 9–10, 40–42.

11. Reminiscences of Marcus Cohn, 31 July 1967, 7–8, JLFP, CUOHROC; Editorial, "Who Is Public Enemy No.1?" *Collier's* 105 (25 May 1940): 78; Barnouw, *The Golden Web*, 174.

12. On the background to the Newspaper-Radio Investigation, see Mickie Edwardson, "Convergence, Issues, and Attitudes in the Fight Over Newspaper-Broadcast Cross-Ownership," *Journalism History* 33 (Summer 2007): 79–92; Clifford Jene Leabo, "The 1941 Newspaper-Radio Hearings—FCC Gambit" (M.A. thesis, University of Minnesota, 1972); Joon-Mann Kang, "Franklin D. Roosevelt and James L. Fly: The Politics

of Broadcast Regulation, 1941–1944," *Journal of American Culture* 10 (Summer 1987): 23–33; and Harvey Levin, "Cross-Channel Ownership of Mass Media: A Study in Social Valuation" (Ph.D. dissertation, Columbia University, 1953).

13. James Lawrence Fly, Memorandum to Franklin Roosevelt, 23 December 1940, 2, Box 17, Folder White House, Fly Papers, Columbia, emphasis in original; James Lawrence Fly to Franklin Roosevelt, 27 March 1941, ibid.

14. Federal Communications Commission, Order No. 79, *Federal Register* 6 (22 March 1941): 1580.

15. Editorial, "Newspaper Ownership Issue: Let's Have It Out," *Broadcasting* 20 (24 March 1941): 9; "FCC Action Against Multiple, Newspaper Ownership Is Seen," *Broadcasting* 20 (10 March 1941): 10; Sol Taishoff, "FCC Starts Newspaper Ownership Drive," *Broadcasting* 20 (24 March 1941): 7–8; *FM: A Bulletin of News and Notes on the Advancement of Frequency Modulation* 50 (4 April 1941): 1, Box 1, Folder 10, Dorrance Papers, LAB; *FM: A Bulletin of News and Notes on the Advancement of Frequency Modulation* 53 (25 April 1941): 6, Box 1, Folder 11, ibid.

16. W. E. Macfarlane to Hulbert Taft, 1 April 1941, Box 21, Folder 1, Series XI-173—*Chicago Tribune*, Business Manager Files, 1926–1955, Tribune Archives; Editorial, "Newspapers and Radio," *Editor & Publisher* 74 (29 March 1941): 26; Editorial, "A Straw in the Wind," *Editor & Publisher* 74 (5 April 1941): 20. There is an extensive collection of critical newspaper coverage of the investigation from papers across the country collected in Box 29, Fly Papers, Columbia.

17. Sol Taishoff, "Newspaper Stations Gird to Check FCC," *Broadcasting* 20 (31 March 1941): 7–8, 42; Walter Schneider, "Newspaper Radio Group Seeks $200,000 Fund," *Editor & Publisher* 74 (26 April 1941): 24, 111; Jack Gould, "Ethridge Resigns Radio Survey Post," *New York Times*, 14 May 1941, 22; Mark Ethridge, Speech to NAB Convention, Jefferson Hotel, St. Louis, 14 May 1941, 3, Box 15, Folder Mark Ethridge, Fly Papers, Columbia; "Radio v. New Deal," *Time* 37 (26 May 1941): 17; Jack Gould, "Fly Says N.A.B. Aims at Corner on 'Pull,'" *New York Times*, 16 May 1941, 44; "Removal of Fly Demanded by N.A.B.," *New York Times*, 17 May 1941, 17; Barnouw, *The Golden Web*, 173. For another significant public attack on Fly and the FCC, see Harold Hough, "Are Newspapers Qualified to Operate Broadcasting Stations?" Address Before the International Circulation Managers Association, Detroit, 17 June 1941, Box 16, Folder 20, MCEC, SHSW; and "Charge of Monopoly in News Disclaimed by Harold Hough," *Broadcasting* 20 (23 June 1941): 12, 19.

18. Federal Communications Commission, Order No. 79-A, *Federal Register* 6 (8 July 1941): 3302; "FCC vs. Press," *Business Week*, 26 July 1941, 32–33.

19. Editorial, "The Radio Inquiry," *Editor & Publisher* 74 (5 July 1941): 20; "Resentment Expressed at Tone of FCC Radio Questionnaire," *Editor & Publisher* 74 (12 July 1941): 3; "ANPA Enters Wide-Open Press Battle," *Broadcasting* 21 (14 July 1941): 7; "Ill-Will Prevails as Press Hearing Looms," *Broadcasting* 21 (21 July 1941): 7–8; Editorial, "Gestapo Tactics," *Broadcasting* 21 (21 July 1941): 30; "The Newspaper-Radio Issue Before the FCC," Newspaper-Radio Committee Pamphlet, 21 July 1941, p. 5, Box 16, Folder 20, MCEC, SHSW.

20. American Newspaper Publishers Association, "Motion to Vacate Order No. 79 and Order No. 79–A and Terminate Proceeding," 14 July 1941, 2, Box 1932, Docket 6051, FCCDCF, NACP; Elisha Hanson to Federal Communications Commission, 14 July 1941, 2, ibid.; *In the Matter of Orders No. 79 and 79–A*, 8 F.C.C. 589 (23 July 1941), 589, 591.

21. As early as 1936, the *Nashville Banner* had warned in editorials that Roosevelt might try to use federal control of radio in an attempt to exert control over newspapers. If the current administration, "possessing the power through its appointees," tried to exert itself over broadcasting, it could move easily to "subtly undermine the press and impair the confidence of the citizens of the nation in it," in essence to "utilize the radio as an effective agency to execute its designs against a free and independent press." Editorial, "Radio Must Be Free," *Nashville Banner*, 25 January 1936, Clipping in Box 43, Folder 38, NBC, SHSW.

22. George Seldes, *Lords of the Press* (New York: Julian Messner, 1938), 254; Statement of Points to Be Relied Upon on Appeal by Defendant, James G. Stahlman, 25 August 1941, 2, 4, Box 989, *Stahlman v. Federal Communications Commission*, No. 8039, U.S. Court of Appeals for the District of Columbia, USCA, NADC. Testimony on the *Banner* application was taken in the case in August 1941 and the matter put in the pending file after the U.S. entered World War II. When the freeze on new station construction was lifted after the war, the FCC denied the *Nashville Banner's* application. See *Nashville Radio Corp.*, 11 F.C.C. 639 (9 October 1946).

23. "Newspaper Inquiry Off to a Wobbly Start," *Broadcasting* 21 (21 July 1941): 9–11, 52–57; Thomas Thatcher, Testimony Before the FCC, 23 July 1941, 14, Box 1932, Docket 6051, FCCDCF, NACP; Elisha Hanson, Testimony Before the FCC, 23 July 1941, 31, ibid.; Editorial, "Newspaper-Owned Radio," *New York Times*, 23 July 1941, C18; Editorial, "ANPA Denies FCC Power," *Editor & Publisher* 74 (19 July 1941): 20; Editorial, "Same Old Story," *Broadcasting* 21 (28 July 1941): 34.

24. Allan Haywood, Testimony Before the FCC, 25 September 1941, 1384–86, Box 1933, Docket 6051, FCCDCF, NACP.

25. Ibid., 1379, 1384, 1387.

26. On engineering expertise and the development of federal radio policy, see Hugh Slotten, *Radio and Television Regulation: Broadcast Technology in the United States, 1920–1960* (Baltimore: Johns Hopkins University Press, 2000). On expert authority more generally, see Andrew Abbott, *The System of Professions: An Essay on the Division of Expert Labor* (Chicago: University of Chicago Press, 1988); Thomas Haskell, ed., *The Authority of Experts: Studies in History and Theory* (Bloomington: Indiana University Press, 1984); and Bruce Seely, *Building the American Highway System: Engineers as Policy Makers* (Philadelphia: Temple University Press, 1987).

27. Alfred McClung Lee, Testimony Before the FCC, 24 July 1941, 264, 270, 272–75, Box 1932, Docket 6051, FCCDCF, NACP. Lee's major published work on the press is Alfred McClung Lee, *The Daily Newspaper in America: The Evolution of a Social Instrument* (New York: Macmillan, 1937).

28. Carl Friedrich, Testimony Before the FCC, 3 October 1941, 1587, 1593–94, 1602–4, Box 1934, Docket 6051, FCCDCF, NACP.

29. Morris Ernst, "Foreword," in James Joyce, *Ulysses* (New York: Vintage, 1990 [1934]), vii. Ernst's major monographs on civil liberties before the Newspaper-Radio Investigation include Morris Ernst and William Seagle, *To the Pure: A Study of Obscenity and the Censor* (New York, Viking, 1928); Morris Ernst and Pare Lorentz, *Censored, or the Private Life of the Movie* (New York: Cape and Smith, 1930); Morris Ernst and Alexander Lindey, *Hold Your Tongue! Adventures in Libel and Slander* (New York: W. Morrow, 1932); and Morris Ernst and Alexander Lindey, *The Censor Marches On: Recent Milestones in the Administration of the Obscenity Law in the United States* (New York: Doubleday, Doran, 1940).

30. Marquis James, "Morris L. Ernst," *Scribner's Magazine* 104 (July 1938): 7–11, 57–58; Fred Roddell, "Morris Ernst," *Life* 16 (21 February 1944): 98, 100; Betty Winfield, *FDR and the News Media* (Urbana: University of Illinois Press, 1990), 145; "Divorce of Radio and Press Urged," *Broadcasting* 20 (17 February 1941): 8.

31. Morris Ernst, Testimony Before the FCC, 2 October 1941, 1398–99, 1401, 1497, Box 1933, Docket 6051, FCCDCF, NACP.

32. Roddell, "Morris Ernst," 102; Morris Ernst, *Too Big* (Boston: Little, Brown, 1940), 293; Morris Ernst, Testimony Before the FCC, 2 October 1941, 1406, Box 1933, Docket 6051, FCCDCF, NACP.

33. Ibid., 1416, 1441, 1407–8, 1526.

34. Hadley Cantril and Gordon Allport, *The Psychology of Radio* (New York: Harper & Brothers, 1935); Paul Lazarsfeld, *Radio and the Printed Page: An Introduction to the Study of Radio and Its Role in the Communication of Ideas* (New York: Duell, Sloan and Pearce, 1940). On Lazarsfeld's career and influence, see Allen Barton, "Paul Lazarsfeld and Applied Social Research: Invention of the University Applied Social Research Institute," *Social Science History* 3 (October 1979): 4–44; William J. Buxton and Charles R. Acland, "Interview with Dr. Frank N. Stanton: Radio Research Pioneer," *Journal of Radio Studies* 8 (Summer 2001): 191–229; Daniel Czitrom, *Media and the American Mind: From Morse to McLuhan* (Chapel Hill: University of North Carolina Press, 1982), chap. 5; Todd Gitlin, "Media Sociology: The Dominant Paradigm," *Theory and Society* 6 (September 1978): 205–53; Bruce Lenthall, *Radio's America: The Great Depression and the Rise of Modern Mass Culture* (Chicago: University of Chicago Press, 2007), chap. 5; David Morrison, "Kultur and Culture: The Case of Theodor W. Adorno and Paul F. Lazarsfeld," *Social Research* 45 (Summer 1978): 331–55; John Durham Peters, "Democracy and American Mass Communication Theory: Dewey, Lippmann, Lazarsfeld," *Communication* 11 (1989): 199–220; and Dan Schiller, *Theorizing Communication: A History* (New York: Oxford University Press, 1996), chap. 2.

35. Paul Lazarsfeld to Hazel Rice, 16 March 1942, 3, Vol. 2351, Reel 203, Correspondence—Censorship—Press-Radio—1942, Entry 2—Dr. Paul F. Lazarsfeld, Office of Radio Research, ACLU Records; Paul Lazarsfeld, Testimony Before the FCC, 29 January 1942, 3040–45, Box 1935, Docket 6051, FCCDCF, NACP.

36. Paul Lazarsfeld, "Some Notes on the Relationship Between Radio and the Press," *Journalism Quarterly* 18 (March 1941): 10–13; Minutes of the Joint Meeting of the National Council on Freedom from Censorship and the Radio Committee, 18 February 1942, 2, Vol. 2350, Reel 203, Correspondence—Censorship—National Council on Freedom from Censorship—1942, Entry 3—Committee Meetings, ACLU Records; Paul Lazarsfeld to Hazel Rice, 16 March 1942, 2, Vol. 2351, Reel 203, Correspondence—Censorship—Press-Radio—1942, Entry 2—Dr. Paul F. Lazarsfeld, Office of Radio Research, ACLU Records.

37. Paul Lazarsfeld to Hazel Rice, 16 March 1942, 2, Vol. 2351, Reel 203, Correspondence—Censorship—Press-Radio—1942, Entry 2—Dr. Paul F. Lazarsfeld, Office of Radio Research, ACLU Records; Newspaper Radio Committee pamphlet, *Are Newspaper Stations Different from Others?* (April 1942), 3, Box 16, Folder 20, MCEC, SHSW.

38. "FCC Press Data Reveal No Distinction," *Broadcasting* 21 (8 December 1941): 10; Louis Caldwell to E. M. Antrim, 4 October 1941, 2, Box 21, Folder 2, Series XI-173 —*Chicago Tribune*, Business Manager Files, 1926–1955, Tribune Archives.

39. William Lindley, "Ralph Casey . . . Journalist, Educator, Social Scientist," *Journalism Educator* 33 (October 1978): 20–24, 43; Ralph Casey, Testimony Before the FCC, 21 January 1942, 2716, 2720, Box 1935, Docket 6051, FCCDCF, NACP.

40. David Weaver, "Frank Luther Mott and the Future of Journalism History," *Journalism History* 2 (Summer 1975): 44–47; Frank Luther Mott, *American Journalism: A History of Newspapers in the United States Through 250 years, 1690–1940* (New York: Macmillan, 1941).

41. Frank Luther Mott, Testimony Before the FCC, 21 January 1942, 2803, 2813–14, 2833, Box 1935, Docket 6051, FCCDCF, NACP.

42. David Ciepley, "Why the State Was Dropped in the First Place: A Prequel to Skocpol's 'Bringing the State Back In,'" *Critical Review* 14 (2000): 157–213.

43. Arthur Garfield Hays, *Let Freedom Ring* (New York: Horace Liveright, 1928); Judy Kutulas, *The American Civil Liberties Union and the Making of Modern Liberalism, 1930–1960* (Chapel Hill: University of North Carolina Press, 2006), chap. 4.

44. Arthur Garfield Hays, Testimony Before the FCC, 30 January 1942, 3131–32, 3157, Box 1936, Docket 6051, FCCDCF, NACP.

45. Ibid., 3138–43.

46. Roscoe Pound, Testimony Before the FCC, 6 February 1942, 3360, Box 1936, Docket 6051, FCCDCF, NACP.

47. Morton Horwitz, *The Transformation of American Law, 1870–1960: The Crisis of Legal Orthodoxy* (New York: Oxford University Press, 1992), 219–22; James Landis, *The Administrative Process* (New Haven, Conn.: Yale University Press, 1938), 46; Thomas McCraw, *Prophets of Regulation: Charles Francis Adams, Louis D. Brandeis, James M. Landis, Alfred E. Kahn* (Cambridge, Mass.: Belknap Press of Harvard University Press, 1984), 212, 152; Edward Purcell, *The Crisis of Democratic Theory: Scientific Naturalism and the Problem of Value* (Lexington: University of Kentucky Press, 1973), 86–89.

48. Roscoe Pound, Testimony Before the FCC, 6 February 1942, Box 1936, 3386, 3397–98, Docket 6051, FCCDCF, NACP.

49. Ibid., 3410–13; "Dean Pound Raps Press Ownership Ban," *Broadcasting* 22 (9 February 1942): 9, 48.

50. Harold Hough, Petition to Federal Communications Commission, 20 January 1942, 2, Box 1935, Docket 6051, FCCDCF, NACP; Sydney Kaye to James Fly, 29 December 1941, 1, ibid.

51. Leabo, "The 1941 Newspaper-Radio Hearings—FCC Gambit," 104–7; *Stahlman v. Federal Communications Commission*, 126 F.2d 124 (1942), 127; Editorial, "FCC Court-Nipped," *Broadcasting* 22 (2 February 1942): 32; Louis Caldwell to E. M. Antrim, 14 February 1942, 2, Box 21, Folder 2, Series XI-173—*Chicago Tribune*, Business Manager Files, 1926–1955, Tribune Archives. See also "Court Rules FCC Cannot Bar Newspaper Ownership of Radio," *Editor & Publisher* 75 (31 January 1942): 3, 34; "Court Clips FCC Press-Radio Authority," *Broadcasting* 22 (2 February 1942): 12.

52. Newspaper-Radio Committee, *Freedom of the Press: What It Is, How It Was Obtained, How It Can Be Retained* (March 1942), 1, Pamphlet 4306, LAB.

53. "FCC Working on Final Report Covering Press-Radio Hearing," *Broadcasting* 22 (30 March 1942): 11, 58; Editorial, "Radio-Press Impasse," *Editor & Publisher* 75 (23 May 1942): 20; George Biggers to George Burbach, 7 May 1943, 1, Box 109, Folder Radio and Television, Burbach, George, 1942–1943, Pulitzer Papers, LOC.

54. NBC sold the Blue network to the American Broadcasting System, which soon became the American Broadcasting Company, or ABC.

55. *National Broadcasting Co., Inc. v. United States*, 319 U.S. 190 (1943), 226; Editorial, "Fact Against Talk," *Broadcasting* 24 (31 May 1943): 30; Editorial, "Usurping Congress," *Broadcasting* 24 (7 June 1943): 32.

56. "Resolution Passed by the National Council on Freedom from Censorship on Press-Radio Censorship," 18 February 1942, Vol. 2351, Reel 203, Correspondence—Censorship—Press-Radio—1942, Entry 3—Press-Radio Research, ACLU Records; Lewis Mumford, *Technics and Civilization* (New York: Harbinger, 1963 [1934]), 241; Lewis Mumford to Hazel Rice, 24 March 1942, Vol. 2351, Reel 203, Correspondence—Censorship—Press-Radio—1942, Entry 5—Kirsh Memo, ACLU Records; H. L. Mencken to Hazel Rice, 20 March 1942, ibid.; Walter Prichard Eaton to Hazel Rice, 20 March 1942, ibid.

57. Statement of Policy Concerning the Ownership of Radio Stations by Newspapers, 30 March 1942, Vol. 2350, Reel 203, Correspondence—Censorship—National Council on Freedom from Censorship—1942, Entry 5—Members, ACLU Records; "See No Peril in Press-Radio Link," *Editor & Publisher* 75 (11 April 1942): 4.

58. Barry Karl, *The Uneasy State: The United States from 1915 to 1945* (Chicago: University of Chicago Press, 1983), 160–62, 181.

59. Harold Hough, Testimony in U.S. House of Representatives, 77th Cong., 2nd sess., *Proposed Changes in the Communications Act of 1934, Hearings Before the Committee on Interstate and Foreign Commerce on H.R. 5497* (Washington, D.C.: Government

Printing Office, 1942), 361; "Fly Opens FCC Case Against Sanders Bill," *Broadcasting* 22 (15 June 1942): 14; Harold Hough, Testimony in U.S. Senate, 78th Cong., 1st sess., *To Amend the Communications Act, Hearings Before the Committee on Interstate Commerce on S. 814* (Washington, D.C.: Government Printing Office, 1944), 385, 402.

60. Brinson, *The Red Scare*, chap. 2; Barnouw, *The Golden Web*, 174; "FCC Inquiry Voted as Cox Assails Fly," *New York Times*, 20 January 1943, 33; Editorial, "Cox's Round," *Broadcasting* 24 (25 January 1943): 30; "Fly Charges Plot to Wreck the FCC," *New York Times*, 5 July 1943, 1, 26; "Unfairness Is Charged in Cox Investigation of FCC," *New York Times*, 22 August 1943, E8; Louis Caldwell to Miller McClintock, 7 July 1943, Box 31, Folder 3, Series XI-173—*Chicago Tribune*, Business Manager Files, 1926–1955, Tribune Archives.

61. Eugene Cox and Eugene Garey, Testimony in U.S. House of Representatives, 78th Cong., 1st sess., *Study and Investigation of the Federal Communications Commission, Hearings Before the Select Committee to Investigate the Federal Communications Commission, Acting Under H. Res. 21* (Washington, D.C.: Government Printing Office, 1943), 1, 8–9.

62. Brinson, *The Red Scare*, 82–83; Barnouw, *The Golden Web*, 175–76.

63. "Stronger Probe into FCC Actions Seen," *Broadcasting* 25 (4 October 1943): 8, 7; Barnouw, *The Golden Web*, 179.

64. Bill Bailey, "Committee Split May End Probe of FCC," *Broadcasting* 26 (21 February 1944): 9, 58; "Cox Sees Industry Threat; Garey Quits," *Broadcasting* 26 (28 February 1944): 9, 64; Editorial, "The House Fiasco," *Broadcasting* 26 (6 March 1944): 34; U.S. House of Representatives, 78th Cong., 2nd sess., *Investigation of the Federal Communications Commission, Final Report of the Select Committee to Investigate the Federal Communications Commission, Pursuant to H. Res. 21*, House Report 2095 (Washington, D.C.: Government Printing Office, 1945), 51, 17; Bill Bailey, "Lea Probe Demands Sweeping Law Change," *Broadcasting* 28 (8 January 1945): 13, 60–61.

65. "Fly Says FCC Not Inclined to Reopen Newspaper Divorcement Controversy," *Broadcasting* 24 (8 March 1943): 41; Editorial, "Bound and Gagged," *Broadcasting* 24 (3 May 1943): 40; "FCC Seen Determined to Delay Newspaper Ownership Answer," *Broadcasting* 25 (1 November 1943): 16; "FCC Newspaper Decision Before Holidays," *Broadcasting* 25 (6 December 1943): 9–10; Reminiscences of Pete Shuebruk, 16 August 1967, 17, JLFP, CUOHROC; Louis Caldwell to Elbert Antrim, 3 December 1943, Box 21, Folder 2, Series XI-173—*Chicago Tribune*, Business Manager Files, 1926–1955, Tribune Archives.

66. Reminiscences of Harry Plotkin, 27 December 1967, 30–31, JLFP, CUOHROC.

67. Chafee's major pre-World War II scholarly work on civil liberties is Zechariah Chafee, "Freedom of Speech in War Time," *Harvard Law Review* 32 (June 1919): 932–73; Chafee, "A Contemporary State Trial—The United States versus Jacob Abrams et al.," *Harvard Law Review* 33 (March 1920): 747–74; Chafee, *Freedom of Speech* (Rahway, N.J.: Harcourt, Brace, 1920); and Chafee, *Free Speech in the United States* (Cambridge, Mass.: Harvard University Press, 1941). *Free Speech in the United States* was a revision of his

1920 *Freedom of Speech*, a work historian Jerold Auerbach calls the "seminal twentieth-century treatise on the subject." Jerold Auerbach, "The Patrician as Libertarian: Zechariah Chafee, Jr. and Freedom of Speech," *New England Quarterly* 42 (December 1969): 531. See also Jonathan Prude, "Portrait of a Civil Libertarian: The Faith and Fear of Zechariah Chafee, Jr.," *Journal of American History* 60 (December 1973): 633–56; David Rabban, *Free Speech in Its Forgotten Years* (New York: Cambridge University Press, 1997), chap. 7; and Donald Smith, *Zechariah Chafee, Jr.: Defender of Liberty and Law* (Cambridge, Mass.: Harvard University Press, 1986).

68. Rabban, *Free Speech in Its Forgotten Years*, 300–303, 316–26, 335, 342–55.

69. Zechariah Chafee, Testimony Before the FCC, 3 October 1941, 1717–19, Box 1934, Docket 6051, FCCDCF, NACP.

70. Ibid., 1722, 1725–26. These points have been elucidated in a broader perspective in C. Edwin Baker, *Advertising and a Democratic Press* (Princeton, N.J.: Princeton University Press, 1994).

71. Zechariah Chafee, Testimony Before the FCC, 3 October 1941, 1712, Docket 6051, FCCDCF, NACP.

72. Ibid., 1713.

73. Memorandum from James Lawrence Fly to Franklin Roosevelt, re: Newspaper Ownership of Radio Stations, 14 December 1943, Reel 13, Folder Federal Communications Commission, July 2, 1943–1944, *President Franklin D. Roosevelt's Office Files, 1933–1945, Part 4: Subject Files* (Bethesda, Md.: University Publications of America, 1994); "Press Ownership 'Tolerated' by FCC," *Broadcasting* 26 (3 January 1944): 9; Editorial, "Into the Land of Bondage," *Broadcasting* 26 (3 January 1944): 10; "Press Ownership May Go to Congress," *Broadcasting* 26 (10 January 1944): 9, 54; Sol Taishoff, "Press-Ownership Ban Dropped by FCC," *Broadcasting* 26 (17 January 1944): 9–10.

74. "Defers Limiting Newspaper Radio," *New York Times*, 31 December 1943, 10; Federal Communications Commission, Newspaper Ownership of Radio Stations, Notice of Dismissal of Proceeding, *Federal Register* 9 (18 January 1944): 702–3.

75. Editorial, "Newspapers: Free, White and Eligible," *Broadcasting* 26 (17 January 1944): 10; Sol Taishoff, "Press-Ownership Ban Dropped by FCC," *Broadcasting* 26 (17 January 1944): 9; Editorial, "Comdr. Courageous," *Broadcasting* 26 (22 May 1944): 36; Editorial, "'Flyocracy'," *Broadcasting* 26 (14 February 1944): 40; Editorial, "No Discrimination," *Editor & Publisher* 77 (22 January 1944): 30; James F. Foley, "The Newspaper-Radio Decision," *Federal Communications Bar Journal* 7 (February 1944): 11–17.

76. "Craven Sparked Drive for Press in FCC," *Editor & Publisher* 77 (5 February 1944): 16; "Comdr. Craven to Join Cowles' Station," *Broadcasting* 26 (22 May 1944): 7, 58; "Dynasty in Radio," *Business Week*, 4 November 1944, 81–84. Former FCC Commissioner Clifford Durr was not kind toward Craven when asked about him some years later. In an oral history interview, Durr remarked that, "in the first place, Craven was not—this can't go down in the history books, but we might say here, he was not a man whose character impressed me very much . . . he was stupid and I don't think he had

too much character." Reminiscences of Clifford Durr, 17 September 1967, 22–23, JLFP, CUOHROC.

77. James Fly, Testimony in *Hearings Before the Select Committee to Investigate the Federal Communications Commission Acting Under H. Res. 21*, 3919; Bill Bailey, "Newspaper Problem Not Settled, Says Fly," *Broadcasting* 26 (26 June 1944): 11, 30; Editorial, "Still It's Unsettled," *Broadcasting* 26 (26 June 1944): 40.

78. Brinkley, *The End of Reform*, 6.

79. *National Broadcasting Co., Inc. et al. v. United States et al.*, 228.

Chapter 5. Media Corporations and the Critical Public: The Struggle over Ownership Diversity in Postwar Broadcasting

1. "Radio and War," Address by Archibald MacLeish at 20th Annual NAB Convention, Cleveland, 11 May 1942, 7, Box 10, Folder 7, NAB, SHSW.

2. Gerd Horten, *Radio Goes to War: The Cultural Politics of Propaganda during World War II* (Berkeley: University of California Press, 2002), 90, 117; James Baughman, *The Republic of Mass Culture: Journalism, Filmmaking, and Broadcasting in America Since 1941* (Baltimore: Johns Hopkins University Press, 2006 [1992]), chap. 1; Howard Blue, *Words at War: World War II Era Radio Drama and the Postwar Broadcasting Industry Blacklist* (Lanham, Md.: Scarecrow Press, 2002).

3. Broadcasters' Victory Council, Newsletter No. 6, 10 March 1942, 1, Box 3, Folder 11, Dorrance Papers, LAB; Byron Price, Address to the Cleveland City Club, Office of Censorship, Press Release PR-43, 20 March 1943, 4, 2, Box 1, Folder Censorship, January 1, 1943 to [blank], FCC-RID, NACP; Edwin Emery, *History of the American Newspaper Publishers Association* (Minneapolis: University of Minnesota Press, 1950), 241–42.

4. Lizabeth Cohen, *A Consumers' Republic: The Politics of Mass Consumption in Postwar America* (New York: Vintage, 2003), 114–18; Elizabeth Fones-Wolf, *Selling Free Enterprise: The Business Assault on Labor and Liberalism, 1945–1960* (Urbana: University of Illinois Press, 1994), 37–44; Ellen Schrecker, *Many Are the Crimes: McCarthyism in America* (Princeton, N.J.: Princeton University Press, 1998).

5. Justin Miller, Opening Remarks at All-Media Conference on Freedom of Expression, Washington, D.C., 26 June 1947, 2, 3, 1, Box 96, Folder 2, NAB, SHSW.

6. Justin Miller, "Attacks on Freedom of Communication," Address to American Society of Newspaper Editors Convention, Washington, D.C., 23 April 1949, 10, 16, Box 1, Folder 7, NAB, SHSW.

7. Ibid., 22–23.

8. Robert U. Brown, "FM Offers Opportunities To Newspaper Publishers," *Editor & Publisher* 77 (26 February 1944): 7, 32; "Publishers Told FM Offers Outstanding Opportunity," *Editor & Publisher* 77 (29 April 1944): 15; "Publishers Told of FM Opportunities," *Broadcasting* 26 (1 May 1944): 7–8; Jerry Walker, "Newspapers' Interest in FM Fight Sought," *Editor & Publisher* 78 (14 April 1945): 82; Jerry Walker, "One-Third of Stations Have Press Affiliation," *Editor & Publisher* 81 (20 March 1948): 40; "Daily to

Provide First Video Station to Texas," *Editor & Publisher* 79 (29 June 1946): 44; "Radio-Paper Combine Trend Grows," *Broadcasting* 32 (28 April 1947): 13, 75.

9. Arthur Hays Sulzberger to Edwin H. Armstrong, 18 December 1943, Box 1, Folder Sulzberger, Arthur Hays to Edwin Howard Armstrong, Armstrong Papers, Columbia; "Advertising Policy of WQXR," 3, Box 1, Folder WQXR-FCC Hearings (1946) (4 of 6), Sanger Papers, Columbia; Eli Jacobi to WQXR, 18 July 1946, Box 1, Folder WQXR-FCC Hearings (1946) (2 of 6), ibid.; "Good Taste in Ads Is Aim of Times Station," *Editor & Publisher* 78 (31 March 1945): 28; Elliott Sanger, *Rebel in Radio: The Story of WQXR* (New York: Hastings House, 1973), 88–103.

10. Morris Ernst, Address to Eleventh Annual Convention of the American Newspaper Guild, 8 August 1944, 2, Box 25, Folder Free Speech, Fly Papers, Columbia; Morris Ernst, *The First Freedom* (New York: Macmillan, 1946), 154; Harry Lorin Binsse, "Our Dire Need for Diversity," *Commonweal* 43 (22 March 1946): 570–72; Morris Ernst, "Freedom to Read, See, and Hear," *Harper's* 191 (July 1945): 51–53.

11. For an overview of the Commission, see Stephen Bates, *Realigning Journalism with Democracy: The Hutchins Commission, Its Times, and Ours* (Washington, D.C.: Annenberg Washington Program in Communications Policy Studies of Northwestern University, 1995).

12. The Hutchins Commission's vice chairman was Zechariah Chafee, Harvard Law Professor and a key witness in the FCC's 1941–1944 Newspaper-Radio Investigation. The other members were John M. Clark (Professor of Economics, Columbia University), John Dickinson (Professor of Law, University of Pennsylvania), William Hocking (Professor Emeritus of Philosophy, Harvard University), Harold Lasswell (Professor of Law, Yale University), Archibald MacLeish (former Assistant Secretary of State), Charles Merriam (Professor of Political Science, University of Chicago), Reinhold Niebuhr (Professor of Ethics and Philosophy of Religion, Union Theological Seminary), Robert Redfield (Professor of Anthropology, University of Chicago), Beardsley Ruml (Chairman, Federal Reserve Bank of New York), Arthur Schlesinger (Professor of History, Harvard University), and George Shuster (President, Hunter College).

13. Commission on the Freedom of the Press, *A Free and Responsible Press* (Chicago: University of Chicago Press, 1947), 1, 43, emphasis in original.

14. Furman Lee Cooper to FCC, 3 September 1945, Box 246, File 45-4, FCCOED-GC, NACP.

15. Federal Communications Commission, Newspaper Ownership of Radio Stations, Notice of Dismissal of Proceeding, *Federal Register* 9 (18 January 1944): 703.

16. For a case-by-case study of FCC decisions on newspaper-radio combinations during this period, see John August Grams, "An Analysis of Federal Communications Commission Actions in the Licensing of Newspaper-Affiliated Broadcasting Stations to 1970" (Ph.D. dissertation, University of Wisconsin, 1973), chaps. 3–4.

17. *Stephen R. Rintoul,* 11 F.C.C. 108 (9 December 1945), 113–14; "Newspaper, Station Monopoly Case Heard," *Broadcasting* 29 (15 October 1945): 94; "Publisher's WSRR Ownership Given Official FCC Approval," *Broadcasting* 29 (24 December 1945): 71.

18. *The Observer Radio Co. et al.*, 11 F.C.C. 354 (19 June 1946), 363; *Meadville Tribune Broadcasting Co., et al.*, 11 F.C.C. 666 (28 October 1946), 669, 670.

19. *Beatrice Cobb et al.*, 11 F.C.C 672 (28 October 1946); *Peacock and Peacock et al.*, 11 F.C.C. 679 (30 October 1946); *Nashville Radio Corp. et al.*, 11 F.C.C. 639 (9 October 1946); *Voice of Augusta, Inc. et al.*, 11 F.C.C. 733 (27 November 1946); *Green Bay Broadcasting Co. et al.*, 11 F.C.C. 822 (23 December 1946); *City of Sebring, Fla. et al.*, 11 F.C.C. 873 (8 January 1947); *Miller, Miller, Penney & Penney*, 11. F.C.C. 236 (2 May 1946); *Arkansas-Oklahoma Broadcasting Corp.*, 3 Pike and Fischer Radio Regulation 479 (1946); *Commonwealth Broadcasting Corp. et al.*, 11 F.C.C. 1179 (25 April 1947); *Southern Tier Radio Service, Inc. et al.*, 11 F.C.C. 171 (20 March 1946), 181; "Paper Ownership, Community Activities Play Part in Binghamton, N.Y. Grant," *Broadcasting* 30 (14 January 1946): 44; *James A. Noe (WNOE) et al.*, 13 F.C.C. 448 (26 January 1949); *Norman Broadcasting Co.*, 5 Pike and Fischer Radio Regulation 120 (29 June 1949), 138, 143.

20. *Laurence W. Harry, et al.*, 13 F.C.C. 23 (14 July 1948), 30; "Ohio Papers Battle FCC 'Intimidation,'" *Editor & Publisher* 81 (7 February 1948): 10; Mrs. Hoyt Oberlin to Federal Communications Commission, 6 February 1948, 1–2, Box 2734, Docket 7356, FCCDCF, NACP.

21. William Locke to FCC, 27 November 1945, Box 2736, ibid.

22. *Laurence W. Harry, et al.*, 13 F.C.C. 23 (14 July 1948), 38, 41. A lengthy court battle followed the FCC's decision when the papers filed an appeal. The federal appeals court sided with the FCC in 1950, asserting that "Monopoly in the mass communication of news and advertising is contrary to the public interest." *Mansfield Journal Co. (FM) v. Federal Communications Commission*, 180 F.2d 28 (1950), 33; "Definition of Freedom," *New Republic* 122 (6 December 1950): 9–10; James Butler, "Radio Can Be Denied on 'Monopoly' Ground," *Editor & Publisher* 83 (28 January 1950): 9; Editorial, "Price of Freedom," *Broadcasting* 39 (9 October 1950): 48; Howard Gilbert, "Newspaper-Radio Joint Ownership: Unblest Be the Tie That Binds," *Yale Law Journal* 59 (June 1950): 1342–50. The newspapers' clashes with radio continued after the unsuccessful applications and appeals. The *Lorain Journal* refused to carry the program logs of WEOL and WEOL-FM, the stations that received the Lorain licenses, as paid advertisements and told local merchants they could not continue to advertise in the newspaper if they purchased any advertising on the radio. Federal attorneys filed a Sherman Act complaint against the paper, charging it with engaging in "combination and conspiracy in restraint of the interstate commerce of competitive news and advertising media and of their advertisers." The paper responded with a First Amendment defense ultimately dismissed in federal court, and it was ordered to cease discriminating against advertisers and the radio station. *United States v. Lorain County Journal*, 92 F. Supp 794 (1950), 795. The paper unsuccessfully appealed this decision to the Supreme Court, which ruled that the paper was in violation of the Sherman Act and that its business practices were not protected from regulation by the First Amendment. *Lorain Journal Co. et al v. United States*, 342 U.S. 143 (1951); John Lopatka and Andrew Kleit, "The Mystery of *Lorain*

Journal and the Quest for Foreclosure in Antitrust," *Texas Law Review* 73 (May 1995): 1255–1306.

23. *Scripps-Howard Radio, Inc. et al.*, 13 F.C.C. 473 (27 January 1949), 503; *Scripps-Howard Radio, Inc. v. Federal Communications Commission*, 189 F.2d 677 (1951), 683; "S-H Radio Asks Review of FCC Paper Policy," *Editor & Publisher* 84 (18 August 1951): 52; Earl Abrams, "FCC Newspaper Policy," *Broadcasting* 41 (13 August 1951): 29.

24. Joseph Morrison, *Josephus Daniels: The Small-d Democrat* (Chapel Hill: University of North Carolina Press, 1966), chap. 2; Susan Douglas, *Inventing American Broadcasting, 1899–1922* (Baltimore: Johns Hopkins University Press, 1987), chap. 8; Robert McChesney, *Telecommunications, Mass Media, and Democracy: The Battle for Control of U.S. Broadcasting, 1928–1935* (New York: Oxford University Press, 1993), 180–86; Josephus Daniels, Testimony Before the FCC, 18 July 1946, 322–23, Box 2827, Docket 7504, FCCDCF, NACP; A. J. Fletcher, Testimony Before the FCC, 12 August 1946, 633, 640, Box 2826, ibid.; A. J. Fletcher, Testimony Before the FCC, 17 July 1946, 95, Box 2827, ibid.; *Capitol Broadcasting Co., Inc. et al*, 11 F.C.C. 859 (6 January 1947).

25. Ambrose McCoy to T. J. Slowie, 14 August 1947, 1, Box 2480, Docket 7025, FCCDCF, NACP; Ernest Dupre to T. J. Slowie, 15 August 1947, 1–2, 4, ibid.; City of Providence, Resolution of the City Council, No. 545, 15 August 1947, 1, ibid.; Rhode Island House of Representatives, Resolution of Protest to the Federal Communications Commission, 27 May 1947, ibid.; *Providence Journal Co.*, 12 F.C.C. 267 (15 October 1947).

26. *Orlando Daily Newspapers, Inc. et al.*, 11 F.C.C. 760 (6 December 1946); *Midland Broadcasting Co. et al.*, 12 F.C.C. 611 (26 January 1948); *Le Mond, Jones and Fisher et al.*, 11 F.C.C. 919 (14 February 1947), 927.

27. Wilmer Smith, Testimony Before the FCC, 21 March 1946, 300, Box 2466, Docket 7003, FCCDCF, NACP; *The Sandusky Broadcasting Co. et al.*, 11 F.C.C. 1383 (28 June 1947), 1395.

28. *Hanford Publishing Co. et al*, 11 F.C.C. 1431 (28 June 1947).

29. Christopher Sterling and Michael Keith, *Sounds of Change: A History of FM Broadcasting in America* (Chapel Hill: University of North Carolina Press, 2008), chaps. 2–3.

30. News Syndicate Company was the legal name of the corporation applying for the license; *New York Daily News* was the entity most New Yorkers understood as the applicant. I use the terms accordingly in this chapter.

31. Philip Roth, *The Plot Against America* (Boston: Houghton Mifflin, 2004), 125, 305.

32. Alexander Pekelis, "Group Sanctions Against Racism," *New Republic* 113 (29 October 1945): 571; "Anti-Bias Meeting Set," *New York Times*, 19 January 1946, 9; "2,200 at Protest Rally," *New York Times*, 25 January 1946, 21.

33. Anna Mars to FCC, 7 July 1946, Box 2011, Docket 6175, FCCDCF, NACP; George Ehrlich to FCC, 8 July 1946, ibid.

34. Pamphlet, "FM: Prospectus and Plans for Peoples Radio Station in the Greater

New York Area," undated, Box 1889, Docket 6013, FCCDCF, NACP; Peoples Radio Foundation, "What Is Peoples Radio Foundation?" ibid.; Eugene Konecky, *The American Communications Conspiracy* (New York: Peoples Radio Foundation, 1948), 108–9.

35. Jack Anderson Spanagel to FCC, 10 July 1946, emphasis in original, Box 2625, Docket 7221, FCCDCF, NACP; Walter Kraus to FCC, 17 July 1946, ibid.; Pete Seeger and Lee Hays to FCC, 28 March 1946, Box 2626, Docket 7221, FCCDCF, NACP. The PRF was not without its detractors. A particularly vitriolic campaign came from citizens who charged that the group was a communist-led organization trying to worm its way into American life. The genesis of the campaign was an article in the *Chicago Journal of Commerce* on 1 July1946. The paper ran its attack on the PRF as the sixth installment of an eleven-part series of articles published in late June and early July 1946 alleging Communist infiltration in government, labor unions, the press, and the culture industries. The paper called the PRF a "Fifth Column front" and urged readers to write letters to the government in opposition. "This is more than a business matter," the *Journal of Commerce* warned. It "affects the whole country and the world. Public officials should speak out on it publicly. The Fifth Column wants an FM channel so that it may propagandize for its masters in Moscow." A number of readers, mostly from the northern Midwest, wrote letters to the FCC to protest the PRF application in New York City. See Andrew Avery, "Peoples Radio Foundation Seeks FM Outlet in N.Y. For Moscow Propaganda," *Chicago Journal of Commerce*, 1 July 1946, 1, 5. For listener responses from conservatives, see Charles Ziegenhagen to Scott Lucas, 2 July 1946, Box 2625, Docket 7221, FCCDCF, NACP; Ernest Voges to FCC, 8 July 1946, ibid.; and Milton Petersen to Harry Truman, 1 July 1946, ibid.

36. Bernard Silverman to FCC, 2 July 1946, Box 2625, Docket 7221, FCCDCF, NACP; Thomas Lockard to FCC, 8 July 1946, Box 2010, Docket 6175, FCCDCF, NACP; Ruth Oreck to FCC, 11 July 1946, Box 2625, Docket 7221, FCCDCF, NACP, emphasis in original.

37. Spencer Blakeslee, *The Death of American Antisemitism* (Westport, Conn.: Praeger, 2000), chap. 5; Morris Frommer, "The American Jewish Congress: A History, 1914–1950" (Ph.D. dissertation, Ohio State University, 1978), 520–27; John P. Jackson, Jr., "Blind Law and Powerless Science: The American Jewish Congress, the NAACP, and the Scientific Case Against Discrimination, 1945–1950," *Isis* 91 (March 2000): 94, 103–4; Stuart Svonkin, *Jews Against Prejudice: American Jews and the Fight for Civil Liberties* (New York: Columbia University Press, 1997), chap. 4.

38. Petition to the Federal Communications Commission Opposing the Grant of an FM Radio License to the New York Daily News, 26 June 1946, 1, Box 2010, Docket 6175, FCCDCF, NACP.

39. Sondra Vitrio to FCC, 1 July 1946, 2, Box 2010, Docket 6175, FCCDCF, NACP; Tessa Weinstein to FCC, 7 July 1946, ibid.; M. Stowe to FCC, 9 July 1946, Box 2011, Docket 6175, FCCDCF, NACP; Mary Dudziak, *Cold War Civil Rights: Race and the Image of American Democracy* (Princeton, N.J.: Princeton University Press, 2000), 1–9.

40. American Jewish Congress, Petition for Intervention, 14 March 1946, 2, Box

2010, Docket 6175, FCCDCF, NACP; News Syndicate Company, Answer to Petition of the American Jewish Congress for Intervention, 22 April 1946, 1, ibid.

41. F. M. Flynn, Testimony Before the FCC, 9 July 1946, 261, Box 1882, Docket 6013, FCCDCF, NACP; Percy Russell, Testimony Before the FCC, 9 July 1946, 287, ibid.; J. Alfred Guest, Statement Before the FCC, 9 July 1946, 288, ibid.

42. Will Maslow, Testimony Before the FCC, 9 July 1946, 298, 300, ibid.; Bernard Fein, Testimony Before the FCC, 9 July 1946, 305, ibid.; Percy Russell, Testimony Before the FCC, 9 July 1946, 306, 308, ibid.; Joseph Brodsky, Testimony Before the FCC, 9 July 1946, 306, 310–11, ibid.

43. Louis Caldwell, Testimony Before the FCC, 18 July 1946, 1404–5, Box 1884, Docket 6013, FCCDCF, NACP.

44. Will Maslow, Testimony Before the FCC, 18 July 1946, 1407–8, ibid.

45. Will Maslow, Testimony Before the FCC, 27 June 1947, 79, Box 1882, Docket 6013, FCCDCF, NACP; Will Maslow, Testimony Before the FCC, 12 January 1948, 69, Box 1893, Docket 6013, FCCDCF, NACP.

46. Joseph Brodsky, Testimony Before the FCC, 16 July 1946, 1080–81, 1083–84, Box 1883, Docket 6013 Files, NACP.

47. Alexander Pekelis, Testimony Before the FCC, 18 July 1946, 1458, 1460, 1532–33, Box 1884, Docket 6013, FCCDCF, NACP.

48. American Jewish Congress, Memorandum in the Nature of the Proposed Findings Submitted at the Direction of the Federal Communications Commission by the American Jewish Congress, 12 November 1946, 8–9, 15, 98, Box 2010, Docket 6175, FCCDCF, NACP; "Daily News Denies Race Bias Charges," *New York Times*, 13 November 1946, 3.

49. Alexander Pekelis, Letter to the Editor, *New York Times*, 27 November 1946, 24; Zechariah Chafee, Jr., *Government and Mass Communications*, vol. 2 (Chicago: University of Chicago Press, 1947), 639.

50. See for example "Radio Witness Admits Survey of News Errs," *New York Daily News*, 1 October 1946, 29; "The News Pushes Fight on Prejudice Charge," *New York Daily News*, 2 October 1946, 28; "News Is Not Biased, Radio Hearing Told," *New York Daily News*, 4 October 1946, 27; "News Denies Bias, Challenges FCC Right to Rule on Papers," *New York Daily News*, 13 November 1946, 11; "Brief Offered Assailing News FM Application," *New York Daily News*, 17 November 1946, 20; "The News Won't Appeal Turndown on FM," *New York Daily News*, 29 April 1948, 16.

51. F. M. Flynn, Testimony Before the FCC, 3 October 1946, 3326, 3328, 3336, Box 1886, Docket 6013, FCCDCF, NACP; Winifred Mallon, "Daily News Denies Race Bias Charge," *New York Times*, 4 October 1946, 21; News Syndicate, Reply Brief in the Matter of the Commission's Jurisdiction Over Newspaper Content, undated, 2, 49, Box 2010, Docket 6175, FCCDCF, NACP.

52. Winifred Mallon, "FCC Hearings Open in Daily News Case," *New York Times*, 1 October 1946, 9; Arthur Krock, "In the Nation," *New York Times*, 15 November 1946, 21.

53. Clipping, John S. Knight, "Would Our 'Liberals' Restrict the Freedom of Others to Speak?" *Chicago Daily News*, 19 October 1946, Box 103, Folder 6, NAB, SHSW; Charles Whited, *Knight: A Publisher in the Tumultuous Century* (New York: Dutton, 1988), 162; "General Censorship Threat Seen by 'News' in AJC Stand," *Broadcasting* 31 (16 December 1946): 42.

54. John S. Knight, "Do We Have Freedom of Speech in the United States?" Speech at 24th Annual Convention of the National Association of Broadcasters, Chicago, 23 October 1946, 5–6, Box 25, Folder—Free Speech, Fly Papers, Columbia.

55. Memorandum Opinion, Decided 9 April 1947, Released 13 June 1947, 3, 5, 7–9, Box 1893, Docket 6013, FCCDCF, NACP.

56. Will Maslow, Testimony Before the FCC, 27 June 1947, 82, Box 1882, Docket 6013, FCCDCF, NACP; Percy Russell, Testimony before the FCC, 27 June 1947, 87–88, ibid.

57. "FM Radio Channel Denied Daily News," *New York Times*, 5 November 1947, 54; Editorial, "The Newspaper-Radio Issue," *New York Times*, 11 November 1947, C26; Winifred Mallon, "5 FM Grants Here Set Aside by FCC," *New York Times*, 18 December 1947, 58; "N.Y. News Appeals FCC's FM Ruling," *Editor & Publisher* 80 (29 November 1947): 46.

58. *WBNX Broadcasting Co. Inc. et al.*, 12 F.C.C. 837 (7 April 1948), 839, 841–43, 851.

59. *WBNX Broadcasting Co. Inc. et al.*, 12 F.C.C. 805 (7 April 1948); "Newspaper Yields to FM Radio Ban," *New York Times*, 29 April 1948, 44; Elizabeth Fones-Wolf, *Waves of Opposition: Labor and the Struggle for Democratic Radio* (Urbana: University of Illinois Press, 2006), 160.

60. John Abel, Charles Clift, and Frederic Weiss, "Station License Revocations and Denials of Renewal, 1934–1969," *Journal of Broadcasting* 14 (Fall 1970): 411–21; Robert Horwitz, *The Irony of Regulatory Reform: The Deregulation of American Telecommunications* (New York: Oxford University Press, 1989), 157–65.

61. Richard J. Meyer, "Educational Broadcasting and Charles A. Siepmann," *International Review of Education* 10 (1964): 211–12; Federal Communications Commission, *Public Service Responsibility of Broadcast Licensees* (Washington, D.C.: Government Printing Office, 1946). On the Blue Book, see Michael Socolow, "Questioning Advertising's Influence Over American Radio: The Blue Book Controversy of 1945–1947," *Journal of Radio Studies* 9 (December 2002): 282–302.

62. Editorial, "F(ederal) C(enshorship) C(ommission)," *Broadcasting* 30 (18 March 1946): 58; Charles Siepmann, *Radio's Second Chance* (Boston: Little, Brown, 1946), 222, 9, emphasis in original.

63. Hearst Radio, Inc., Petition for Reconsideration of the Commission's Action in Designating the Renewal Application of WBAL for Hearing in Consolidation with the Application of Public Service Radio Corporation, for Reconsideration and Grant of Renewal Application of WBAL and for Other Relief, 13 December 1946, 6, Box 2766, Docket 7400, FCCDCF, NACP; "Pearson, Allen Ask WBAL Facilities," *Broadcasting* 31 (23 September 1946): 15.

64. On Pearson's career, see Herman Klurfeld, *Behind the Lines: The World of Drew*

Pearson (Englewood Cliffs, N.J.: Prentice Hall, 1968); and Oliver Pilat, *Drew Pearson: An Unauthorized Biography* (New York: Harper's Magazine Press, 1973).

65. Drew Pearson, Testimony Before the FCC, 10 February 1948, 2847–48, Box 2771, Docket 7400, FCCDCF, NACP.

66. Cindy Aron, *Working at Play: A History of Vacations in the United States* (New York: Oxford University Press, 1999), chap. 4; Pilat, *Drew Pearson*, 51–53; Andrew Rieser, *The Chautauqua Movement: Protestants, Progressives, and the Culture of Modern Liberalism* (New York: Columbia University Press, 2003), 262; Edward Ross to Paul Pearson, quoted 262.

67. Drew Pearson, Testimony Before the FCC, 10 February 1948, 2849–52, Box 2771, Docket 7400, FCCDCF, NACP.

68. Robert Allen, Testimony Before the FCC, 26 January 1948, 2301, 2303, Box 2770, Docket 7400, FCCDCF, NACP; Robert Allen, Testimony Before the FCC, 27 January 1948, 2463, 2483–84, 2491, ibid.; Robert Allen, Testimony Before the FCC, 28 January 1948, 2534–35, ibid.

69. Elizabeth Holt Downs, Testimony Before the FCC, 30 January 1948, 2605, 2607–8, Box 2770, Docket 7400, FCCDCF, NACP.

70. Charles Siepmann, *The Radio Listener's Bill of Rights: Democracy, Radio, and You* (New York: Anti-Defamation League of B'Nai B'Rith, 1948), 7, 11.

71. Charles Siepmann, "Radio's Operation Crossroads," *The Nation* 163 (7 December 1946): 645.

72. Hearst Radio, Inc., Petition for Reconsideration of the Commission's Action in Designating the Renewal Application of WBAL for Hearing in Consolidation with the Application of Public Service Radio Corporation, for Reconsideration and Grant of Renewal Application of WBAL and for Other Relief, 13 December 1946, 9, 10, 11, 13, Box 2766, Docket 7400, FCCDCF, NACP; "FCC Delays WBAL Renewal Hearing; Hearst Files Plea," *Broadcasting* 31 (30 September 1946): 75; Rufus Carter, "WBAL Hearing Issues Announced," *Broadcasting* 31 (25 November 1946): 15, 101; Rufus Carter, "Did FCC Staff Distort Blue Book Facts?" *Broadcasting* 31 (16 December 1946): 15, 89; "WBAL Asks FCC to Publish 'Correction' on Its Blue Book," *Broadcasting* 32 (27 January 1947): 17.

73. Michael Curley to FCC, 3 January 1947, Box 2766, Docket 7400, FCCDCF, NACP; John Rutherford to FCC, 7 January 1947, ibid.; Robert Fich to FCC, 10 February 1947, ibid.; "Proclamation by Mayor Thomas D'Alessandro, Jr., Designating the Month of September, 1947 as 'WBAL' Month in Baltimore," 7 August 1947, Box 2773, Docket 7400, FCCDCF, NACP.

74. Norman Williams to FCC, 17 December 1946, 1–3, Box 2766, Docket 7400, FCCDCF, NACP; Betty Sachs to Charles Denny, 22 December 1946, 1, ibid.

75. William Dempsey, Testimony Before the FCC, 26 January 1948, 2180–81, Box 2770, Docket 7400, FCCDCF, NACP; Editorial, "Here Lies the Blue Book," *Broadcasting* 34 (19 January 1948): 48; *Hearst Radio, Inc. v. Federal Communications Commission*, 167 F.2d 225 (1948), 226.

76. *Hearst Radio, Inc. et al.*, 15 F.C.C. 1149 (14 June 1951), 1177, 1179, 1181, 1183.

77. Ibid., 1183, 1187.

78. Ronald Coase, "The Federal Communications Commission," *Journal of Law and Economics* 2 (October 1959): 11.

79. Konecky, *The American Communications Conspiracy*, 110–11, 117.

80. Ibid., 58.

81. Ibid., 118, 111.

82. Ibid., 112, 59, 129, 146.

83. James Baughman, *Television's Guardians: The FCC and the Politics of Programming, 1958–1967* (Knoxville: University of Tennessee Press, 1985), 12, 19; Susan Brinson, *The Red Scare, Politics, and the Federal Communications Commission, 1941–1960* (Westport, Conn.: Praeger, 2004), 114.

Conclusion: The Persistence of Print: Newspapers and
Broadcasting in the Age of Television

1. Robert McCormick, Speech Broadcast on WGN-TV, 5 July 1949, 1, 3, Transcript in Box 132, Folder WGN—Radio and Television, 1946–1949, Series I-60—Robert R. McCormick, Business Correspondence, 1927–1955, Tribune Archives.

2. Arch Oboler, "Arch Oboler Sounds Requiem for Radio," *Variety* 157 (3 January 1945): 71; Merlin Aylesworth, "Radio Is Doomed . . . But Its Stars Will Be Tops in Television," *Look* 13 (26 April 1949): 66; Electronic Industries Association, *Electronic Market Data Book, 1970* (Washington, D.C.: Electronic Industries Association, 1970), 6; James Baughman, *The Republic of Mass Culture: Journalism, Filmmaking, and Broadcasting in America Since 1941* (Baltimore: Johns Hopkins University Press, 2006 [1992]), 30–31; Jack Gould, "What TV Is—And What It Might Be," *New York Times*, 10 June 1951, SM10.

3. Interview with William S. Hedges, 4 October 1951, 81–82, Box 2, Folder Oral History Project: "30 Years in Broadcasting: A Limited View of One Man Watching the Growth of an Industry," Hedges Papers, SHSW; James Lawrence Fly, Letter to the Editor, *Look* 13 (7 June 1949): 6.

4. Susan Douglas, *Listening In: Radio and the American Imagination* (Minneapolis: University of Minnesota Press, 2004 [1999]), chap. 9; Michael Brian Schiffer, *The Portable Radio in American Life* (Tucson: University of Arizona Press, 1991), chaps. 9–11; Electronic Industries Association, *Electronic Market Data Book, 1970*, 6, 16.

5. George Parker, "Radio Devices Broaden Detroit News Service," *Editor & Publisher* 79 (30 November 1946): 40; Tim Kiska, *A Newscast for the Masses: The History of Detroit Television News* (Detroit: Wayne State University Press, 2009), chap. 2; "Daily to Provide First Video Station in Texas," *Editor & Publisher* 79 (29 June 1946): 44; "KSD Inaugurates Commercial Video Service in St. Louis," *Broadcasting* 32 (10 February 1947): 14; Joseph Pulitzer, Jr., Memo to George Burbach, 12 February 1947, 3, Box 113, Folder Radio and Television, Television, Facsimile, FM, 1945–47, Pulitzer Papers, LOC.

6. "Newspapers Launch TV Net," *Business Week*, 24 June 1950, 21; Reminiscences

of Frank Atkinson Arnold, November 1950 and January and June 1951, 85, RPP, CUOHROC.

7. Bernard Berelson, "What 'Missing the Newspaper' Means," in Paul Lazarsfeld and Frank Stanton, eds., *Communications Research 1948–1949* (New York: Harper & Brothers, 1949), 125–26; Jerry Walker, "Newspapers and TV Are Complementary," *Editor & Publisher* 85 (9 March 1952): 12; James Baughman, "Wounded But Not Slain: The Orderly Retreat of the American Newspaper," in David Paul Nord, Joan Shelley Rubin, and Michael Schudson, eds., *A History of the Book in America*, vol. 5, *The Enduring Book: Print Culture in Postwar America* (Chapel Hill: University of North Carolina Press, 2009): 119–34.

8. Editorial, "Is This U.S.A. or –," *Broadcasting* 29 (15 October 1945): 54; Statement of Richard T. Leonard, Printed in U.S. Senate, 80th Cong., 1st sess., *To Amend the Communications Act of 1934, Hearings Before a Subcommittee of the Committee on Interstate and Foreign Commerce on S.1333* (Washington, D.C.: Government Printing Office, 1947), 583.

9. *Bamberger Broadcasting Services, Inc., et al.*, 11 F.C.C. 1242 (8 May 1947), 1254; Susan Brinson, *The Red Scare, Politics, and the Federal Communications Commission, 1941–1960* (Westport, Conn.: Praeger, 2004); Robert Horwitz, *The Irony of Regulatory Reform: The Deregulation of American Telecommunications* (New York: Oxford University Press, 1989).

10. Reminiscences of Fred Friendly, 30 October 1967, 2, JLFP, CUOHROC; Clarence Dill, Interviewed by Ed Craney, Butte, Montana, 21 July 1964, 22–23, Oral History Transcript AT-15, LAB.

11. Steven Classen, *Watching Jim Crow: The Struggles over Mississippi TV, 1955–1969* (Durham, N.C.: Duke University Press, 2004); Michael Stamm, "Questions of Taste: Interest Group Liberalism and the Campaigns to Save Classical Music Broadcasting in Post-World War II Chicago," *Historical Journal of Film, Radio and Television* 25 (June 2005): 291–309; Erwin Krasnow, Lawrence Longley, and Herbert Terry, *The Politics of Broadcast Regulation* (New York: St. Martin's, 1982), 206–10; Sterling Quinlan, *The Hundred Million Dollar Lunch* (Chicago: J. Philip O'Hara, 1974).

12. Walter Kerr, "The Problem of Combinations," *Saturday Review* 21 (12 October 1968): 82–83.

13. Nicholas Johnson, "The Media Barons and the Public Interest: An FCC Commissioner's Warning," *The Atlantic* 221 (June 1968): 43, 50; Nicholas Johnson, *How to Talk Back to Your Television Set* (New York: Bantam, 1970); Howard Junker, "The Greening of Nicholas Johnson," *Rolling Stone*, 1 April 1971, 32–39.

14. *Multiple Ownership of Standard, FM, & TV Broadcast Stations*, 22 F.C.C. 2d 339 (25 March 1970); Jules Witcover, "Post Assails TV Challenge," *Washington Post*, 17 May 1974, A1, A18; William Claiborne, "FCC Held Aware of Nixon's Wishes," *Washington Post*, 18 May 1974, A3; Harvey Zuckerman and Roy Mason, "The Great Cross-Media Ownership Controversy," *American Bar Association Journal* 60 (December 1974):

1570–74; Joseph Spear, *Presidents and the Press: The Nixon Legacy* (Cambridge, Mass.: MIT Press, 1984), 129–34.

15. *Multiple Ownership*, 50 F.C.C. 2d 1046 (31 January 1975); *Multiple Ownership*, 53 F.C.C. 2d 589 (5 June 1975), 589; *National Citizens Committee for Broadcasting v. Federal Communications Commission*, 555 F.2d 938 (1977), 954; *Federal Communications Commission v. National Citizens Committee for Broadcasting et al.*, 436 U.S. 775 (1978).

16. Robert McChesney, *The Problem of the Media: U.S. Communication Politics in the 21st Century* (New York: Monthly Review Press, 2004), chap. 7; *Prometheus Radio Project v. Federal Communications Commission*, 373 F.3d 372 (2004). For good discussions of the poles in the cross-ownership debate, see Richard Kapler, *Cross Ownership at the Crossroads: The Case for Repealing the FCC's Newspaper/Broadcast Cross Ownership Ban* (Washington, D.C.: Media Institute, 1997) for the deregulatory argument; and Douglas Gomery, *The FCC's Newspaper-Broadcast Cross-Ownership Rule: An Analysis* (Washington, D.C.: Economic Policy Institute, 2002) for the case that the cross-ownership ban should be retained.

17. C. Edwin Baker, *Media Concentration and Democracy: Why Ownership Matters* (New York: Cambridge University Press, 2007), 190.

18. Robert Entman and Steven Wildman, "Reconciling Economic and Non-Economic Perspectives on Media Policy: Transcending the 'Marketplace of Ideas,'" *Journal of Communication* 42 (Winter 1992): 5–19.

19. Address by Morris Ernst to Eleventh Annual Convention of the American Newspaper Guild, 8 August 1944, 3, Box 25, Folder Free Speech, Fly Papers, Columbia; Raymond Nixon, "Trends in Daily Newspaper Ownership Since 1945," *Journalism Quarterly* 31 (Winter 1954): 7; Benjamin M. Compaine and Douglas Gomery, *Who Owns the Media? Competition and Concentration in the Mass Media Industry*, 3rd ed. (Mahwah, N.J.: Erlbaum, 2000), 9; Bryce Rucker, *The First Freedom* (Carbondale: Southern Illinois University Press, 1968).

20. For analyses and critiques of this position, see Baker, *Media Concentration and Democracy*, chap. 3; and Robert McChesney, *Rich Media, Poor Democracy: Communication Politics in Dubious Times* (New York: New Press, 1999), chap. 3.

21. Scott Gant, *We're All Journalists Now: The Transformation of the Press and Reshaping of the Law in the Internet Age* (New York: Free Press, 2007); Yochai Benkler, *The Wealth of Networks: How Social Production Transforms Markets and Freedom* (New Haven, Conn.: Yale University Press, 2006), 29–30.

22. On concentration in the various information and media industries in the Internet age, see Eli Noam, *Media Ownership and Concentration in America* (New York: Oxford University Press, 2009). Noam's data is exhaustive, though focused almost exclusively on the post-1984 period.

23. Mark Lloyd, *Prologue to a Farce: Communication and Democracy in America* (Urbana: University of Illinois Press, 2006), chap. 9.

24. For thoughtful analyses of the travails of and possibilities for journalism in the Internet age, see Leonard Downie, Jr., and Michael Schudson, "The Reconstruction of American Journalism," *Columbia Journalism Review* 48 (November/December 2009): 28–51; and Robert McChesney and John Nichols, *The Death and Life of American Journalism: The Media Revolution That Will Begin the World Again* (New York: Nation Books, 2010).

Index

Acknowledgments

Neil Harris of the University of Chicago provided invaluable guidance and mentorship in the early development of this book. Advice, criticism, and support from George Chauncey, Amy Dru Stanley, and Adrian Johns influenced the book in countless ways, and I had the good fortune at Chicago of also working with Mae Ngai and Bill Novak.

At the University of Pennsylvania Press, my series editors Pamela Laird and Mark Rose have encouraged the project from its earliest stages of revision into book form and have been wonderful to work with. I owe a particular debt to Richard John, who invited me to give a talk at the Newberry Library several years ago, and who has remained an incisive critic and advocate since. Richard has read countless drafts of the manuscript, and his comments and suggestions have helped to shape the work into the book that it is today. My editor, Bob Lockhart, has provided unfailing good cheer and counsel throughout the writing process. Alison Anderson graciously shepherded the book through the production process.

Many others have generously offered indispensable assistance, advice, and criticism along the way: David Bailey, James Baughman, Sam Becker, Jane Briggs-Bunting, Michael Brillman, Michael Carriere, Frank Chorba, Mike Czaplicki, Hazel Dicken-Garcia, Lucinda Davenport, Kirsten Fermaglich, Lisa Fine, Kathy Roberts Forde, Douglas Gomery, Joanna Grisinger, Molly Hudgens, Bob Hunter, Mark Kornbluh, Steve Lacy, Grant Madsen, Ev Meade, Matt Millikan, John J. Pauly, Mark Pedelty, Chris Russill, Aaron Shapiro, Jim Sparrow, Christopher Sterling, Susan Strasser, David Suisman, Dwight L. Teeter, Jr., Al Tims, Derek Vaillant, and Ellen Wu. Erik Helin and Andrew Struska provided skilled research assistance.

All responsibility for errors of fact, omission, and interpretation is my own.

Chapter drafts have been presented to audiences at Michigan State

University, the American Journalism Historians Association, the Business History Conference, the Policy History Conference, the Hagley Museum and Library, the University of Minnesota, the University of Chicago, the Popular Culture Association, the Law and Society Association, and the Newberry Library.

Earlier versions of some material appeared in "Newspapers, Radio, and the Business of Media in the United States," *OAH Magazine of History* 24 (January 2010): 25–28; and "The Sound of Print: Newspapers and the Public Promotion of Early Radio Broadcasting in the United States," in Susan Strasser and David Suisman, eds., *Sound in the Age of Mechanical Reproduction* (Philadelphia: University of Pennsylvania Press, 2009), 221–41.

This book would not have been possible without the generous financial support of several institutions and organizations: the Department of History and the Social Sciences Division at the University of Chicago; the School of Journalism and Mass Communication and the College of Liberal Arts at the University of Minnesota; the Department of History and the College of Communication Arts & Sciences at Michigan State University; and the Gilder Lehrman Institute of American History.

Staff members at various archives and libraries provided assistance with locating materials, and I owe thanks to those at the Rare Book and Manuscript Library and the Oral History Research Office at Columbia University; the Manuscript Division and the Motion Picture, Broadcasting, and Recorded Sound Division at the Library of Congress; the Bancroft Library at the University of California, Berkeley; the Herbert Hoover Presidential Library in West Branch, Iowa; and the State Historical Society of Wisconsin. I would like to express particular gratitude to David Pfeiffer at the National Archives in College Park, Maryland; Michael Henry at the Library of American Broadcasting at the University of Maryland; Eric Gillespie at the Colonel Robert R. McCormick Research Center in Wheaton, Illinois; and Frank Conaway at the University of Chicago's Regenstein Library.

And finally, I'd like to acknowledge my family for unstinting support as I worked on this book. Thanks to Wanda Smith, Lusik Sarkissian, Teni Sarkissian, Carole Stamm, and Molly Stamm. Michael Smith kindly bought me a new computer that helped immensely with the writing. Diane Stamm generously put me up in Washington and provided great company during my research trips there.

I owe much to my mother, Michell Smith, and I hope that giving her a finished copy of this book offers some small recompense for all that she has done for me.

And finally, I would like to thank Ani Sarkissian, for really just about everything.